The Battles of Kings Mountain and Cowpens

The American South is so identified with the Civil War that people often forget that the key battles from the final years of the American Revolution were fought in Southern states. The Southern backcountry was the center of the fight for independence, but backcountry devotion to the Patriot cause was slow in coming. Decades of animosity between coastal elites and backcountry settlers who did not enjoy accurate representation in the assemblies meant a complex political and social milieu throughout this turbulent time.

The Battles of Kings Mountain and Cowpens focuses on the battles of the Southern backcountry. With careful attention to political, social, and military history, Walker concentrates on the communities and events unacknowledged by most accounts of the Revolutionary War.

In five concise chapters bolstered by government documents, auto-biographical excerpts, correspondence, and diaries, *The Battles of Kings Mountain and Cowpens* gives students of the American Revolution an important new perspective on the role of the south in the resolution of the fighting.

For additional documents, images, and resources please visit *The Battles of Kings Mountain and Cowpens* companion website at www.routledge.com/cw/criticalmoments.

Melissa Walker is Professor of History at Converse College.

Critical Moments in American History
Edited by William Thomas Allison, Georgia Southern University

The Battles of Kings Mountain and Cowpens

The American Revolution in the Southern Backcountry

Melissa Walker

Routledge
Taylor & Francis Group

NEW YORK AND LONDON

First published 2013
by Routledge
711 Third Avenue, New York, NY 10017

Simultaneously published in the UK
by Routledge
2 Park Square, Milton Park, Abingdon, Oxon OX14 4RN

Routledge is an imprint of the Taylor & Francis Group, an informa business

© 2013 Taylor & Francis

Library of Congress Cataloging in Publication Data
Walker, Melissa, 1962–
    The battles of Kings Mountain and Cowpens: the American
    Revolution in the Southern backcountry/by Melissa Walker.
    p. cm.
    Includes bibliographical references.
    1. King's Mountain, Battle of, S.C., 1780. 2. Cowpens, Battle of,
    Cowpens, S.C., 1781. I. Title.
    E241.K5W28 2012
    975.7'03—dc23   2012031045

ISBN: 978-0-415-89560-6 (hbk)
ISBN: 978-0-415-89561-3 (pbk)
ISBN: 978-0-203-08186-0 (ebk)

Typeset in Bembo and Helvetica Neue
by Florence Production Ltd, Stoodleigh, Devon

Printed and bound in the United States of America by
Walsworth Publishing Company, Marceline, MO.

This book is dedicated to my students at
Converse College—past, present, and future.

Contents

Series Introduction

Welcome to the Routledge *Critical Moments in American History* series. The purpose of this new series is to give students a window into the historian's craft through concise, readable books by leading scholars, who bring together the best scholarship and engaging primary sources to explore a critical moment in the American past. In discovering the principal points of the story in these books, gaining a sense of historiography, following a fresh trail of primary documents, and exploring suggested readings, students can then set out on their own journey, to debate the ideas presented, interpret primary sources, and reach their own conclusions—just like the historian.

A critical moment in history can be a range of things—a pivotal year, the pinnacle of a movement or trend, or an important event such as the passage of a piece of legislation, an election, a court decision, a battle. It can be social, cultural, political, or economic. It can be heroic or tragic. Whatever they are, such moments are by definition "game changers," momentous changes in the pattern of the American fabric, paradigm shifts in the American experience. Many of the critical moments explored in this series are familiar; some less so.

There is no ultimate list of critical moments in American history—any group of students, historians, or other scholars may come up with a different catalog of topics. These differences of view, however, are what make history itself and the study of history so important and so fascinating. Therein can be found the utility of historical inquiry—to explore, to challenge, to understand, and to realize the legacy of the past through its influence of the present. It is the hope of this series to help students realize this intrinsic value of our past and of studying our past.

William Thomas Allison
Georgia Southern University

Figures

Acknowledgments

The seeds for this book were sown at my interview for a teaching position at Converse College in January 1996. Joe P. Dunn, Dana Professor of History and chair of the department of history and politics, suggested that I might be interested in including field trips to nearby Revolutionary War battlefields in some of my courses. Over the next few years, I did just that. Eventually, I developed a course for our January term called The American Revolution in the Southern Backcountry. Each time I taught the course, my students and I tramped over the landscapes where John Sevier, Daniel Morgan, Nathanael Greene, Alexander Chesney, and hundreds more men fought in bitter cold and blazing heat. In 2007 and 2009, with my colleague Edward Woodfin, I directed a National Endowment for the Humanities Landmarks in American History and Culture workshop for school teachers on the same topic.

Over the years, I have had the opportunity to learn from many of the masterful historians cited in these pages including Lawrence Babits, Marvin Cann, Walter Edgar, George Fields, Cynthia Kierner, and Michael Scoggins. The staffs at Historic Brattonsville (site of the Battle of Huck's Defeat), Kings Mountain National Military Park, Cowpens National Battlefield, and Ninety Six National Historic Site have been generous in sharing their time and their knowledge with my students and me. John Robertson led my first guided battlefield tour at Cowpens, and he continues to be a resource on every visit. I am grateful to all these fine professionals.

Thanks to William Allison who asked me to contribute a manuscript to the "Turning Points" series, and especially for his careful reading of the initial draft. His suggestions made it a better book. I am grateful to Converse College for a sabbatical leave that allowed me to finish this project in a timely manner. I hope it will benefit many Converse students who enroll in my American Revolution course in future years. Thanks to Eddy Woodfin for reading portions of the manuscript, and to my husband, Chuck Reback, who not only tolerated my distraction but read the entire manuscript and saved me from many careless errors.

I dedicate this book to my students who have taught me as much about history and human nature as I have taught them.

Timeline

"National" events		Southern colonial and backcountry events
1754–63	French and Indian War	
1758–61		Cherokee War
1761–63		Struggle between South Carolina royal governor and its assembly over the extent of assembly's power.
1763	February 10—Treaty of Paris marks the official end of the French and Indian War October—Proclamation of 1763 forbids migration west of the crest of the Appalachian Mountains	
1764	Parliament enacts various Navigation and Revenue Act including Sugar Act and Currency Act	
1765	March—Stamp Act and Quartering Act passed Stamp Act protests October—Stamp Act Congress	Stamp Act Protests in southern colonies
1766	Stamp Act Repealed March—Declaratory Act	
		May—Word of Stamp Act's repeal reaches southern colonies
	June—Townshend Acts	
1767–68	First round of American Boycotts of British goods	South Carolina Regulator Movement Begins North Carolina Regulator Movement Begins South Carolina creates Committee of 39 to enforce boycotts March—Truce between South Carolina Regulators and Moderators
1769		South Carolina Judiciary Act Addresses Regulator demands
1770	March—Boston Massacre	South Carolina Assembly appropriates money for defense of John Wilkes South Carolina Assembly installs statue honoring William Pitt

1771		Royal government effectively ends in South Carolina though royal governor does not depart
		March—Battle of Alamance results in defeat of North Carolina Regulators
1773	Tea Act	
	Tea Act protests and boycotts	Tea Act protests and boycotts
	December—Boston Tea Party	December—South Carolina Tea is unloaded and stored for safekeeping.
1774	March–June—Passage of the Coercive (Intolerable) Acts	
	September 5–October 26—First Continental Congress Meets	North and South Carolina send delegates to First Continental Congress.
	October 20—First Continental Congress passes "the Association," a prohibition on trade with Britain	In South Carolina, Committee of ninety-nine organizes Provincial Congress.
1775		Georgia organizes a Provincial Congress and ratifies the Association
		South Carolina organizes Committee of Safety to oversee colony's defense
	April 19—Battles of Lexington and Concord	April—Committee of Safety Seizes British supply of munitions in Charles Town
	May—Second Continental Congress	North and South Carolina and Georgia send delegates to Second Continental Congress.
	June—Formation of Continental Army; George Washington named commander in chief	June—South Carolina Provincial Congress ratifies the Association and authorizes formation of military units under command of Committee of Safety; issues Circular Letter to the districts of the states outlining its positions on British authority.
	June—Battle of Bunker Hill in Boston results in Patriot defeat.	Summer—Royal government effectively ends in North Carolina and Georgia
		Summer—Representatives of the South Carolina Committee of Safety and North Carolina Whigs seek backcountry support
		July—Seizure of Port Charlotte from British
		September—Treaty of Ninety Six forestalls armed conflict between Whigs and Loyalists in South Carolina backcountry
		November Whig forces take Fort Johnson in South Carolina.
	November—Lord Dunmore's Proclamation	November—First battle of Ninety Six.
		November/December—Snow Campaign
1776	January—Publication of *Common Sense*	
	March—British evacuate Boston.	March—South Carolina adopts state constitution.
		April—North Carolina Provincial Congress issues Halifax Resolves authorizing delegates to Second Continental Congress to vote for independence. First state to do so.
		June–Whig victory—Battle of Sullivan's Island
	July—Declaration of Independence adopted	August—news of the Declaration reaches southern colonies
	September—British occupy New York City	July–October—Cherokee campaign in South Carolina
	December—Washington's forces are victorious at Battle of Trenton in New Jersey	

1777   January—Patriot victory at Princeton,
New Jersey

May—Cherokee cede all South Carolina lands to the colony
in the Treaty of DeWitt's Corner

September—British victory at Battle of
Brandywine in Pennsylvania
September—British occupy the American
capital at Philadelphia
October—American victory at Saratoga
in New York
December—Washington's army enters
winter quarters at Valley Forge

1778   February–French-American treaty of
alliance signed
June—British abandon Philadelphia and
return to New York

December—British occupy Savannah

1779   February—Patriot victory over Loyalist forces at Kettle
Creek in Georgia
May 11–12—First Battle of Charleston—British withdraw

July—British burn Fairfield and Norwalk,
Connecticut

October—American attempt to recapture Savannah fails

1780   Winter–spring—British invade South Carolina.
April—Governor Rutledge flees South Carolina.
April 1—Siege of Charles Town begins
April 14—Whig defeat—Battle of Monck's corner
May 12—Surrender of Charles Town to British
May 29—Battle of the Waxhaws
June 3—Clinton revokes original terms of parole.
June 18—British troops burn Hill's Ironworks
June 20—Whigs rout Loyalist forces at Ramsour's Mill,
North Carolina

July—French troops arrive in Rhode Island
to aid the American cause

July 12—Whig victory at Battle of Huck's Defeat
July 13—First battle of Cedar Springs—Whig victory
August 16—American defeat at Battle of Camden
August 18—Whig victory at Musgrove's Mill

October—George Washington appoints
Nathanael Greene as commander of the
southern branch of the Continental Army

October 7—Battle of Kings Mountain

1781   January 17—American victory at the Battle of Cowpens
January 17—early March—The "race to the Dan"

March—Articles of Confederation Adopted

March 15—General Greene is defeated at Guilford
Courthouse in North Carolina
April 25—General Greene is defeated at Hobkirk's Hill in
South Carolina
May 22–June 19—General Greene lays siege to British
garrison at Ninety Six; ultimately withdraws and British
abandon fort.

		June 6—Whigs recapture Augusta, Georgia
		September 8—General Greene defeated at Eutaw Springs, South Carolina
	October 19—Cornwallis surrenders at Yorktown, Virginia	
1782		July—British evacuate Savannah
		Backcountry fighting between Whigs and Loyalists continues
	November 30—British and Americans sign preliminary peace treaty	November 14—Battle of James Island, South Carolina is last Southern engagement; British victory
		December 14—British leave Charleston
1783	September 3—Treaty of Paris formally concludes the war and recognizes American independence	
	November—British troops leave New York City	

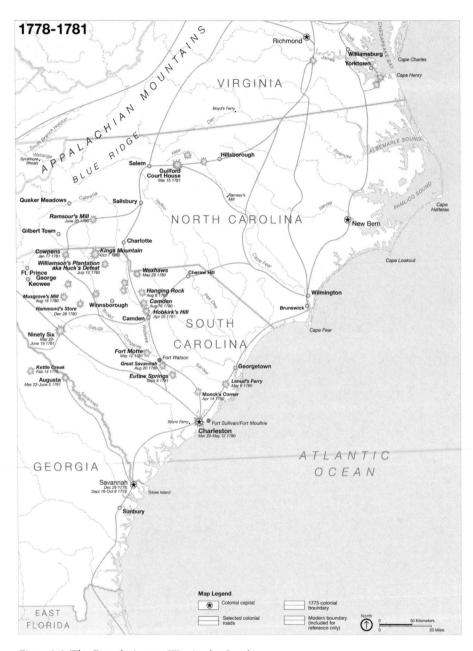

Figure 1.1 The Revolutionary War in the South

CHAPTER 1

The Southern Backcountry Before the American Revolution

*The settlers who swarmed into the
backcountry before and after the Cherokee
War created a distinct society in South
Carolina, a society out of touch with
Charleston . . .*
Robert Stansbury Lambert, South Carolina
Loyalists in the American Revolution

*We are Free-Men—British Subjects—Not
Born Slaves—We contribute our Proportion
in all Public Taxations, and discharge our
Duty to the Public, equally with our Fellow
Provincials Ye[t] We do not participate with
them in the Rights and Benefits which they
Enjoy, tho' equally entitled to them.*
Rev. Charles Woodmason, South Carolina
"Regulator's Remonstrance"

In May 1780, after a long siege, British troops under the command of General Henry Clinton captured Charles Town and roughly 5,000 Continental soldiers. A month later, Clinton's successor as commander of the southern army, General Charles Cornwallis, wrote that the British had put "an end to all resistance in South Carolina." It seemed that British victory, at least over the Southern colonies, was imminent. Scarcely more than a year later, Cornwallis surrendered to George Washington at

Yorktown ending the last large-scale confrontation of regular troops in the long war for American independence. The surprising reversal in British fortunes was largely the result of bitter warfare in the Carolina backcountry and two turning point battles—at Kings Mountain and Cowpens. This book is the story of that backcountry conflict and those turning point battles.[1]

The American South is so identified with the Civil War that people often forget that the key battles from the final years of the American Revolution were fought in Southern states. Nearly 20 percent of total combat deaths from the entire Revolutionary War occurred in South Carolina. The Southern backcountry may have been at the center of the fight for independence, but backcountry devotion to the Patriot cause was slow in coming. For decades before the American Revolution, social, political, and religious animosities had smoldered between coastal elites who controlled the colonial governments in North and South Carolina and backcountry settlers who did not enjoy adequate representation in their colonial assemblies or legal systems sufficient for maintaining law and order. Seething conflicts between lowcountry and backcountry citizens would help shape the character of the Revolutionary War in the South. The backcountry war was more like a civil war than a war between nations; it was a fight between Americans and Americans. For example, only one soldier at the Battle of Kings Mountain was British: the Scotsman Patrick Ferguson. All the rest of the combatants—on both sides—were Americans. Throughout the war, the numbers of "redcoats" on the Southern battlefields remained relatively small. To understand this war between Americans and Americans, it is necessary to understand something about Southern colonial life before the Revolution.[2]

THE SOUTHERN BACKCOUNTRY

Eighteenth-century Southerners referred to the area more than fifty miles inland from the coast as the backcountry. The distinction between lowcountry and backcountry was rooted in geography. Lowcountry terrain was just that: close to sea level. Tidewater streams and swamps traversed the lowcountry's coastal plain. By contrast, the backcountry included sand hills, piedmont, and large expanses of hardwood and pine forests. The far western reaches of the backcountry stretched into the foothills of the Appalachian Mountains.[3]

The Southern backcountry of South Carolina and North Carolina was colonized beginning in the 1740s by Scots-Irish, English, German, Swiss, Welsh, Moravian, and Huguenot settlers. The vast majority of backcountry settlers entered by the "back door," arriving not from the coast, but via the Great Philadelphia Wagon Road or the Great Indian Trading Path from Pennsylvania and Virginia. Georgia's frontier was settled a bit later, and many of its newcomers were North and South Carolinians fleeing the violence of the Cherokee War and the Regulator Movements. Between 1763 and 1773, the provincial governments gained millions of acres from the Indians, and royal officials in Georgia and South Carolina used generous land grants to lure new settlers to the backcountry. South Carolina was also known for its relative religious tolerance. Most of the determined backcountry settlers in that colony rejected Anglican worship for one of the several dissenting Protestant sects: Presbyterian, Baptist, or Methodist. By the 1760s, about 35,000 white people lived in the South Carolina back-country alone. Some backcountry settlers were squatters, eking out a living on land to which they did not hold title. A few engaged in lively and profitable trade with the Indians, but most were yeoman farmers and artisans who earned a living through subsistence and market-oriented pro-duction of wheat, tobacco, hemp, butter, and livestock that they sold in Charles Town, Wilmington, or Savannah. Many of these backcountry farmers had ambitions of becoming slave-owning planters. By the time of the Revolutionary War, slaves made up about one-fifth of the backcountry population.[4]

The distances that separated backcountry settlers from the lowcountry founders of the far Southern colonies generated tensions. Few roads connected the backcountry settlements to the coastal towns, and overland travel was arduous and time-consuming. It took at least a week to travel from the backcountry settlement of Ninety Six, South Carolina, to Charles Town, and two weeks from the frontier settlements at Long Canes, further west. Backcountry settlers had some contact with Charles Town where they traveled to trade, and backcountry news was sometimes featured in the Charles Town newspapers. Nonetheless, many backcountry folk lived an isolated existence in territory where most homesteads were primitive and widely scattered with few of the legal or social controls found in the more densely populated coastal regions.[5]

ANXIETY IN THE BACKCOUNTRY—THE 1750S

In the backcountry, settlers lived in an uneasy truce with native Americans. In the mid-eighteenth century, the Cherokee and Catawba Indian nations resided in the Carolina backcountry while the Creeks occupied Georgia's frontiers. All three groups had early forged a trading partnership with the British, but tensions between white settlers and Indians persisted. A small nation, numbering only about 1,700 in the mid-eighteenth century, the Catawba subsisted through a combination of hunting, fishing, and farming. After the arrival of the Europeans, they also engaged in a vigorous trade. A few decades of conflict with white settlers nevertheless took its toll on the small nation, and their numbers dwindled. In 1763 South Carolina's

The Cherokee Indians in the Southern Backcountry

By the time Europeans began to explore the southeastern part of North America, the Cherokee were the most powerful of the Indian tribes residing in the region. At one time, the Cherokee nation controlled at least 140,000 acres in the southeast. They combined hunting and gathering with agriculture to supply their needs. Men hunted and fished while women cultivated the land and gathered wild food. They lived in settled villages that governed themselves democratically; political power was decentralized, and villages were largely autonomous, but the nation acted in a united way for most military actions.

The Cherokees first came into contact with Europeans in 1540 when an expedition led by Spaniard Hernando de Soto passed through their territory. A second Spanish expedition led by Juan Pardo in 1567 established six forts in Cherokee country, but the Indians rose against the Spanish, killing the soldiers stationed there and burning all the forts forcing the Spanish to retreat to the coast. Only with the arrival of English settlers in the seventeenth century did the Cherokee come to have sustained contact with Europeans. First they developed trade relationships with Virginians, and after the establishment of Carolina (later divided into North and South Carolina), European trade became an integral part of the Cherokee economy.

Throughout the eighteenth century, European disease and intermittent warfare with other tribes, often on behalf of the British, took a toll on the Cherokee nation, but they remained the most powerful tribe in the southeast. The incursion of increasing numbers of white settlers chipped away at Cherokee territorial integrity as well as they were pressured to cede increasing amounts of land to whites. In 1738 and 1739, nearly half the Cherokee population died in a smallpox epidemic. With blessings from the Cherokee, the British built forts in Cherokee country to defend against other tribes and the French, including Fort Loudoun in present-day Tennessee and Fort Prince George in modern-day South Carolina. These forts would be at the epicenter of Cherokee involvement in the revolutionary ferment.

Indian agent, John Stuart, negotiated the Treaty of Augusta. Ratified by the South Carolina Assembly, the treaty granted the Catawba a reservation in the north central part of the colony. The fact that colonial officials allowed the Catawba to remain permanently in the colony indicates that whites did not see the few Catawba as a significant threat to their security or their land-hungry ambitions.[6]

The Cherokee were far more numerous than the Catawba, and they had a long history of interdependent relations with the British. In 1693, a group of Cherokee journeyed to Charles Town to sign a treaty of friendship and ask for firearms to protect themselves against other Indian nations, an event that marked the beginning of the nation's sustained contact with the British. Over time, the desire for guns and iron tools led the Cherokee to develop a vigorous trade in deerskins with the Europeans. By 1710, 50,000 deerskins a year were being exported from Charles Town, most of them the product of Cherokee hunting. The possession of firearms and iron tools enabled the Cherokee to become more productive hunters and farmers, but their increasing thirst for deerskins also caused them to encroach on other tribes' hunting territories. In the 1710s and 1720s, the Cherokee fought wars with all of the neighboring Indian nations: the Shawnee, Creeks, and Catawba. Trade continued to grow throughout the mid-eighteenth century; by 1747, the value of deerskin shipments from Charles Town equaled the combined total of shipments of indigo, beef, pork, lumber, and naval stores. A looming deer shortage escalated the friction between natives and whites and between the Cherokee and other nations.[7]

For their part, the British not only enjoyed the fruits of the deerskin trade, but they also valued the buffer that the Cherokee provided between British settlers and Indians further west. For this reason official royal policy was to maintain good relations with the powerful southeastern nation, a policy not particularly popular with backcountry settlers. John Stuart, the Superintendent of Indian Affairs, saw whites as the chief threat to peace, and he pursued measures to protect the welfare of Indians and maintain their landholdings. To prevent abuse by traders, he successfully lobbied the British government to license traders, restrict the sale of rum, and fix prices for trade goods, putting him at odds with backcountry settlers.[8]

By the mid-eighteenth century, backcountry distrust of the Crown's management of Indian relations escalated even as the Cherokee suffered a precipitous population decline due to disease and inter-tribal warfare. Roughly 8,000 Cherokee warriors lived in towns scattered in the Southern mountains, where they faced increasing pressure from the hordes of white settlers moving in around them. In 1755, the secretary to the royal governor of South Carolina toured the backcountry. He reported in the previous year alone, 300 families from Pennsylvania had arrived in the area around the Saluda River. The encroachment of white settlers on backcountry land was a source of frustration for the Indians, but in the near term, the Cherokee believed the Creeks on their Western frontier posed a bigger threat than white colonists. They prevailed upon their British trading partners for protection, and the British built and staffed two forts, Fort Prince George near Keowee and Fort Loudoun in East Tennessee. The Cherokee would come to regret inviting British troops into the heart of their tribal territory.[9]

THE CHEROKEE WAR—1759–62

In the 1750s, French officials and traders made a concerted effort to undermine the Anglo–Cherokee relationship, and tensions mounted between the great European power and the strongest native nation in the southeast. When the French and Indian War broke out, the British expected the Cherokee to fight enemies of the Crown, and officially the tribe remained an ally of the British. Some warriors, however, joined the French cause. Yet fighting between the British and their native allies and the French and their native allies was only one facet of the backcountry hostilities during the French and Indian War. In this period, tensions on the edge of white civilization led to trouble. For example, in 1758, a group of Virginia frontiersmen killed some thirty Cherokee warriors who were returning home after fighting with British forces attacking Fort Dusquesne. Then in 1759, English soldiers garrisoned in the Lower Towns (the South Carolina towns of the Cherokee) raped some Cherokee women. In his study of British–Cherokee relations, historian Tom Hatley said that "Cherokee discontent built slowly like a thundercloud at the foot of the mountain." The Cherokee took revenge by attacking isolated Carolina settlements, an action that in turn led to reprisals from the colonists. Isolated backcountry fighting in 1759 prompted South Carolina's Royal Governor, William Henry Lyttleton, to launch an expedition to Fort Prince George, the British garrison at Keowee in the Lower Towns. He seized a number of tribal leaders and held them as hostages, using them as leverage to negotiate a peace treaty. The treaty did not hold. Early in 1760, Cherokee warriors surrounded Fort Prince George, lured an officer outside the walls and killed him. The English troops inside the fort retaliated by killing the Cherokee hostages. The resulting conflict became known as the Cherokee War.[10]

Attacks and counter-attacks escalated throughout 1760 and 1761, marked by barbarous assaults on both sides. In one attack in early 1760,

Cherokees ambushed a wagon train of about 250 settlers trying to flee to safety in Augusta. Forty people were killed or captured, most of them women and children. The victims included the grandmother of John C. Calhoun (a future South Carolina political leader and vice president of the United States). Eyewitness accounts reported that bodies left at the scene were "inhumanely butchered." The colonists met brutality with brutality. After a large number of Indians were killed during a 1760 siege near Ninety Six, Governor Lyttleton said, "We have now the Pleasure Sir to fatten our Dogs with their Carcasses, and to Display their Scalps, neatly ornamented on the Top of our Bastions." Two Indians killed in an attack on Rebb's Fort had their bodies "cut to Pieces and given to the Dogs, so much [were] the Back-Settlers exasperated at their Perfidy and Barbarity."[11]

As the war dragged on, the South Carolina Assembly offered a bounty on Indian scalps encouraging an escalation of violence. Many white settlers moved into crowded makeshift forts where disease was rampant, and they appealed to Charles Town for help. Other backcountry settlers abandoned their homes for safer settlements closer to the coast. A former missionary to the Cherokee, William Richardson, wrote, "If some speedy assistance is not afforded the frontiers will, we are afraid, be immediately deserted . . ." The South Carolina Assembly appropriated relief funds for the refugees, but some of the owners of private forts embezzled the funds. The winter of 1760–1761 proved particularly hard for both sides; the Cherokee people suffered from hunger while about 1,500 whites spent the winter crowded into backcountry garrisons where their

> Reverend William Richardson, former missionary to the Cherokee, wrote, "If some speedy assistance is not afforded the frontiers will, we are afraid, be immediately deserted."

ranks were ravaged by food shortages and smallpox. The homes and farms abandoned by refugees were looted and seized by both thieves and militiamen. The fighting finally ended in summer 1761 when a force of British regulars and South Carolina militia marched into the Cherokee country and defeated them, burning villages and destroying fields and orchards and livestock. At last, exhausted and their ranks decimated by hunger, disease, and warfare, the Indians sued for peace. A treaty was signed in December 1761, marking the beginning of a steady erosion of Cherokee territorial holdings. The tribe would soon lose additional land in the 1763 Treaty of Augusta, the same agreement that created the Catawba reservation, which established new eastern boundaries for the Cherokee nation, stripping them of most of their South Carolina landholdings.[12]

PERSISTENT CHAOS AND VIOLENCE—THE SOUTH CAROLINA REGULATOR MOVEMENT

Even after the Cherokee War ended, a chaotic state of affairs persisted in the backcountry. The war had left many settlers destitute, especially of food, because they had been unable to plant and harvest crops. After the war, some people no longer bothered to cultivate crops, fearing they might be destroyed in future warfare. Contemporary observers reported that some people found stealing easier than working for a living. Respect for property rights seemed to have vanished during the war as even members of the militia stole from abandoned homesteads. Sizable settlements of people characterized by respectable backcountry folk as "lower sorts" lurked in isolated forests where they operated as bandit groups, stealing and extorting from respectable folk. They tortured people in an effort to learn where money was hidden, often applying hot coals to the feet until the victims divulged whatever information the bandits wanted. Thugs stole horses, and they raped and kidnapped women and girls, sometimes forcing them to become mistresses to the outlaws from whom they learned to be "bold in Sin." Merchants and tavern owners were coerced into fencing stolen goods; those who refused to cooperate with the thieves became targets themselves. As the 1760s wore on, the crime wave escalated.[13]

One example of the heinous behavior of the outlaw gangs was the attack on Savannah River merchant John "Ready Money" Scott. Scott was famous for paying for goods in cash, an unusual practice in a society where bartering was more common. Knowing that he kept large amounts of money on his property, four men attacked Scott and his wife, throwing snuff in Mrs. Scott's eyes to curb her resistance. They hit Scott on the head, then bound and blindfolded him, before burning him with a hot iron until he revealed where he had hidden his money. Another gang, dressed as Indians, invaded the home of aging backcountry storekeeper Dennis Hayes. They bound him, took £3,000 worth of goods, and raped Mrs. Hayes and their ten-year-old daughter.[14]

Historians have struggled to understand the causes of the dreadful violence that plagued the South Carolina backcountry in the 1760s. The pre-eminent modern historian of South Carolina, Walter Edgar, argues that the crime problem in the Carolina backcountry was part of "a larger pattern of lawlessness on the frontier from northern Georgia to western Pennsylvania." In his study of the South Carolina Regulator Movement, historian Richard Maxwell Brown says that backcountry disorder was symptomatic of a "fundamental social disunity." He emphasizes the essential divisions among the diverse backcountry settlers and between backcountry settlers and the privileged lowcountry citizens. There is no doubt that the devastation wrought by the Cherokee War played a large role in the "disunity" of the backcountry.[15]

Whatever its roots, the uncontrolled violence exacerbated the social, political, and religious animosities that had smoldered between coastal elites and backcountry settlers for decades. South Carolina was a wealthy colony, and Charles Town was the fourth largest city in the British North America, but backcountry settlers felt far removed from the cosmopolitan prosperity of the provincial capital. The lowcountry was well organized with an established court and law enforcement system and ample representation in the colonial assembly. The backcountry, however, was not so fortunate. They had no law enforcement except the justices of the peace who heard civil cases. With no courts or administrative offices in the backcountry, settlers were forced to travel to Charles Town to register a deed, swear out a warrant, or file a lawsuit. An occasional visit from a tax assessor was likely to be the frontier resident's only contact with government. In spite of the lack of services the backcountry received from the provincial government, the Provincial Assembly taxed crude backcountry farms at same rate as the wealthy plantations of the lowcountry, and Charles Town officials dictated that backcountry men organize themselves into militia units to aid in defense of the colony. Yet even as they fulfilled these citizenship duties, the backcountry residents found themselves politically marginalized; in South Carolina, for example, the backcountry districts boasted fully 80 percent of the colony's white population, but they had only two representatives in the colonial assembly. Backcountry citizens had requested additional seats in the assembly, but the colonial government, led by the royal governor, refused to create new counties—and thus new assembly seats—until the backcountry settlers agreed to support the Anglican Church. Since many of them were members of "New Light" or Calvinist Protestant sects—mostly Baptists and Presbyterians—there was little chance of that happening.[16]

Lowcountry/backcountry tensions escalated in the wake of the breakdown of good order in the backcountry. Because of the lack of a court system, marauders were rarely prosecuted. Even when they did face trial, few of the perpetrators of backcountry violence paid for their crimes. Six members of one bandit gang captured and sent to Charles Town for trial were convicted for a variety of crimes. However, Royal Governor Montagu pardoned five of them, enraging the backcountry's law-abiding citizens.[17]

Finally in 1767, respectable backcountry folk had had enough. Since repeated appeals to the colonial government in Charles Town for assistance with law enforcement had been ignored, leading backcountry men decided to take the law into their own hands. In doing so, they were joining an established tradition in frontier America—vigilantes who acted outside the legal system to restore law and order. Their motivations were hardly simple, however. The leading men were also ambitious, and they believed that punishing the outlaws would indeed return peace and safety to backcountry people but they also expected to restore the stability that would make economic prosperity possible. In other words, they believed that quelling the lawlessness would make it possible for the ambitious among them to prosper again. The respectable folk who organized themselves and took "the most vigorous measures to clear the country of the whole gang" came to be known as the South Carolina Regulators. The Regulators launched all-out war on the backcountry outlaws. They burned bandit hideouts and whipped those they caught. They rounded up gang members and their families, tying them to trees and lashing them. They ambushed gangs with gunfire. They even held their own trials and executed the worst of the criminals.[18]

The Regulators included many of the most prominent citizens of the backcountry including small planters and men of more substantial means, and many of them went on to hold government appointments and elective offices and to accumulate considerable wealth. Historians estimate that while somewhere upwards of 3,000 to 6,000 men participated in the movement at various times, an active nucleus of 500 performed most of vigilante activity. Among the best known names were James Mayson of Ninety Six and William Wofford from the area that would soon become the Spartan District. Militia commander Robert Cunningham was also a Regulator.[19]

> Anglican minister Charles Woodmason wrote, "[F]or many Years past, the Back Parts of this Province hath been infested with an infernal Gang of Villains, who have committed such horrid Depredations on our Properties and Estates—Such Insults on the Persons of many Settlers and perpetrated such shocking Outrages thro'out the Back Settlements, as is past Description."

In November 1767, the Regulators submitted to the Commons House a sharply worded statement of grievances, drafted by Charles Woodmason, a fiery Anglican missionary to backcountry congregations. Woodmason had long been a critic of the wildness and immorality he witnessed among backcountry residents, and he was ardent in his support of Regulator attempts to restore order. In addition to a statement of grievances, the document he authored outlined twenty-three requests intended to provide the backcountry with institutions that would restore

Charles Woodmason, Backcountry Missionary

An Anglican missionary to backcountry settlements in the 1760s, Charles Woodmason recorded his observations of backcountry life and culture in a travel journal. English-born, Woodmason emigrated to Charles Town in 1752. He acquired land in the Pee Dee River basin, and established a plantation cultivated by slaves. He also established a store on a branch of the Black River. Woodmason became a church and political leader, being elected a church warden, a militia commander, and a justice of the peace. This period of prosperity and success did not last; Woodmason's fortunes took a turn for the worse after he returned to England in 1762 to settle the estate of the wife he had left behind. In his absence, his land and property was sold to satisfy his debts. The man who returned to South Carolina a year later was forced to rebuild his life from reduced circumstances.

Through influential friends, Woodmason was appointed to more than one official government position, and he became a popular fixture in Charles Town society until he made the mistake of applying for a position as an official distributor of the infamous revenue stamps required by the Stamp Act. Woodmason had not anticipated the harsh reaction that Stamp Tax would provoke among many of his fellow South Carolinians. Soon the popular man-about-town became a pariah, a target for the popular indignation at British intrusions upon colonial self-government. In 1765, Woodmason decided to leave the tense atmosphere of Charles Town. He applied for a position as an itinerant Anglican minister in the sparsely-settled frontier of upper St. Marks Parish. After his ordination, he embarked on a new career, saving souls for the Anglican church and rescuing backcountry folk from the evils of the dissenting religions that were gaining favor on the frontier.

Shocked at what he saw as the depravity of many backcountry residents, Woodmason lamented, "It will require much Time and Pains to New Model and form the Carriage and Manners, as well as Morals of these wild Peoples." He said,

> Most of these People had never before seen a Minister, or heard the Lords Prayer, Service or Sermon in their Days. I was a Great Curiosity to them— And they were as great Oddities to me. After Service they went to Revelling Drinking Singing Dancing and Whoring—and most of the Company were drunk before I quitted the Spot—They were as rude in their Manners as the Common Savages, and hardly a degree removed from them. Their Dresses almost as loose and Naked as the Indians, and differing in Nothing save Complexion . . .

Woodmason's journal provides today's reader with a rich, if sometimes unflattering and unfair, portrait of the backcountry in the eighteenth century. Woodmason would eventually become furious at the Charles Town government's neglect of backcountry affairs, especially in the wake of the violence that pervaded the region after the Cherokee War. He fiercely defended the Regulator Movement and criticized elite Charles Town political leaders.[20]

law and order. Among them: a system of courts and courthouses and jails. Woodmason wrote,

> . . . [F]or many Years past, the Back Parts of this Province hath been infested with an infernal Gang of Villains, who have committed such horrid Depredations on our Properties and Estates—Such Insults on the Persons of many Settlers and perpetrated such shocking Outrages thro'out the Back Settlements, as is past Description.

He chided the assembly for ignoring previous requests for help, but

> instead of Public Justice being executed on many of these Notorious Robbers (who have been taken by us at much Labour and Expence and Committed) and on others (who with great difficulty and Charge have been arraigned and convicted) We have to lament, that such have from Time to Time been pardon'd and *afresh* set loose among Us, to repeat their Villanies . . .

Because of the assembly's inaction and Governor Montagu's pardon of convicted bandits, Woodmason explained, "many among Us have been obliged to punish some of these Banditti and their Accomplices in a proper Manner."[21] In language strikingly similar to that that had been used by various Charlestonians during the Stamp Act protests two years earlier, he wrote, "We are *Free-Men*—British Subjects—Not Born *Slaves*—We contribute our Proportion in all Public Taxations, and discharge our Duty to the Public, equally with our Fellow Provincials Ye[t] We do not participate with them in the Rights and Benefits which they Enjoy, tho' equally entitled to them." In short, the Regulators blamed the backcountry unrest on the colonial government which had ignored the needs of their backcountry brethren for years.[22]

Offended by the tone of the petition and by the fact that its author, Woodmason, had been a supporter of the Stamp Act, the Commons House first tabled the petition. The imperial crisis was becoming intertwined with the provincial one. After some delay and apologies from the Regulators for giving offense, the Commons House authorized two companies of mounted Rangers to help Regulators restore order, something they managed to accomplish within a few months. Using intelligence from the Regulators, the Rangers captured many outlaws and flogged or hanged them. The most notorious were sent to Charles Town for trial. If convicted, they faced hanging or branding. By March 1768, the backcountry outlaws had been defeated. In April, the Assembly passed an act creating circuit courts in the backcountry. Many settlers breathed a sigh of relief, hoping that tranquility would soon reign.[23]

Unfortunately, even after the Rangers were disbanded and courts were authorized, the Regulators did not stop their extralegal activities. Many Regulators believed there were still "Rogues, and other Idle worthless, vagrant people" who needed to be punished or driven from the back-country. In 1768, the Regulators gathered in the Saxe Gotha District on Congaree Creek and passed a "Plan of Regulation," a document that functioned as the law of the backcountry for nearly three years. Regulators began to interfere with the colonial courts by refusing to allow repre-sentatives of the court in Charles Town to serve warrants, and they attacked people to settle old scores and to punish those who criticized the Regulator movement. The vigilantes even began to extend their reach beyond those violating the laws to those violating community mores. Historian Tom Hatley points out that many of the targets of Regulator discipline were backcountry hunters and traders whose rough lifestyles made them little more than "white Indians" in the minds of their neighbors. The Regulators were especially suspicious of men who had liaisons with Indian women or people who lived on the margins of Cherokee country. Likewise, women who lived "wild" lives could become targets; for example, women suspected of fornication or adultery were whipped. Men were punished for failing to support their families. The Regulators tried to force those they saw as idle or vagrant to work against their will, and they prevented prosecution of Regulator leaders who had broken the law. Historians of vigilante movements have noted that these movements often spiral out of control in a manner similar to the trajectory of the Regulator movement. Once men have exercised extralegal authority, they are reluctant to give it up.[24]

It took a counter-vigilante movement called the Moderators to end the tyranny of the Regulators. The Moderators were made up of respect-able backcountry folk who had been attacked by the Regulators. John Musgrove, a planter from the Saluda River and Jonathan Gilbert, a justice of the peace from Beaverdam Creek, recruited men to help them suppress the Regulators. In March 1769, a stand-off ensued between the two groups. About 600 armed men from each side faced off near the junction of the Bush and Saluda Rivers. Cool heads prevailed at last; Richard Richardson from the Santee area and William Thompson of Orangeburg managed to negotiate a truce. Under pressure from the royal governor, the Commons House passed a new Circuit Court Act in 1769 that established additional courthouses and jails in Beaufort, Camden, Cheraw, Georgetown,

Orangeburg, and Ninety Six. The Regulator Movement fell silent, but backcountry settlers had deep-seated memories of the turmoil. These memories would resurface during the American Revolution.[25]

NORTH CAROLINA'S REGULATORS

North Carolina's backcountry was also home to a Regulator movement, one precipitated by similar tensions but with different catalyzing events. In contrast to their southern neighbor, North Carolina's backcountry districts boasted well-organized governments. Backcountry settlers nonetheless felt marginalized in provincial politics and abused by local officials. As in South Carolina, the Western counties were underrepresented in the provincial assembly. Westerners also had little control over local officials who were appointed by the governor. Local officials often used threats against settlers' land titles to charge excessive rents. They demanded payment of taxes in specie (gold coins or British currency), difficult to obtain for backcountry residents who relied on a barter economy. Judges and other court officials charged excessive fees. The eastern landowners who dominated their assembly levied high taxes on frontier farmers.[26]

The animosities burst into open revolt in 1767 when the assembly voted public funds to build an opulent new "palace" for Royal Governor William Tryon. Over the next two years, armed bands began to attack corrupt or abusive local officials. Backcountry North Carolina farmers organized themselves into a group called Regulators who aimed to "regulate" local affairs. The provincial government responded by standardizing fees and reining in local officials but also by attacking the protesters. In May 1771 at the Battle of Alamance, Regulator forces clashed with militia controlled by the provincial government. Governor Tryon ordered the ringleaders tried at Hillsborough where six Regulators were hanged. The governor's crackdown was effective; the North Carolina Regulator Movement was thoroughly suppressed, and many former Regulators moved to Georgia or East Tennessee to start new lives. However, because Governor Tryon had become a symbol of excess and abuse by royal officials, he was soon transferred to New York. He was succeeded by Josiah Martin, a diplomatic former army officer who was able to soothe some of the coastal/backcountry tensions in North Carolina.[27]

The violent events that had engulfed the backcountry in the 1760s would have repercussions for years to come. Thanks to the Cherokee War, backcountry residents had developed a well-organized militia system and guerilla tactics suitable for frontier fighting. They were adept at using small skirmishes, ambushes, and squads of mobile rangers to achieve military objectives and keep the enemy off-balance. The Regulator Movements in North and South Carolina also sowed seeds of bitter enmity both among backcountry settlers and between backcountry and lowcountry folks that would persist into the years of the Revolution. Meanwhile, in Charles Town and New Bern and Savannah, another kind of trouble was brewing: trouble between colonists and the mother country.[28]

CHAPTER 2

Imperial Crisis in the South

The fear of slaves on the one hand, and the military potential of mobilizing slaves on the other, gave a peculiar twist to the logic of war [in the southern colonies].
     Ray Raphael, *A People's History of the American Revolution: How Common People Shaped the Fight for Independence*

Threats of arbitrary impositions from abroad—& instigated Insurrections at home—are sufficient to drive an oppressed people to the use of arms.
     South Carolina General Committee

The Regulator Movements coincided with the early years of the imperial crisis. Both the response of colonial governments to the backcountry crisis and the personal grudges forged during those years would have important implications for the choices backcountry residents made during the American Revolution. While backcountry folks resented the coastal elites who insisted on lording over them, they were also becoming disillusioned with British government. After all, British officials had initially refused to set up courts and give them assembly representation. By the time of the imperial crisis, backcountry folks were used to being self-reliant, to worshipping without interference from the Church of England, and to dispensing their rough frontier justice. It would prove difficult for both the British and the opponents of British rule to control these backcountry folk.[1]

THE GROWING CONFLICT WITH MOTHER ENGLAND

In 1763, when the Treaty of Paris marked the official end of the French and Indian War, South Carolina seemed the least likely colony to move toward severing ties with the British government. The merchants of Charles Town were prospering from trade with London, Bristol, Liverpool, and Glasgow while rice and indigo planters grew rich from exporting their crops to England. Backcountry farmers were often grateful for the land grants they had received from England. But things turned around in the next thirteen years as the British government attempted to rein in the increasingly autonomous colonies. Not only did the British bungle attempts to bring the colonists back into the fold, but a number of fiery South Carolina patriots whipped up revolutionary sentiment. In this period, as later in South Carolina's history, events were shaped to a large degree by a few persuasive and magnetic personalities who helped push South Carolina toward independence. South Carolina nonetheless maintained a large Loyalist population.[2]

In South Carolina, tensions in relations between the British and the colonists appeared even before the Treaty of Paris was signed. The first conflict involved the amount of power that the Commons House (also called the Provincial Assembly), the colony's elected legislature, would wield. In December 1761, Royal Governor Thomas Boone arrived in South Carolina with instructions from the London Board of Trade to revise election laws in ways that would reduce the power of the Commons House. The legislature, however, refused to act on his instructions. Boone soon found an opportunity to retaliate. When Christopher Gadsden, a merchant and militia captain who was an outspoken critic of royal government in the colony, was elected to fill a vacant position in the assembly in 1762, Boone refused to administer the oath of office. He dissolved the assembly, accusing it of violating the election act. New elections were held, and defiant South Carolina voters again elected Gadsden by an overwhelming margin. The Commons House now demanded an apology from the governor; he refused. No public business was done in South Carolina during 1762 and 1763 because of this power struggle between the Commons House and the governor. South Carolinians resented other attempts by the British government to assert authority over them. During the French and Indian War, England had appointed regular British army officers to command colonial troops. Colonial soldiers chafed at the condescending arrogance with which they were treated by their superior officers.[3]

In contrast to the colonies farther up the eastern seaboard, at first the Southern colonists raised few alarms about the Navigation Acts. The Sugar Act and other legislation designed to raise revenue for the British did not distress South Carolina, in part because it included concessions for the rice trade. The Stamp Act proved to be another matter entirely. Imposed by Parliament in 1765 to raise revenue to pay for the costs of billeting a standing army in the North American colonies, the Stamp Act required that all printed material produced in the colonies be manufactured on paper embossed with a revenue stamp. More galling, the law required that the Stamp Tax be paid in British currency rather than paper money produced in the colonies. Like their fellows in other colonies, southerners were enraged by the Stamp Act. It constituted a direct tax, a tax levied by the Crown on individuals, rather than an indirect tax on goods. Moreover, the Stamp Tax affected all segments of the population from artisans and seamen to lawyers and laborers. Revenue stamps were required on newspapers, legal documents, books, playing cards, and apprenticeship agreements. Even marriage licenses had to include a revenue stamp in order to be valid.[4]

Southern cities erupted when news of the new tax reached the colonies. Local newspapers were flooded with letters to the editor protesting the new tax. The Charles Town newspapers also reprinted the speeches and tracts of Stamp Act opponents from up and down the East Coast. Legislators denounced the Stamp Act, arguing that the colonists had a legal right to tax themselves through their provincial assemblies and that any other direct tax on the population was unlawful. In response to an appeal from the Massachusetts Assembly, the South Carolina Commons House elected three representatives to the Stamp Act Congress, a meeting of representatives from all the colonies scheduled to meet in New York City in October to plan collective action. Meanwhile, the common folks took their own action. A loosely organized group of Charles Town Whigs calling themselves the Sons of Liberty organized demonstrations asserting their "rights as Englishmen." They argued that because they did not have voting representatives in Parliament, they were being taxed without their consent. Protestors erected a gallows and hung an effigy of a stamp collector. When a shipment of the infamous revenue stamps arrived in Charles Town Harbor in the fall of 1765, acting Royal Governor William Bull ordered them secured so that the mob would not seize and destroy them. Fearing for their lives, the Charlestonians who had been appointed to serve as stamp tax collectors took refuge on a ship in the harbor. For nine days, a mob roamed the city searching the homes of

Whigs, Patriots, or Rebels; Loyalists or Tories?

The multitude of names given to people on both sides of the revolutionary conflict can be confusing, and the labels themselves are loaded with ideological meaning. Today, we most commonly refer to those who supported the cause of independence as Patriots, a term that denotes someone who loves, honors, and defends his country. During the revolutionary era, however, southerners who supported independence were usually called Whigs. The term Whig referred to a seventeenth- and eighteenth-century British political party that was suspicious of the concentration of political power and believed it was necessary to jealously guard individual liberties. Whigs favored a constitutional monarchy and a separation of powers; they called for the superiority of Parliament over the monarch. They also supported toleration of Protestants who dissented from the Anglican Church. In the revolutionary era, British Whigs were opposed to the government of Lord North, prime minister from 1770 to 1782. As the most visible British policymaker, North became a symbol of British tyranny to many Americans; American opponents of British policy in the colonies often called themselves Whigs in order to identify themselves as champions of republican government and individual liberties. To the British, of course, those who resisted British government were simply rebels, men engaged in treason against the legitimate government.

The terms used for those who opposed independence carried similar ideological implications. They usually called themselves Loyalists to signify their loyalty to the Crown. Their enemies, the Whigs, called them Tories. In England, Tories were politically conservative and supported the supremacy of the monarchy and the Anglican Church. Lord North was a Tory; thus Americans who opposed British policy and advocated independence came to identify Americans who fought to maintain British control with North's party.

anyone suspected of supporting the Stamp Act, and protestors staged a funeral procession for "American Liberty" complete with a coffin. After a few days the stamp tax collectors returned to shore and resigned their positions. North Carolina and Georgia saw similar protests. In Wilmington, citizens successfully pressured the Stamp Tax collector to resign. In Georgia, "Sons of Liberty" confronted the royal governor with demands that he not enforce the Stamp Tax; he resorted to locking the stamps away for safekeeping, hoping that the tumult would eventually subside.[5]

The controversy disrupted political life in the Southern colonies for months. Trade and legal business ground to a halt in South Carolina because Boone's successor as royal governor, William Bull, refused to reopen the courts or the port without the use of stamps for official business. A committee of the Assembly drafted an official response to the crisis, petitioning the king to protect the Commons House's right to tax the colony and make its own laws. Things were at an impasse until word reached Charles Town of the repeal of the Act in May 1766. Opponents celebrated with a grand illumination fueled by candles in windows of the city's houses.[6]

The actions taken by Parliament after it repealed the Stamp Act were at first little more than an irritation to most southerners. They largely ignored the Declaratory Act that asserted England's right to tax the colonies, but they were annoyed by the Currency Act, which said colonial currency would not be accepted as legal tender. The Currency Act led to a shortage in the colonial money supply, but the act did not spur loud objections. Then a new round of revenue acts passed in 1767, the Townshend Acts, caused another eruption of protest. Artisans, planters, and merchants resisted the Townshend Acts of 1767 with non-importation agreements and economic pressure against merchants who refused to sign them. In November 1768, the Massachusetts Assembly's circular letter (a letter circulated to the legislatures in other colonies) urging collective action against the Townshend Acts arrived in Charles Town. Royal Governor Charles Grenville Montagu warned the South Carolina Commons House to ignore the letter. House members ignored him and deliberated the collective action advocated by other colonies. The governor responded by dissolving the assembly, and he did not call the House into session until June 1769. Meanwhile most members of the Commons House had signed the non-importation agreement, and they were soon joined by many rank and file citizens. One study estimates that nearly half of all South Carolinians participated in the boycotts to protest the Townshend Acts. Assembly members met and created a committee of thirty-nine planters, merchants, and artisans to implement the agreement, which they mostly did by force and intimidation. The Committee of thirty-nine was one of several extra-legal organizations that functioned as something of a shadow government during the imperial crisis.[7]

At this stage in the imperial crisis, the primary vehicles for resistance to British policy were non-importation agreements, that is, boycotts of British goods. The success of boycotts depended on consumers being willing to forego the purchase of imported goods, sometimes at great personal inconvenience. Most imported items were purchased by women who managed household consumption. Manufactured cloth was the most commonly imported British product.

When women boycotted British cloth, they were forced to weave the cloth themselves, an enormously time-consuming task. Thus, the boycott's success depended on cooperation from women. Participating in the boycott was an inherently political action, and in an age when women had no legally-recognized political voice, the first political act of many women was to say "no" to the purchase of British goods and the payment of British taxes. The revolutionary ferment altered women's daily work lives and inspired many to see the domestic sphere as a location for political action.[8]

Revenue acts were only one source of colonists' exasperation with the Mother Country. The actions of dishonest judges and customs officers appointed by the British government also angered some colonists. Many customs officers took bribes to look the other way in enforcing the Navigation Acts while they punished honest merchants by enforcing petty

"Our Rights As Englishmen"

Americans who objected to British taxation policies often complained that the mother country was violating their "rights as Englishmen." At the outset of the imperial crisis, colonists believed themselves to be British citizens who owed their allegiance to king and country. They took pride in being citizens of the mightiest and freest nation in the world. Since the signing of the Magna Carta in 1215, English people had boasted the broadest range of individual rights of any people in the world, rights that evolved and expanded over the next five centuries.

The British constitutional system, built on centuries of legislation, case law, common law, judicial rulings, and petitions, was grounded in the idea of the supremacy of law. The purpose of law, in the British view, was to protect citizens against arbitrary authority—that is, any action that would limit, violate, or remove a citizen's rights without due process of law. In this system, legal processes existed to correct violations. In the colonies in particular, colonial legislatures had gradually succeeded in enshrining the idea that taxes should only be levied by representatives of the people (that is, by elected legislatures). Most Americans did not object to the idea that the British government could tax them indirectly—through duties on imports and exports, for example—but they were incensed at taxes that they were forced to pay directly to the British government, such as the Stamp Tax. Many colonists also believed that their rights were violated by the imposition of vice-admiralty courts, military-style courts that heard cases in which navigation laws were alleged to have been violated. Vice-admiralty courts did not use juries, leading American merchants who faced charges in these courts to object that they were being denied their due process rights. Finally, many Americans interpreted both the stationing of British troops in the colonies and the Coercive Acts that interfered with the operation of civilian-controlled government in Massachusetts as signs that the British intended to take away their rights and freedoms as Englishmen.

rules and seizing vessels for small infractions. An example was the 1767 seizure of two vessels belonging to Henry Laurens, Charles Town's richest merchant. Laurens sued, claiming that his property had been wrongfully seized. The case came before a vice-admiralty court, a juryless court that had jurisdiction over cases involving maritime activities. Vice-admiralty courts were a sore point with the colonists since they saw the courts as arbitrary and as a denial of their English rights to a jury trial. In this case, however, Laurens triumphed. The vice-admiralty judge released one vessel and let the customs officer keep the other. Laurens filed a successful damage suit against the customs officer. The official retaliated by confiscating another of Laurens's ships, offering to return it if Laurens would relinquish the damages awarded by the court. Laurens sued again, and the vice-admiralty judge released the vessel because of the customs officer's scheming. Though he ultimately won his cases, the episode radicalized the once loyal Henry Laurens into open opposition to British policy. He wrote four pamphlets about the case and the dangers that customs officials and vice-admiralty courts posed to American liberties and property.[9]

The actions of British officials were infuriating, but the colonists also instigated conflict. In 1770, South Carolina's assembly took two actions that angered the British government. First, the Commons House appropriated £1,500 for the Society of the Gentleman Supporters of the Bill of Rights. The money was to be used for the legal defense of English newspaperman John Wilkes, an ardent Whig who was accused of libeling King George. The colonial governor protested that the colonists did not have the right to appropriate money (paid out of their own taxes) without the approval of the governor and his council. The governor refused to release the funds, and in retaliation, the Assembly refused to pass a tax bill that year, effectively blocking the colonial government's revenue stream. The South Carolinians' second cheeky action was the Commons House's purchase and installation of a marble statue of William Pitt, the member of the British Parliament who had been instrumental in negotiating the repeal of the Stamp Act. Carved by English sculptor Joseph Wilton, the sculpture portrayed Pitt dressed in a toga with one arm holding the Magna Carta and the other extended upward. On July 5, 1770, it was erected at the intersection of Broad and Meeting streets. An inscription on its base read,

> In grateful memory of his services to his country in general and to America in particular, the Commons House of Assembly of South Carolina unanimously voted this statue of the Hon. William Pitt, Esq. who gloriously exerted himself by defending the freedom of Americans, the true sons of England, by promoting a repeal of the

Stamp Act in the year 1766. Time will sooner destroy this mark of their esteem than erase from their minds their just sense of his patriotic virtue.

Charlestonians' blatant celebration of efforts to undermine Parliamentary authority seemed impudent in eyes of colonial authorities. Both the appropriation for Wilkes's defense fund and the one for the Pitt statue struck at the heart of the issues dividing the colonists and the Mother Country—colonists' right to control their own taxes through their elected representatives.[10]

Between 1769 and 1771, Governor Montagu dissolved the South Carolina Commons House four times, each time holding new elections in an effort to seat a legislature more favorably disposed to Crown policies. His actions fueled the suspicions of South Carolina's citizens that he and other representatives of the British government were conspiring to deprive colonists of their rights as Englishmen. For all practical purposes, royal government in South Carolina ceased to exist in 1771, the last year in which any legislation was passed. From that point, various extralegal bodies of Whigs acted as the civil government of the colony until the adoption of a constitution in 1776. As historian Walter Edgar put it, "Most South Carolinians simply ignored the British establishment and went about creating an alternative government."[11]

As the preceding examples suggest, in the South Carolina lowcountry, local issues—issues about how the elected South Carolina assembly could spend its own tax money—were at least as important in escalating the imperial crisis as the issues of whether Parliament could tax the colonists. In the backcountry, too, local issues shaped the rising crisis and citizens' responses. In his community study of the Waxhaws, historian Peter N. Moore said,

> Neighborhood tensions that had festered over the previous decade informed patterns of resistance, dividing Whigs from Loyalists, and making neutrality increasingly difficult to maintain.

> A statue of William Pitt placed in Charles Town was inscribed: "In grateful memory of his services to his country in general and to America in particular, the Commons House of Assembly of South Carolina unanimously voted this statue of the Hon. William Pitt, Esq. who gloriously exerted himself by defending the freedom of Americans, the true sons of England, by promoting a repeal of the Stamp Act in the year 1766. Time will sooner destroy this mark of their esteem than erase from their minds their just sense of his patriotic virtue."

In its timing, its impact, and the patterns of its allegiances, the
Revolutionary War in the Waxhaws was very much a product of
the home front.[12]

In Georgia, revolutionary ferment developed more slowly than in
North or South Carolina because of the competence and political skills
of the royal governor. Governor James Wright managed to maintain
control until 1775 by keeping the most radical elements in the provincial
assembly in check. The Georgia assembly sent petitions demanding repeal
of the Stamp Act and the Townshend duties to London, and they also
adopted non-importation agreements, but Wright shut down the assembly
to prevent more drastic measures such as the election of an ardent Whig
as speaker of the assembly. In 1773, Wright was able to purchase some
temporary goodwill with most Georgians by acquiring a large land cession
from the Creeks. The popularity of the land cession proved temporary
because some Creeks, resisting the cession, launched frontier attacks in
late 1773. Wright negotiated a peaceful settlement to the fighting,
infuriating backcountry Georgia residents who had hoped Wright would
use the conflict as an excuse to seize still more land. In the midst of this

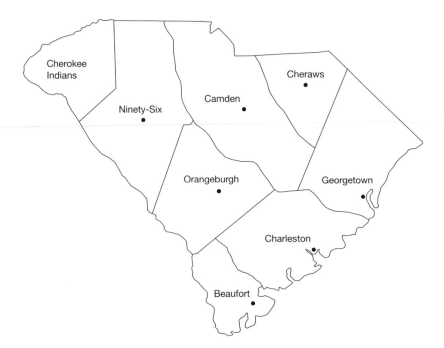

Figure 2.1 Election Districts in South Carolina—1769

dispute, Georgians largely ignored the Tea Act, the next major flashpoint in British–colonial relations.[13]

THE TEA ACT

The simmering tensions between the British government and her North American colonists came to a boil again with the passage of the Tea Act in 1773. The Tea Act was not intended to raise revenue; in fact, it imposed no new taxes. An early version of a corporate bailout, the Tea Act granted a monopoly on tea sales in all British colonies to the foundering British East India Company. Colonial agents were to act on the company's behalf in selling £18 million pounds of tea at a bargain price. The Act actually made British East India Company tea less expensive than that imported from the Dutch. For the colonists, however, the problem was that the sale of tea exclusively by authorized British agents would undercut colonial merchants. Whigs leaders saw the Act as a ploy to get them to abandon their opposition to British taxation by encouraging them to purchase the cheaper tea. When news of the Tea Act arrived in South Carolina followed by a shipment of tea on the *London* on December 1, 1773, Charles Town's Sons of Liberty called for a mass meeting to protest importation of the tea. Fearing reprisals from an unruly mob, the merchants designated as agents of the British East India Company announced at the meeting that they would not accept the tea. Others present agreed not to purchase or consume the tea and to encourage others to do likewise. To avert violence, Lt. Governor Bull confiscated the tea. It was unloaded from the *London* and stored in the basement of Charles Town's Exchange Building where it stayed until it was sold in 1776 to finance the purchase of war materiél by the patriots.[14]

Southern Whigs took steps to ensure that all people complied with the boycotts. At the Charles Town mass meeting protesting the Tea Act, delegates established a General Committee to enforce its resolutions not to purchase or consume British East India Company tea. This organization succeeded the Committee of thirty-nine as a shadow government. When word of the better-known Tea Act protest, the Boston Tea Party, reached Charles Town, Whig leaders expressed support of their Massachusetts brethren. Months later, many Southerners were shocked and outraged when word arrived of the Coercive Acts, also known as the Intolerable Acts. Intended to punish Massachusetts for the actions of the Tea Party protestors, the Coercive Acts closed the port of Boston until the British East India Company received restitution for the tea that had been thrown

Women and the Boycott of Tea

It quickly became apparent to southern Whigs that the boycott on tea and other British goods would never succeed without the cooperation of women. Not only were women the principal household purchasing agents, but they also regularly incorporated tea drinking rituals into their social occasions. As a result, Whig leaders seeking to enforce the boycott made it a point to issue appeals directly to Southern women. Reverend William Tennent, III, of South Carolina addressed the women of the colony in a newspaper editorial, calling on them to save the colony from the "Dagger of Tyranny" by giving up tea. He wrote, "Yes, ladies, you have it in your power more than all Your Committees and Congresses to strike the stroke" by giving up the trivial pleasures of drinking tea.[15]

Women themselves embraced this new political role. One Southern woman wrote to another during the boycotts following the Tea Act that she and her friends "commenced perfect statesmen" in the wake of the Act. In short, she meant that their boycott of British tea was a political act—the act of statesmen. The Tea Act also sparked the first women's political writing in Southern newspapers. "The Planter's Wife" wrote in the *South Carolina Gazette,* "Every mistress of a family may prohibit the use of tea and East India goods among her family." Southern women also organized to express support for the boycott. On October 25, 1774, Mrs. Penelope Barker organized a meeting of fifty-one women in Edenton, North Carolina. Together they formed an alliance wholeheartedly supporting the American cause against "taxation without representation." Their petition proclaimed that they would boycott tea because they were "determined to give memorable proof of their patriotism" and could not be "indifferent on any occasion that appears nearly to affect the peace and happiness of our country . . . it is a duty that we owe, not only to our near and dear connections . . . but to ourselves." Political organizing of this type scandalized many women and men in America and England alike, but these examples illustrate the extent to which the imperial crisis was politicizing daily life.[16]

into the harbor, thus crippling the Massachusetts economy. The Coercive Acts also altered the form of Massachusetts government in order to give the British more control, limiting the power of town meetings and allowing the British to appoint most government officials. Another element of the Coercive Acts was the Quartering Act that required all the North American colonies to pay for the support of British troops deployed to maintain order and British control.[17]

Southern Whigs feared that Coercive Acts were harbingers of future attacks on liberties. North Carolinians sent food and supplies to Massachusetts after Boston Harbor was closed. Defying the royal governor's order, North Carolina also elected its own provincial congress. Passage of Coercive Acts also captured the attention of Georgia Whigs who had recently been distracted by controversies over Creek lands. South Carolina's General Committee called for a meeting of representatives from all parts of the colony in Charles Town on July 6, 1774, to consider appropriate action and develop plans to enforce non-importation agreements. In response to a request from New England Whigs, the General Committee elected five lowcountry leaders to serve as delegates at this first Continental Congress. North Carolina also sent delegates, but Georgia did not.[18]

> "The Planter's Wife" wrote in the *South Carolina Gazette*, "Every mistress of a family may prohibit the use of tea and East India goods among her family."

The British were fast losing control of their North American colonies. At South Carolina's General Meeting, delegates elected a Committee of Ninety-Nine composed of 15 merchants, 15 mechanics, and 69 planters to serve as the governing body of the colony. Over the objections of royal officials, the Commons House appropriated funds to cover expenses of delegates to the First Continental Congress. The Committee of Ninety-Nine held elections for a provincial congress, made up of 187 delegates. The lowcountry was allocated 132 seats while the backcountry, with 60 percent of the white population, was allocated only 55 seats. Once again lowcountry elites were acting to ensure that they maintained control of the colony.[19]

The Provincial Congress became the third extralegal governing body of South Carolina. At its first meeting in Charles Town in early 1775, it adopted a non-importation agreement, chose five delegates to the Second Continental Congress, and prepared to resist British aggression. The Provincial Congress sought to consolidate its control of the colony by seizing official British government mail. By reading this mail, officials learned that the British intended to use force to restore authority, and the Provincial Congress voted to take more urgent action. The first overt act of Revolution occurred in Charles Town on April 21, 1775 when a secret committee of the Provincial Congress seized 1,600 pounds of gunpowder, 800 guns, and 200 cutlasses that belonged to the British government. The munitions had been stored in the Old Statehouse at the corner of Meeting and Broad Streets. Though the British were never able to identify and prosecute the culprits, they saw it as an act of rebellion.[20]

In Georgia, Whigs also convened a provincial congress in January 1775, and the new body ratified the Continental Association, an agreement developed by the First Continental Congress to boycott British goods until the mother country addressed colonial grievances. In-fighting inhibited the efforts of Georgia Whigs to determine on a course of action until news of the battles of Lexington and Concord galvanized support for Whig cause.[21]

AFRICAN-AMERICANS, INDIANS, AND THE IMPERIAL CRISIS

As the imperial crisis escalated, Southern Whigs worried that the British would incite African-Americans and Indians to rise against them. Fears of slave insurrections were especially acute in South Carolina, which was importing about 2,000 slaves a year during imperial crisis. Slaves constituted 59 percent of the colony's 174,500 inhabitants, and in the lowcountry, blacks outnumbered whites by nearly two to one. White South Carolinians carried vivid memories of the terrifying 1739 Stono Rebellion that resulted in the deaths of nearly 50 whites; a slave uprising was the deepest fear of many southerners.[22]

Slaves were politicized by the discussion of the imperial crisis that was taking place all around them, particularly discussions of John Locke's assertion that all men possessed natural rights to life, liberty, and property. Whig leaders used the language of slavery to appeal to supporters, comparing their own subjugation to English rule to the position of their slaves. For example, in June 1769, the editor of the South Carolina Gazette wrote, "we are real SLAVES as those we are permitted to command." The famous African seaman Olaudah Equiano witnessed the celebrations of the repeal of the Stamp Act in Charles Town, and he testified that many white sailors and artisans wore blackface to indicate their slavery to King George and strode through the streets chanting, "Liberty, Liberty." Slaves quickly learned to apply concepts of rights to themselves. A few weeks after the blackface parade, black South Carolinians began to echo that chant until slave patrols halted gatherings of blacks. Many in Charles Town worried that the city's slaves were "not under good regulation." British officials played on these fears; in 1766, Lieutenant Governor William Bull, Jr, warned the Assembly that 107 Colleton County slaves had left their plantations and were organizing an insurrection.[23]

Southern whites' anxieties that the British might exploit unrest among the black population were exacerbated by various events. In 1772, in the Somerset case, a British court ruled that slavery was unconstitutional in England and Wales on the grounds that "the state of slavery is of such a nature, that it is incapable of being introduced on any reasons, moral or political; but only positive law, which preserves its force long after the reasons, occasion, and time itself from whence it was created, is erased from memory: it's so odious, that nothing can be suffered to support it, but positive law." The decision sent shock waves through the American colonies as rumors of impending rebellions struck fear in the hearts of Southerners. On May 29, 1774, the *South Carolina Gazette* reported that London was sending a shipment of 78,000 guns and bayonets to the colonies "to put into the hands of N★★★★★s [Negroes], the Roman Catholics, the Indians, and Canadiens" all over North America. The next May, the South Carolina General Committee ordered Charles Town residents to organize a nightly patrol in order to "guard against any hostile attempts that made be made by our domesticks." In July 1775, the Pitt County, North Carolina Committee of Safety responded to a rumor of an insurrection plot by ordering patrollers to shoot any group of four or more African-Americans who were off their masters' plantations without permission. Anxieties about slave rebellions reached a fever pitch in the South in November 1775 when Virginia's royal governor, Lord Dunmore, issued his famed proclamation offering to free all indentured servants and Negroes who were willing to bear arms alongside British troops.[24]

> The South Carolina General Committee ordered Charles Town residents to organize a nightly patrol in order to "guard against any hostile attempts that made be made by our domesticks."

If lowcountry whites worried that the British might incite slaves to rise against them, backcountry settlers feared the potential of Indian attacks provoked by the British. Colonists themselves exacerbated these fears by continuing to encroach on Indian lands, thus encouraging native support of the British. For example, in 1775, North Carolina purchased a vast tract of land in the Appalachian Mountains for £10,000 of trade goods, prompting Indian opponents of previous land cessions to vow to resist white encroachment on Cherokee lands. As we have already seen, a comparable land cession from the Creeks in Georgia in 1773 had created similar problems. On the Southern frontier, tensions between white settler and Indians were running high.[25]

The Whigs were able to secure Catawba support for their cause, but their efforts to keep the Cherokee and Creeks neutral were largely unsuccessful. The Whigs were also correct in their belief that the British were seeking to retain their alliances with Native Americans. British agents tried to garner the support of Cherokees, Creeks, Choctaws, and Chickasaws. These four tribes boasted a fighting force of about 14,000. Early in 1776, John Stuart, the Indian superintendent for the Southern district, sent his brother Henry to Cherokee country with a supply of ammunition. His mission was to court Cherokee support of the British.

Henry Stuart reported that the Cherokee believed "it seemed to be the intention of the white people to destroy them from being a people." Henry Stuart implied that the Crown's Indian agents could succeed in unifying and controlling them, the Indians could potentially help the British retain control of the Southern colonies. However, uniting the four tribes would prove to be a difficult challenge. In fact, divisions within tribes proved to be at least as much an obstacle to British ambitions as intertribal animosities. Rifts among the Creeks and Cherokees led to divided allegiances among them when the Revolutionary War broke out. The Choctaws also faced internal divisions. They had fought their own civil war from 1747 to 1750, and they had been allies with the French until the end of the French and Indian War resulted in French expulsion from North America. Choctaw relations with the British had been strained by forced land cessions and bad behavior by the Indian agent assigned to them. They were also at war with Creeks, a war the British had encouraged. In short, the internecine state of tribal affairs, complicated by the inconsistent actions of British Indian agents would combine to undermine British efforts to secure alliances with southern Indians.[26]

By early 1775, royal officials in the Southern colonies found themselves increasingly powerless as Whigs undermined their authority at every turn. For their part, Whig opponents of British policy needed to obtain widespread support from Southern whites if they hoped to deter Britain's legislative power in the long term. The next few months would find both sides engaged in a campaign to win hearts and minds, especially in the backcountry.

CHAPTER 3

Revolutionary War and the Challenge of Winning Hearts and Minds

Eight months before the colonies declared their independence from Great Britain, the South Carolina backcountry was embroiled in a violent conflict between Whigs and Loyalists.

Rachel N. Klein, Unification of a Slave State: The Rise of the Planter Class in the South Carolina Backcountry, 1760–1808

In the month of Nov'r 1775, the South Carolina Militia . . . laid siege to a Fort erected by the rebels [Whigs] at Ninety-Six; . . . which continued for the space of three days and three nights—at the expiration of which the Rebels were forced to surrender and give up the Fort and Artillery.

Colonel David Fanning, Loyalist

In early 1775, Whig speakers in the South's coastal cities worked to raise anti-British sentiments to a fever pitch. News of the battles of Lexington and Concord in Massachusetts radicalized many southern Whigs, and events unfolded quickly in the spring and summer of 1775. In May 1775, the South Carolina Provincial Congress voted to raise three regiments of 500 men each. They also created a Council of Safety with virtually unlimited power to function as the executive power of the colony. The Congress also formed an Indian Department charged with countering British Indian agent John Stuart's efforts to secure Cherokee support for the Crown. On June 3, the Provincial Congress enacted a "Continental Association"—a pact in which signatories agreed to fight for recognition of their rights by the British; anyone who refused to subscribe to the association was defined as an enemy of the liberty of the colonies. Then on June 6, 1775, the Provincial Congress authorized formation of additional military units: two permanent regiments of foot soldiers and a regiment of rangers, mounted troops. The rangers would patrol the backcountry. Two prominent backcountry men—William Thomason and James Mayson—would lead the Rangers, and frontiersmen and militia from the backcountry staffed this regiment.[1]

WINNING HEARTS AND MINDS TO THE WHIG CAUSE

Because not all southerners supported the Whig cause, opponents of British policy enlisted impassioned rhetoric about their rights as Englishmen in their war of words. On June 30, the South Carolina Provincial Congress issued "A Circular Letter To The Committees In The Several Districts And Parishes Of South Carolina." The document outlined the offenses of the British at the battles of Lexington and Concord and defended the actions of both the Second Continental Congress and the South Carolina Provincial Congress as "important and justifiable steps to place your lives, liberties and properties, in a state of some security against the iron hand of tyranny . . ." If rhetorical persuasion did not quell dissent, the Council of Safety was prepared to silence critics by force. For example, William Wragg, an opponent of the Whigs, was banished to his plantation and ultimately hanged. Charles Town Whigs forced fellow citizens to comply with non-importation agreements. The Whigs also played on fears of slave revolts and Indian attacks to rally support. For example, in a widely publicized move, the Council of Safety ordered Thomas Jeremiah, a free black man who was a slaveholder and a harbor pilot, hanged after he was accused of plotting a slave insurrection and supporting the British.[2]

While vocal opponents of the actions of the Provincial Congress were easily silenced in Charles Town, pacifying critics in the backcountry proved more difficult. Historians differ on the extent to which back-country residents had chosen sides by 1775. Some have argued that backcountry folk were rather lethargic about the entire dispute with the Crown until they were forced to choose sides while other historians have maintained that most backcountry residents had declared allegiances by April 1775. Whatever the case, there is no doubt that there was a vocal opposition to Whig actions among backcountry citizens.[3]

Understanding that backcountry support was crucial to their cause, South Carolina's Provincial Congress dispatched a delegation to the hinterland to explain to backwoodsmen that they needed to join the Revolution because their liberties were threatened by King George and Parliament. The five members of the delegation included the Presbyterian minister William Tennent, Baptist minister Oliver Hart, Council of Safety member William Henry Drayton, and two prominent backcountry Whigs, Joseph Kershaw and Richard Richardson. In addition to the inclusion of two leading backcountry citizens, the choice of ministers from so-called dissenting sects (non-Anglicans) was calculated to appeal to the frontiersmen. Members of the delegation, who usually split up to make stump speeches in backcountry communities, received a mixed response. In July 1775, the Council of Safety ordered leading backcountry planter and militia captain Thomas Fletchall to assemble his men to sign the Association. One of Fletchall's men, David Fanning, reported, "Col'n Thomas Fletchall . . . present[ed] two papers for the Inhabitants to sign one was to see who was friends to the King and Government, and the other was to see who would join the Rebellion . . . There was 118 men signed in favor of the King . . ." Fletchall wrote Henry Laurens, president of the Council of Safety, declaring that not one of his men had signed the association and that he "utterly refuse[d] to take up arms against my king." He was joined by other influential citizens in decrying the actions of the Provincial Congress. Historian Rachel Klein has observed that Fletchall's Loyalism was particularly disturbing to Whigs because of his influence with fellow citizens.[4]

The delegation sometimes used threats to gain signatories to the Association, and their efforts met with mixed success. German settlers on the Congaree River refused to listen until Drayton and Tennent threatened them with dire consequences, resulting in 15 men signing the Association. A few days later at the Saluda River, Council of Safety delegates convinced only one person in their audience to sign. At King's Creek, Thomas "Burnfoot" Brown, a man whose legs had been tarred and held over a fire by a Patriot mob earlier in the summer, leaving him permanently crippled, denounced the Whigs as savages. Opposition to the Whig cause was especially intense around the frontier village of Ninety Six, the intersection of three major backcountry trading roads. The village of 100 settlers probably got its name because it was roughly 96 miles from the Cherokee trading town of Keowee. At Ninety Six,

Drayton debated several prominent backcountry Loyalists including Patrick and Robert Cunningham, Thomas Fletchall, and Moses Kirkland, all of whom refused to sign the Association. By contrast, the delegation was warmly received by Scots-Irish settlers east of the Saluda River, especially the ardent Whigs in the Spartan District who agreed to organize a new regiment of militia, the first of several additional volunteer units formed in the New Acquisition District as a result of the visits by the delegation.[5]

In the same period, Whig leaders from North Carolina cultivated support from their own backcountry settlers. Many leading Whigs had been among the coastal elites whom the Regulators blamed for the abuses against backcountry settlers, increasing backcountry men's skepticism about the Whig cause. Royal Governor Martin received assurances from some Regulator leaders that they would be loyal to the Crown, but Whigs used a combination of persuasion and intimidation and employed the influence of Calvinist and Presbyterian ministers to win over backcountry settlers to the Whig cause. Whigs drove many North Carolina Loyalists (often former Regulators) from their homes, making it hard for Governor Martin to mobilize a Loyalist militia.[6]

At the same time that Drayton and his delegation were trying to win the hearts and minds of backcountry citizens to the Whig cause, the South Carolina Council of Safety sent Major James Mayson to secure Fort Charlotte, a frontier outpost on the Savannah River, for the Whigs. In July 1775, he was successful, and he took the captured supplies thirty miles northwest to Ninety Six. Fearing that the munitions might be used against Loyalists, Robert and Patrick Cunningham and Joseph Robinson led Loyalist militiamen in a march to seize the supplies from Mayson's men. They placed Mayson under arrest for stealing Crown property on July 17, releasing him a few days later. In a situation indicative of the extent to which backcountry loyalties constantly shifted is the case of Moses Kirkland. Kirkland had served with Mayson at Fort Charlotte, but he apparently became worried about Whig intentions for the ammunition because he joined the Loyalist cause at this point.[7]

As the summer wore on, pressure on backcountry residents who refused to support the Whig cause increased. The Council of Safety blocked Loyalists from coming into Charles Town to do business, a form of economic pressure that was devastating to many poorer people who declined to sign the Continental Association. Drayton ordered the arrest of several prominent backcountry people who refused to comply with the terms of the Association. When the Loyalist opposition persisted, Drayton decided to try to neutralize them. He set up a negotiating session with the opposition, resulting in the Treaty of Ninety Six, signed September 16, 1775. The Treaty required non-associators to remain neutral in the conflict between Whigs and the English in return for being left alone by the Council of Safety. For a time, it seemed that conflict in the backcountry had been averted.[8]

CHOOSING SIDES

Historians have devoted considerable effort to identifying the factors that shaped citizens' decisions about whether to become Whigs or Loyalists. Historian Ray Raphael has noted that backcountry Loyalists shared the republican values of the revolutionaries and that Loyalists rarely justified their loyalty to the Crown on ideological grounds. Nor did Loyalists and Whigs divide neatly on religious or class lines. Some Loyalists were slaveholders, some were not. Some were Anglicans, some were not. Most Loyalists were recent arrivals to the southern backcountry, having migrated to the backcountry from Europe or another colony fewer than 15 years before, but other recent arrivals became revolutionaries. The backcountry divisions often reflected those of the old Regulator/Moderator conflict; most Regulators became Whigs, and most Moderators became Loyalists, but even this generalization does not hold in every case. In his history of the Loyalist movement in South Carolina, Robert Stansberry Lambert says that magistrates and justices of the peace who had had their power usurped by the Regulators often carried that resentment into the revolutionary years and as a result became Loyalists. Lambert also notes that veterans of British military service in the French and Indian War—as opposed to service in local militias—tended to remain loyal. Most Loyalists were Scots-Irish or German, but most Whigs were Scots-Irish as well.[9]

In the end, historian Rachel Klein says, "neighborhood affiliation, reinforced by ethnic, religious, and familial ties influenced the initial division between Whigs and loyalists."

Or, as Raphael put it, "This was a conflict of interests and personalities, not ideologies." The most ardent Loyalists and the most ardent Whigs were men of influence in their communities, and less prominent men followed their lead because it served personal interests. Rising backcountry slaveholders, men with political and military ambitions, often became Whigs because coastal Whigs recognized their ambitions and rewarded their choice to become Whigs. For their part, some Loyalists harbored deep-seated resentments against Whigs. For example, in early 1775, Robert Cunningham and Moses Kirkland were sympathetic to the Whig cause, but they became vocal Loyalists later that year; Andrew Pickens would later observe that they changed their minds after neither of them were chosen by the Council of Safety to lead a backcountry regiment. Robert

Cunningham's distant relative, William "Bloody Bill" Cunningham, did not become one of the most dreaded Loyalist militia leaders in the back-country until a band of Whigs killed his lame epileptic brother. Other men switched sides, depending on which side seemed to have the upper hand. William Green of South Carolina began the war as a captain in a Whig militia. When the British took Charles Town in 1780, he switched sides and joined a Loyalist militia. In October 1780, he fought on the British side at the Battle of Kings Mountain, but after that defeat he moved to North Carolina and joined the Whigs again.[10]

THE END OF ROYAL GOVERNMENT IN THE SOUTH

The royal governors of the Southern colonies struggled in vain to maintain their authority. In July 1775, following South Carolina's lead, a provincial congress assumed control of Georgia's affairs, and Governor Wright conceded that he could no longer enforce his authority. North Carolina's second provincial assembly met in April 1775 to elect delegates to the Second Continental Congress and to appoint a Council of Safety. By the end of May, beleaguered Royal Governor Josiah Martin had taken shelter in the British garrison at Fort Johnston for his own safety. In July, he fled to the *H.M.S. Crozier*, anchored off the North Carolina coast, where he would remain until the ship sailed in September 1776. Three days after he abandoned Fort Johnston, Whig forces seized it.[11]

Meanwhile in Charles Town, Royal Governor William Campbell tried to regain control of his colony. To prevent Patriots from taking over Fort Johnson, the principal fortification that guarded Charles Town Harbor, in September 1775 Campbell sent a landing party to neutralize or destroy the battery of cannons there. Soldiers dismantled the guns and left them at the fort unattended. Soon after, a contingent of Whig militia arrived and were delighted to discover that they could reassemble the guns. Soon the liberty flag was flying over Fort Johnson. This overt act of war com-mitted under the governor's nose did not bode well for British control. Also in the fall of 1775, the Council of Safety was able to seize Sullivan's Island from the British. Governor Campbell responded by formally dissolving the South Carolina assembly, closing Crown offices in Charles Town, and fleeing to the British warship *Tamar* in the harbor, taking the colony's seal with him. His intention was to hinder colonial actions, since official paperwork needed the colonial seal. He lived on the ship for two months hoping to restore Crown control to the colony, but that left the Provincial Congress with a free hand to run Charles Town. Governor Campbell also allowed some British ships to make raids on upriver plantations, carrying off goods and slaves. The British harbored runaway slaves, refusing Council of Safety demands that they be returned to their owners. In retribution, the Charles Town merchants who had been supplying Governor Campbell's ships ceased the sale of supplies leaving Campbell and British officials no choice but to leave the colony.[12]

THE FIRST BATTLE OF NINETY SIX AND THE SNOW CAMPAIGN

Meanwhile tensions persisted in the backcountry. Historian Walter Edgar has called the Treaty of Ninety Six "a calculated move to smoke out the enemies of the Revolution." Subsequent actions by the Whigs suggest that Edgar is right. After Robert Cunningham responded with harsh words to verbal provocations from Drayton, Cunningham was arrested and taken to Charles Town in chains. Soon other prominent Loyalists were arrested and their homes burned. The violations of the Treaty of Ninety Six led to the first bloodshed of war in the South in October and November 1775.[13]

Loyalist military action at Ninety Six was a response to a Council of Safety attempt to pacify the Cherokee on the frontier. Having had grave concerns that the Cherokee would side with the British, the Council made diplomatic overtures to the Indian nation. In September, Drayton warned Lower Town leaders that he met at the Congarees settlement about British treachery. He said, "If they use us, their own flesh and blood in this unjust way, what must you expect who are a Red People?" In the fall of 1775, reacting to rumors that the British Indian Department was urging the Cherokee to rise against backcountry whites, the Council of Safety decided to send the Cherokee 1,000 pounds of gunpowder and 2,000 pounds of lead to use in deer hunting. The Provincial Congress noted, "Experience has taught us, that occasional presents to the Indians has been the great means of acquiring their friendship." [sic] Hearing about the shipment, on November 3 nearly 2,000 Loyalists led by Robert Cunningham's brother Patrick intercepted the wagon train and seized the munitions near Ninety Six. The Council of Safety responded by issuing a declaration stating, "These wicked men [Loyalists], to the astonishment of common sense, have made many of their deluded followers believe, that this ammunition was sent to the Indians, with orders for them to fall upon the frontiers and to massacre the non-associators." The Council of Safety sent militia troops under the command of Major Andrew Williamson to retrieve the supplies from the Loyalists. Williamson and his lieu-tenants were able to recruit nearly 600 volunteers from the vicinity of

Ninety Six. Knowing that the Loyalists had a force of more than 1,500 men, Williamson ordered his men to erect a stockade at Ninety Six. Loyalist forces attacked Williamson and his troops on November 19. At the end of a day of skirmishing and two days of siege, which resulted in the deaths of a Loyalist and four Patriots, things were at a stalemate. Both sides agreed to go home.[14]

Many Loyalists did go home, but Whig troops lingered in the backcountry. They were soon joined by additional forces sent by the Provincial Congress. Furious at the Loyalist uprising, Congress was determined to force backcountry men to support the Whig cause or face the consequences. Late in November, the Council of Safety dispatched troops commanded by Richard Richardson, himself a leading backcountry citizen, into the area between the Broad and Saluda Rivers to pacify backcountry Loyalists. Accounts of the number of men in Richardson's force range from 2,500 to 5,000. Richardson ordered citizens of the Ninety Six District to return the powder and lead intended for the Cherokee and give up the "robbers, murderers, and disturbers of the peace and good order" who had stolen it. Loyalist militia forces fell back to Cherokee Territory in the face of the Whig advance contributing to Whig suspicions that the Cherokees were colluding with the British and Loyalists. Richardson managed to capture a number of Loyalist leaders including Thomas Fletchall, prompting many rank and file Loyalist militia men to join the Whig militia in order to avoid arrest. Surprising the Loyalists in their camp at a place called the Great Canebrake on the Reedy River on December 22, Whig troops routed Cunningham's men. This expedition became known as the Snow Campaign because more than 30 inches of snow fell as Loyalist militiamen were rounded up and forced to choose between serving with the Whigs, remaining on the sidelines, or losing all their property. For a time the Snow Campaign silenced backcountry opposition to Provincial Congress.[15]

> The South Carolina Council of Safety: "These wicked men [Loyalists], to the astonishment of common sense, have made many of their deluded followers believe, that this ammunition was sent to the Indians, with orders for them to fall upon the frontiers and to massacre the non-associators."

One of the men who switched sides as a result of the Snow Campaign, albeit temporarily, was Alexander Chesney. A Scots-Irish immigrant, Chesney had moved with his family to America from County Antrim, Ireland. He was 20 years old in 1775, and he had spent the previous few months serving as a guide for Loyalist refugees and spies. Captured with members of Cunningham's Loyalist militia in the Snow Campaign, he wrote that for his service to the Crown, "I was made a prisoner, my house ransacked, and Kept a prisoner in the Snowy Camp on Reedy River for about a week; Col Richardson released me, but the congress party [the Whigs] held me at enmity and forced me either to be tryed at Richardson's camp or to join the Rebel Army [the Whigs] which latter alternative I chose in order to save my father's family from threatened ruin. [H]e had been made prisoner already for harbouring some loyalists."[16]

Having temporarily intimidated backcountry Loyalists into submission, the Provincial Congress continued to take steps to defend the colony from British aggression. In February and March 1776, fears of attack by Indians, slaves, and the British led to the organization of more militia companies. These units were staffed with a combination of volunteer enlistments and a draft. When they needed to mobilize troops, officers first asked for volunteers. If not enough volunteered, then they conducted drafts that rotated service among eligible local men, always being sure to leave some able-bodied men at home to defend local communities. Draftees could hire substitutes.[17]

Slaves used the disruptions created by revolutionary conflict to their own advantage. Thousands of slaves ran away, offered their services to the British, or founded maroon colonies where they could live independently. When a British fleet anchored at the mouth of North Carolina's Cape Fear River, 150 runaway slaves showed up to volunteer for his majesty's service. In South Carolina, a British captain admitted to harboring runaway slaves on his ship, which was anchored in Charles Town Harbor. The provisional Whig governments fought hard to maintain control of slaves. For example, the revolutionary governments in both South Carolina and Georgia ordered attacks on maroon colonies. Nonetheless, slaves persisted in trying to gain their freedom through military service or simply taking advantage of the social and political disruption wrought by the imperial crisis.[18]

> Loyalist Alexander Chesney said: "I was made a prisoner, my house ransacked, and Kept a prisoner in the Snowy Camp on Reedy River for about a week; Col Richardson released me, but the congress party [the Whigs] held me at enmity and forced me either to be tryed at Richardson's camp or to join the Rebel Army [the Whigs] which latter alternative I chose in order to save my father's family from threatened ruin."

Some free blacks volunteered for service in the Continental Army. When General Washington arrived in Cambridge in 1775 to take command of the Continental Army, he was startled to find black men among the troops and urged an end to recruiting blacks. His senior officers agreed not to accept slaves or most free blacks. Washington conceded that black men already enlisted could remain but he opposed recruiting new black soldiers. Nonetheless, it was hard to hold the line on this policy. Recruiting troops was a persistent problem, so the Continental Congress permitted states to enlist free blacks in order to meet their quotas. By the end of the war, nearly 5,000 blacks had enlisted in the Continental Army, and hundreds more had served in state militias.[19]

In South Carolina, with its black majority, and in neighboring Georgia, the notion of recruiting African-Americans for military service gained little traction. John Laurens, an aide-de-camp to George Washington, developed a plan to free black Carolinians if they would serve in the Continental Army. He outlined his arguments in a 1777 pamphlet entitled *Observations on Slaves and Indentured Servants*. Knowing of Washington's opposition to the idea, he didn't approach the general directly, but instead urged his father to bring the idea to the commander-in-chief. The younger Laurens also asked his father to convince the South Carolina assembly to enact his plan to "transform the timid Slave into a firm defender of Liberty, and render him worthy to enjoy it himself." John Laurens argued, "Men who have the habit of subordination almost indelibly imprinted on them, would have one very essential qualification of soldiers." Henry Laurens embraced the idea and wrote to Washington advocating it, but the commander-in-chief declined to act because he believed the English would quickly follow suit in developing a coherent policy on arming blacks. Washington also argued that offering freedom to some slaves would render it "more irksome" to those who remained in bondage. Henry Laurens introduced the proposal in the South Carolina Assembly where his fellow South Carolinians William Henry Drayton and Daniel Huger reluctantly favored the plan. Huger pointed out that South Carolina couldn't raise any more white troops because whites preferred to enlist in the militia and serve close to home in order to prevent slave insurrections. Debate on the resolution in the South Carolina Assembly was fierce. Many legislators correctly understood that it could open the doors to eventual abolition. Governor John Rutledge denounced the plan, and it was overwhelmingly defeated. One slaveholder explained why he found the idea too threatening: "A strong, deep seated feeling, nurtured from earliest infancy, decides, with instinctive promptness, against a measure of so threatening an aspect." Although South Carolina did not accept blacks in the infantry, the state did enlist them in navy where they would be unarmed and of little threat. In March 1779, the US Congress authorized South Carolina and Georgia to take measures to enlist able-bodied blacks who would be emancipated at war's end, promising that the United States would compensate owners up to $1,000 per slave for the loss of property, but the practice never became widespread. Some blacks, free and enslaved, also served in militia units.[20]

STEPS TOWARD INDEPENDENCE

In early 1776, all three deep south colonies took cautious steps in the direction of independence. On March 26, 1776, South Carolina became the second of the North American colonies to adopt a state constitution. The document, drafted and adopted by the Provincial Congress, stopped short of declaring independence. Calling South Carolina a colony, the constitution outlined British imperial abuses of the colonists and declared that it was "indispensably necessary" for South Carolina to establish its own government to run the colony "until an accommodation of the unhappy differences between Great Britain and America can be obtained." The constitution provided for a two-house general assembly with the Commons House wielding most of the power including the authority to elect the Upper House and to initiate all revenue bills. Both houses were to elect the executive who had veto power and the authority to make war and peace. John Rutledge was elected the first state executive officer. The new constitution made some concessions to the backcountry including disestablishing the Anglican Church, setting up additional backcountry courts, and providing for some backcountry representation in general assembly (although still not representation proportional to the back-country's white population). Men who did not pledge loyalty to the new provincial government were given one year to sell their property and leave the colony. North Carolina became the first colony to authorize its delegates to the Second Continental Congress to sign a declaration of independence when the Provincial Congress issued the Halifax Resolves on April 12.[21]

Meanwhile, the war continued. Throughout 1776 and 1777, as most of the fighting between Whigs and British troops took place in New England, New York, and the mid-Atlantic, the Southern royal governors lobbied the British military command to move the action to the South. They believed it was ripe for British control because of strong Loyalist support in the colony, particularly in the backcountry. Their pleas were largely ignored. In June 1776 the failure of a large British force to retake Sullivan's Island disheartened the Loyalists and gave a valuable psychological boost to the Patriot cause in the South. The British fleet remained off the South Carolina coast until August when they withdrew and sailed northward.[22]

Peter Harris

A Catawba Indian, Peter Harris was born on the tribe's South Carolina reservation. A smallpox epidemic robbed him of his parents when he was only three. A white family from a neighboring community raised him, but when he was grown, he returned to the reservation, married, and started a family. When the Revolutionary War engulfed South Carolina, Harris, like many of his tribesmen, joined the Whig cause. In 1779, he enlisted in the Third South Carolina Regiment, a Whig unit. He fought in the campaign to defend Charles Town where he was wounded, and he later fought in a company of Catawba Indians under Thomas Sumter and was listed on the unit's payroll until 1783.

After the war, a promoter convinced Harris and three other Catawba men to travel to England where they performed traditional dances for English audiences. The promoter cheated them of all promised revenues from the trip and abandoned them with no money. Benevolent British people paid their way home.

Harris received a land grant of 200 acres near Fishing Creek as payment for his service to the Third Regiment. In 1822, at the age of 66, Harris petitioned the state legislature for financial help saying "I'm one of the lingering members of an almost extinguished race . . . I fought against the British for your sake . . . In my Youth I bled in battle, that you might be independant, [sic] let not my heart in my old age, bleed, for the want of your Commiseration." He was granted a pension of sixty dollars a year. Harris died in 1823.[23]

In South Carolina the Council of Safety continued to pursue alliances with the Indians. The Whigs were able to secure the support of the 500 or so Catawba who lived on a reservation near the North Carolina/South Carolina border. The Catawba were far too weak to try the Cherokee strategy of playing one side against the other, and they lived in a Whig stronghold, making the Whigs the more logical choice. Their reservation became a haven for Whigs fleeing British or Loyalist raiders. A small company of Catawba warriors formed a Whig militia company that helped defend Charles Town in the 1776 British attack. Catawba soldiers fought in numerous backcountry skirmishes and battles. After the battle of Camden, the entire tribe abandoned the reservation and fled to Virginia, returning months later to find that all had been looted or destroyed by British and Loyalist troops.[24]

The Cherokee proved less cooperative with the Whigs. In April 1776, commissioners from South Carolina's Indian Department met with Cherokee leaders at Fort Charlotte, but they were unable to achieve an alliance. According to intelligence gathered by the Whigs, John Stuart was continuing his efforts to secure Cherokee and Creek support of the Crown. Learning that the Whigs intended to arrest him, in June 1776, Stuart fled to Florida. That month, a party of Whig rangers who were trying to locate Stuart's deputy, Alexander Cameron, were attacked by the Cherokee who were harboring him. Four militia men were killed, and their commander was captured. Rumors that "whenever any one of the southern colonies should be attacked on the Sea Coast, they [the Cherokee] will attack the same province on the frontier" seemed highly likely.[25]

THE CHEROKEE WAR

In the summer of 1776, encouraged by both the British and by the Shawnee Indians, the Cherokee launched a long-feared series of attacks on backcountry settlements from Georgia to Virginia. The brutality of the attacks upon non-hostile settlers shocked backcountry residents. For example, Anthony and Elizabeth Hampton and their son Preston were killed in front of their home in the Spartan District. Another settler, Narcissa Robinson, was beaten to death and scalped as she collected water from a spring. Anne Armstrong of the Ninety Six District reported that the Cherokee kidnapped her husband John and took him to one of their towns where they "Most inhumanely Butcher'd [him. The] Savages . . . also took the whole of his Stock, and every other necessary support of life," leaving Anne struggling to feed her three children. In the wake of these attacks, panic and dread swept the frontier districts. The Council of Safety sent Whig militia units on a quickly organized counterattack. William Henry Drayton asked them to "cut up every Indian corn-field, & burn every Indian town —and . . . that every Indian taken shall be the slave and property of the taker." In August 1776, a force of 5,000 Whigs from North and South Carolina and Virginia, led by Major Andrew Williamson and Major Andrew Pickens, launched a vicious war against the Cherokee. One detachment set out to destroy the Lower Towns of the Cherokee (those east of the Appalachian Mountains in South Carolina).[26]

> William Henry Drayton: "[C]ut up every Indian corn-field, & burn every Indian town—and . . . every Indian taken shall be the slave and property of the taker."

The Cherokee offered targeted resistance, not massive defensive action, a tactic that enraged the Whigs and led them to attack non-combatants in villages. One militiaman said, "it grieves us that we should not have an engagement to get satisfaction of them Heathens." Williamson's and Pickens's troops destroyed Keowee, near modern-day Clemson, and several other Cherokee towns, burning homes, slaughtering cattle, and destroying crops. Captured Cherokee warriors were killed or sold into slavery. A Whig eyewitness said that he and his fellow troops engaged in "cutting and destroying all things that might be of advantage to our enemies."[27]

Andrew Pickens

In background, religious beliefs, and economic position, Andrew Pickens embodied the typical traits of a backcountry militia commander. A man of Scots-Irish descent, Pickens was born in 1739 in Bucks County, Pennsylvania. When he was 13, he moved with his family to the Waxhaws community in South Carolina. As an adult, he moved to the community of Abbeville near the Georgia border and then established Hopewell plantation on the Seneca River. Facing the danger of Indian attacks, he served in South Carolina's forces during the Cherokee War of 1760–1761. An influential community leader and a Presbyterian elder, Pickens married Rebecca Calhoun. (Rebecca's brother Patrick would be the father of famed nineteenth-century South Carolina political leader John C. Calhoun.)

In his mid-30s when the Revolutionary War broke out, Pickens became a Whig militia captain. He commanded a major force in the Cherokee Campaign of 1776, and he served in several important backcountry engagements including the Whig militia victory in the Battle of Kettle Creek in Georgia in February 1779. After the fall of Charles Town in 1780, Pickens surrendered his command at Ninety Six. Agreeing to abide by General Clinton's liberal parole terms, he and 300 of his men went home to sit out the rest of the war.

Pickens' parole did not last, however. After Tory raiders destroyed most of his property and frightened his family, he informed British officials that they had violated the terms of parole. Rejoining the Whig cause, he saw action at the Siege of Augusta, the Siege of Ninety Six, and the Battle of Eutaw Springs, but perhaps his most important action was as the militia commander at the Battle of Cowpens in January 1781. Pickens also led a campaign in north Georgia against the Cherokee Indians late in the war. This successful offensive led to the Cherokee cession of significant amounts of land between the Savannah and Chattachoochee rivers in Georgia.

Andrew Pickens—along with Francis Marion and Thomas Sumter—is remembered as one of the most important partisan leaders in the Carolinas. After the war, he represented South Carolina in the US House of Representatives. He and his wife Rebecca had twelve children. He died in Oconee County, South Carolina in 1817.

One particularly dramatic battle, often called the "Ring Fight," took place near a Cherokee town called Tamassee where Pickens and a detachment of 25 men who were exploring territory west of the Lower Towns found themselves surrounded by 180 Cherokee warriors. Pickens ordered his men to form a double circle facing outward. One circle fired while the

> Anne Armstrong: "[The] Savages . . . also took the whole of his Stock, and every other necessary support of life"

others reloaded. The fighting quickly became hand-to-hand combat, and Pickens's men were saved only by the timely arrival of reinforcements. While Pickens was attacking the Lower Towns, Williamson's regiment traveled down the Holston River to attack the Cherokee Upper Towns (or Overhill towns, on the Tennessee side of the Appalachian Mountains), and 2,400 North Carolina militia invaded the Cherokee Middle Towns. On September 19, 600 or so Cherokee warriors ambushed Williamson's force in what is now Macon County, North Carolina. The ensuing battle was called the Battle of the Black Hole. A soldier in Williamson's force, Arthur Fairies (pronounced Faris) described the scene, "We marched off into another hollow surrounded by mountains on all sides only [except] the entrance . . . [T]he Indiens was flanked all around us and fired at once."[sic] Though the Whig militia was ultimately able to prevail, Fairies's diary provided a vivid description of the carnage on the battlefield:

> We had a camp near all night on account of burying our dead and on attending the sick and wounded[. A] most dreadful sight to behold our fellow creatures massacred by the Heathens for there was three of our men sculpt [scalped] and one sadly speared . . . the number of the killed is seventeen.

Former Loyalist Alexander Chesney also fought with Williamson in the Cherokee campaign. He wrote,

> We had a severe battle with the Indians near the middle settlements; in the course of the engagement five or six of them concealed behind a log fired at me as I ascended the hill before the others, and one of their balls struck a saplin[g] of about six inches diameter opposite my breast; fortunately the young tree broke the force of the ball and saved my life.

Andrew Williamson himself reported to William Henry Drayton, "I have now burnt down every town and destroyed all the corn, from the Cherokee line [boundary] to the middle settlements."[28]

The Cherokee sued for peace in early October. Nearly 2,000 Cherokee men, women and children had lost their lives in the fighting. On May 20, 1777, the Cherokee signed The Treaty of DeWitt's Corner, which ceded all their remaining South Carolina lands to the colony. Scattered harassment of backcountry folks by Indians continued for months, leading to additional campaigns against them. Not only did the Cherokee Campaign succeed in lessening the Indian threat for a time, but the brutality of the Whig militia also cowed backcountry Loyalists.[29]

Diminishing the Cherokee threat also encouraged additional migration into the backcountry; a land rush ensued as settlers moved in from Pennsylvania and Virginia in droves. The newcomers would soon find themselves caught up in a brutal civil war in the backcountry. Among the new arrivals were many men who would become important Whig leaders in the later years of the war. For example, William Bratton, a prosperous Virginian, moved to the New Acquisition District in the 1770s; he would be a leading figure in the Battle of Huck's Defeat. Belfast native William Hill settled in the Catawba River valley in response to a bounty that the South Carolina government offered to men who would establish ironworks in the colony. He would become a militia colonel who led Whig militia troops in several major battles.[30]

DECLARING INDEPENDENCE

In the middle of the Cherokee campaign, on August 2, 1776, news of the Declaration of Independence arrived in South Carolina. Four of the state's five delegates to the Second Continental Congress had signed it. (The fifth delegate, Thomas Lynch, Sr., was unable to sign because he had been paralyzed by a stroke.) Many Charlestonians were overjoyed and celebrated with a parade by city troops near the Liberty Tree. When the General Assembly reconvened in September, it expressed pleasure with the decision to cut ties to Britain and set about amending the state constitution. The amended document continued to allocate the lion's share of power to lowcountry elites by setting high property qualifications for holding office and allocating only 64 of 202 seats in the Assembly to the Backcountry. The new constitution maintained the disestablishment of the Anglican Church and guaranteed the rights of a free press as well as many individual rights.[31]

A false calm seemed to descend on the southern states from the autumn of 1776 into 1779. Voter turnout for the fall 1776 South Carolina General Assembly election was low. The legislature passed an act requiring male citizens to take an oath of allegiance to an independent South Carolina, but many of the state's men failed to comply. South Carolinians also resisted military service or signed up for three or six month enlistments when they did join. In 1776, 2,000 South Carolinians were serving in the Continental Army; by 1778, most had left the military. Even generous offers of land and cash bonuses did not boost the state's efforts to fill its recruiting quota. In 1778, the General Assembly authorized using blacks in militia, but only as engineers or sailors. The state rapidly turned to the court system to fill its quotas in the Continental Army; military duty became a common sentence for those convicted of vagrancy, harboring deserters, or hunting deer at night with fire. The vast majority of South Carolinians were more than willing to serve in local militia units, but they resisted regular army service that required months or years away from home.[32]

During the escalating crisis with Britain, most members of the colonial assemblies and other elites in North and South Carolina and Georgia had been quick to join the Whig cause. Many assembly members were merchants who had paid heavy bribes or had ships confiscated by corrupt British customs officials. Other lawmakers were committed to maintaining their hard-won control over internal taxation in the colonies, a control threatened by British efforts to impose new taxes. Most Southern Patriots espoused staunch Whig values, fearing the concentration of power in the hands of one branch of the imperial government. In the eyes of many backcountry settlers, however, coastal Patriots' protests against taxation without representation and abuses of imperial power seemed hypocritical. Although they generally shared the Whig suspicion of concentrated power, frontiersman remembered the internal colonial conflicts of the 1760s and feared that they faced greater tyranny at the hands of members of their own colonial assemblies than the distant British Parliament. Other back-country settlers were committed Loyalists, asserting their fealty to the British Crown. Most frontiersmen simply preferred to stay out of the political fray and pursue their own economic advancement. Thousands of backcountry settlers ignored the conflict between Patriots and the mother country during the early years of the war.

Backcountry folks who did not support independence continued to face pressure from their Patriot neighbors, and many Loyalists fled the colony of South Carolina, settling in remote parts of Georgia or Florida. Southern state legislatures took additional steps to quell Loyalist sentiment. In September 1777, the Georgia legislature passed an act to expel "Internal Enemies of the State." In the spring of 1778, the South Carolina Provincial Congress passed a new law requiring males over the age of sixteen to swear allegiance to South Carolina or else forfeit their right to vote, conduct business, or engage in legal transactions. If a man fled the state without taking the oath and then returned, the proscribed penalty was to be death.

In response to this persecution, a large group of backcountry South
Carolina Loyalists succeeded in marching to East Florida, evading various
militia and Continental forces that tried to stop them. They became part
of a force that called itself the South Carolina Royalists that would fight
numerous skirmishes in the backcountry. Other backcountry Loyalists
responded to Whig persecution with violence. For example, in Orangeburg, Loyalists cut off the ears of a magistrate and a Whig militia captain
and burned an assemblyman's house. Voters in the Ninety Six District
signaled their continuing resistance by electing three Loyalists to the state
legislature, including Robert Cunningham, the man whose arrest had
triggered the 1775 Loyalist uprising in that district. Cunningham and his
compatriots did not attend legislative sessions, fearing arrest if they ventured
to Charles Town, but the election of Loyalist assemblymen was nonetheless
a statement of the district's lack of support for independence. Historian
Jim Piecuch says that Whigs' tough policies with regard to Loyalists were
effective in getting many to support the Whig cause or at least not to resist
Whig control, but for every man who toed the Patriot line, there was
another who maintained his right to express Loyalist sentiments.[33]

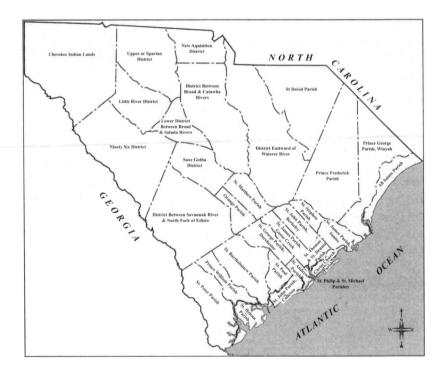

Figure 3.1 Election Districts in South Carolina—1778

After their unsuccessful attempt to seize Sullivan's Island in Charles Town Harbor in 1776, His Majesty's Army largely ignored the deep south colonies, except for continuing efforts to induce southern Indians to take up arms against the Whigs. Likewise the Continental Army paid limited attention to the Southern colonies. Governor Tonyn, the royal governor of Florida, used Loyalists and Indians to conduct cattle raids into Georgia when there was a shortage of supplies. In the summer of 1778, several backcountry militia units from South Carolina and Georgia accompanied Continental troops led by Major General Robert Howe on a campaign to take St. Augustine from the British. Upon reaching Florida, the militia commanders, Andrew Williamson and John Houston, refused to put their troops under Howe's command. As a result of this dispute over military authority, the expedition fell apart before a single shot was fired.[34]

THE BRITISH TURN THEIR GUNS SOUTH

By 1778, the British effort to subdue the rebellious American colonies in New England and the Mid-Atlantic had bogged down, so they turned their attention to the South. After the devastating British defeat at the battle of Saratoga and the American alliance with France, British Undersecretary of the Treasury Charles Jenkinson stepped up his lobbying for a "southern strategy." He made the case that retaining New England was not as important as holding on to the southern colonies. Controlling the South, he argued, was vital to the Crown because the region produced essential products: tobacco, rice, indigo, and naval stores. He acknowledged that New England was a good market for British goods, but not an indispensable one because many of the exports produced by New England duplicated products produced in England. Given the setbacks and stalemate in the northern colonies, British military officials seized on the idea of turning their efforts southward. Aware of many backcountry settlers' ambivalence about the revolutionary effort and their fear of Indian attacks, a threat that could be addressed with strong imperial authority, British officials believed that a large population of Loyalists would support efforts to restore imperial rule. The British also hoped that, because of economic ties, membership in the Anglican Church, and their fear of slave uprisings, many coastal elites would be Loyalists. In short, the British imagined that if they could regain control of the Southern colonies, they might be able to end the American war quickly and retain some, if not all, of their North American territory, an especially attractive prospect in the wake of the Franco-American alliance and impending war with France. General Henry

Clinton, the commander of British forces in North America, was at first skeptical of the Southern strategy, but he eventually embraced it.[35]

In the fall of 1778, the British fleet anchored off the coast of Georgia, carrying a large invasion force. Savannah fell on December 29, 1778. From Savannah, British troops began advancing up the Savannah River toward the town of Augusta, which they quickly seized. Within six weeks of the fall of Savannah, the British army was in control of all of Georgia, and they reinstated the royal governor and royal authority. Early in 1779, the southern commander of the Continental Army, Major General Benjamin Lincoln, launched a campaign to retake the southernmost colony. He ordered backcountry militia forces to join 4,000 Continental troops on that expedition. Backcountry militia under the command of Colonel Andrew Pickens engaged with and defeated Loyalist forces at Kettle Creek on the west bank of the Savannah River, but the larger campaign failed to take either Augusta or Savannah. Georgia would remain under British control for the remainder of the war.[36]

The ultimate southern prize was, of course, Charles Town, yet conquering South Carolina proved more difficult than British officials had anticipated. In May and June 1779, British general Augustine Prevost marched troops overland from Savannah up the South Carolina coast, arriving within a few miles of Charles Town. Many locals eagerly received Prevost and his troops, leading General Clinton to interpret the response as a sign of how the "kings friends" would come forward to aid British troops. Finding that he was outnumbered three to one by General Lincoln's Continental forces, Prevost retreated. In September 1779, a French fleet arrived off the coast of Georgia and, with the aid of American troops, launched a costly attack on the British at Savannah, but they failed to dislodge the King's army and sailed away.[37]

The US Congress had reacted to the loss of Savannah by ordering more troops, ships, and supplies south, but by the fall of 1779, only a fraction of those forces had arrived. General Benjamin Lincoln passed the autumn in an uneasy state. He knew that a new British advance against Continental troops at Charles Town was inevitable, and in November, he complained to General George Washington that he didn't have enough troops to defend Charles Town. Washington did not dispatch additional troops in response. He believed Prevost's small force in Savannah was the only real threat to Lincoln and that Lincoln had sufficient troop strength to defend against them. Events would soon prove the commander-in-chief wrong.[38]

CHAPTER 4

The South's First Civil War

The Fall of Charles Town and its Aftermath

*South Carolina was an easy country to
invade but a hard one to occupy.*
John W. Gordon, South Carolina
and the American Revolution

*The abuse of the British army in taking the
peoples [sic] Horses, Cattle, & provisions
. . . disgusted the inhabitants.*
Robert Gray, Loyalist

Just after Christmas 1779, 8,700 British army troops boarded ships and
set sail from New York. Initially their destination was a secret. Captains
received sealed envelopes; they were instructed not to open the orders
until they were at sea. British North American commander Henry
Clinton's objectives were to regain control of South Carolina and finish
the pacification of Georgia, and he wanted to give the Continental Army
and southern Whigs as little advance notice as possible. The British arrived
off the coast of South Carolina in February 1780 after a harrowing storm-
tossed voyage. They had lost most of their 1,400 horses and some siege
artillery when an ordnance ship sank. The weary army came ashore on
Simmons Island (now Seabrook Island) about 20 miles below Charles
Town. Besides British regulars and Hessian mercenaries, the British
troops included a large contingent of Tories, provincial troops recruited
from New York, New Jersey, and Pennsylvania, and a unit of 70 black

pioneers (laborers, lumbermen, and road builders) from New York. About one in five men in Clinton's South Carolina army was a provincial soldier.[1]

THE FALL OF CHARLES TOWN

Charles Town was defended by just over 5,000 troops under the command of General Benjamin Lincoln. A native of Massachusetts, Lincoln had been a local elected official and militia captain before the Revolution when he was commissioned into the Continental Army as a major general. Wounded in the fighting at Saratoga, he was given time to recover before being appointed head of the southern department of the Continentals in 1779. After the unsuccessful Continental Army attempt to retake Savannah in 1779, Lincoln and his troops had been forced to retreat to Charles Town.[2]

Bowing to pressure from Charles Town's leading men, General Lincoln moved his army within the walls of the city. He knew that his force, a combination of Continental infantry and militia forces, was too small to defend the city against an invading British army, but his pleas to General Washington for additional troops had so far fallen on deaf ears. As Lincoln waited for the inevitable British invasion, he asked Governor Rutledge of South Carolina to provide him with 2,000 additional men in arms, but only about 300 answered Rutledge's call for volunteers. Many backcountry men who had fought in the campaign to liberate Georgia had no interest in fighting to defend Charles Town, home to the lowcountry elites who had long treated them with contempt. Others refused to enlist and leave their families behind on the frontier unprotected from Indian attack. When volunteers failed to materialize, Lincoln then asked the state assembly to arm 1,000 slaves to aid in the city's defense. The legislature declined to arm slaves though later, during the siege, Whig slaveholders volunteered 300 slaves to dig fortification trenches along Charles Town Neck, the narrow strip of land that connected the city to the mainland. Even after he received word that Clinton's forces had departed New York City, George Washington did not act on Lincoln's appeal for additional troops. Not until two months after the British set sail did he order two contingents of relief forces to join Lincoln's defense; most of them would arrive just in time to be captured with the rest of Lincoln's army.[3]

As General Lincoln prepared for the expected attack, the British invasion force spent a grueling six weeks moving from Simmons Island to James Island, a distance of only six miles. They faced persistent harassment from Whig guerillas, and the difficulty of moving troops and supplies through the coastal marshes also slowed the advance. As they made their slow way toward Charles Town, the British committed their own harassment of the civilians who lived on the barrier islands. Young widow Eliza Yonge Wilkinson, holed up on her family's Yonge Island plantation, described the ransacking of her sister's home by a band of British troops:

> I heard the horses of the inhuman Britons coming in such a furious manner, that they seemed to tear up the earth, the riders at the same time bellowing out the most horrid curses imaginable . . . I had no time for thought—they were up to the house—entered with drawn swords and pistols in their hands: indeed they rushed in in the most furious manner, crying out, "Where are these women rebels?" That was the first-salutation! . . . [I]t is not in my power to describe the scene: it was terrible to the last degree; and what augmented it, they had several armed negroes with them, who threatened and abused us greatly. They then began to plunder the house of every thing they thought valuable or worth taking; our trunks were split to pieces, and each mean, pitiful wretch crammed his bosom with the contents, which were our apparel, &c. I ventured to speak to the inhuman monster who had my clothes. I represented to him the times were such we could not replace what they had taken from us, and begged him to spare me only a suit or two: but I got nothing but a hearty curse for my pains; nay, so far was his callous heart from relenting, that casting his eyes towards my shoes, "I want them buckles," said he; and immediately knelt at my feet to take them out . . . The other wretches were employed in the same manner; they took my sister's earrings from her ears, her and Miss Samuells' buckles; they demanded her ring from her finger; she pleaded for it, told them it was her wedding-ring, and begged they would let her keep it; but they still demanded it; and presenting a pistol at her, swore if she did not deliver it immediately, they would fire. She gave it to them; and after bundling up all their booty, they mounted their horses . . . They took care to tell us, when they were going away, that they had favored us a great deal—that we might thank our stars it was no worse.[4]

In such a manner—terrorizing civilians and being terrorized by Whig guerillas—the British forces made their slow way toward Charles Town. On March 10, nearly a month after landing, British troops reached the Ashley River west of Charles Town. Lincoln offered to vacate the city if the enemy would allow him to retain his army; Clinton, of course, refused. Lincoln again discussed removing his troops, but city leaders threatened to fire on the Continentals and throw open the gates of the city to the British if Lincoln tried to withdraw. The net effect of such an action would be to trap Lincoln's army between hostile enemy troops and armed civilians. Lincoln gave in, an action that would prove to be a fateful mistake; the American troops would be trapped on the peninsula between Ashley and Cooper Rivers. Meanwhile, Governor Rutledge and members of his council slipped out of the city in April just before British cut off all escape routes.[5]

For his part, Clinton knew he had the resources to mount an effective siege. He boasted a substantial navy to attack from the sea, and he was soon to be reinforced by British troops from Savannah, bringing his troop strength to 11,000 men. In anticipation of a siege, Lincoln's engineers had erected a formidable series of redoubts and other fortifications across the mile-wide section of Charles Town neck, and the general hoped that these defenses might withstand an assault until reinforcements arrived. Lincoln was also counting on the fleet of five Continental ships guarding the harbor to prevent a British landing, but the American naval commander, Abraham Whipple, balked at making a stand in the harbor. Instead, Whipple agreed to build obstructions in the narrow channel on the Fort Moultrie side of the city. These barriers, however, proved impossible to erect because the channel was deeper and wider than Whipple had believed. Even as plans for harbor defenses fell apart, Lincoln did not abandon Charles Town, believing he could evacuate his army across the Cooper River under cover from Whipple's ships.[6]

The British fleet crossed the bar into the harbor on March 20, but they took no naval action until April 8 when they made a run past Fort Moultrie and into firing range of the city. Now an American escape across the Cooper River was unlikely to succeed. Meanwhile, Clinton's army had crossed the Ashley River and on April 5, the British began firing artillery at the city. On April 10, 1,400 Virginia Continentals arrived to reinforce Lincoln, but they would prove to be powerless to break the siege. The fate of the American army was sealed within a few days when two units of the British army crossed the Cooper River and defeated Whig defenders at Monck's Corner, blocking Lincoln's retreat route. After days of punishing British bombardment, which wreaked havoc on Charles Town, on May 12, General Lincoln surrendered. British soldiers entered the city the next day, capturing 5,700 Americans soldiers and 1,000 sailors. About 2,500 of the prisoners were Continental soldiers. The Americans also relinquished 5,000 muskets and almost 400 valuable artillery pieces, a heavy blow to the undersupplied Continental Army. Casualties were relatively low, however: the Americans lost 225 men, the British 265. Many of South Carolina's leading men were among those captured, including Arthur Middleton and Thomas Heyward, both Declaration of Independence signers. They were sent to a British fortress in Florida.[7]

Lincoln later blamed the capture of his forces on the Continental Congress, saying they wanted him to defend the city to the bitter end, but historian John Ferling maintains that Lincoln did not have orders from commander-in-chief George Washington to hold the city, but instead was intimidated by city leaders. Historian Walter Edgar blames the loss squarely on Lincoln's poor decisions; Edgar remarked that Lincoln "always seemed to count the number of soldiers who might someday be in his command

Boston King

Born a slave in South Carolina around 1760, Boston King's experience was similar to that of many African Americans who sought to gain their freedom by fighting for the British.

As a young man, King learned carpentry, the trade he was practicing when the Revolutionary War broke out. When the British captured Charles Town, King made his way to a Loyalist encampment and offered his services. Soon after, he came down with smallpox when an epidemic swept the Loyalist camp. He survived the illness and eventually joined Cornwallis at Camden. He served as an orderly and a messenger for the British. He was briefly captured twice, once by Loyalists who tried to sell him into slavery and again by an American whaleboat.

When the British evacuated Charles Town, he boarded one of their ships and traveled to New York, one of many African Americans to do so. There he met and married Violet, an enslaved black woman from North Carolina who had also joined the British. The Kings received certificates of freedom from British officials, and their names were entered in the *Book of Negroes*, a register of more than 3,000 slaves who joined the British cause before 1782 and the signing of a provisional cease fire. The Kings joined other refugees on a ship to Nova Scotia where they struggled to rebuild their lives on rocky land unsuited for farming.

King converted to Methodism in 1786, and he soon began to preach to congregations in Nova Scotia. In 1792, Boston King and his wife decided to move to a new British colony in Africa that was established for blacks from London and Canada. The Kings journeyed to Freetown, Sierra Leone. Violet King died soon after they arrived, but Boston thrived. He went to England for additional education under the auspices of the Methodist Church and then returned to Sierra Leone where he worked as a teacher and missionary. He also published his autobiography *Memoirs of the Life of Boston King* in 1798. He remarried and fathered three children. He lived and worked in Sierra Leone until his death in 1802.

rather than those actually present for duty." As a result, in Edgar's view, Lincoln bowed to pressure from city leaders and made the ill-fated decision to remain in Charles Town. Whatever the reasons that Lincoln's army was captured, the loss of virtually the entire southern wing of the Continental Army was a reeling blow to the Patriot cause.[8]

Upon capitulation, General Lincoln accepted General Clinton's terms of surrender, which initially seemed generous. Continental soldiers were to be held until a prisoner exchange could be arranged, but the militia would "be permitted to return to their respective homes, as prisoners on parole; and while they adhered to their parole, were not to be molested by the British troops in person or property." In short, if they stayed out of the fray, paroled militia men were to be left alone; they would not be asked to choose sides.[9]

After the fall of Charles Town, slaves tried to take advantage of the turmoil to gain their freedom. General Clinton announced that he would free slaves who belonged to Whigs but return runaways from Loyalist masters. The British forces soon found themselves "awash in a tidal wave of black refugees." One such man was carpenter Boston King who fled to the British troops in Charles Town to escape a brutal master. In his autobiography, King explained, "To escape his cruelty, I determined to go to Charles-Town, and throw myself into the hands of the English. They received me readily, and I began to feel the happiness of liberty, of which I knew nothing before, altho' I was much grieved at first, to be obliged to leave my friends, and reside among strangers." King and other slaves who found refuge with the British eventually won their liberty.[10]

BRITISH MISTAKES

Once Charles Town fell, the British quickly occupied other strategic locations in the area. Two backcountry forts surrendered when they learned of the fall of Charles Town: the one commanded by Andrew Pickens at Ninety Six and the one led by Joseph Kershaw at Camden. General Clinton sent Major Patrick Ferguson and his American Volunteers (Provincials) to the vicinity of Ninety Six with instructions to recruit and train Loyalist militia. In May, General Clinton wrote, "From every information I receive, and Numbers of the most violent Rebels hourly coming to offer their Services, I have the strongest reasons to believe the general Disposition of the People to be not only friendly to [British] Government, but forward to take up Arms in its support." There were, however, some signs that Loyalist sentiment was mostly superficial. One royal official reported to Clinton that the number of longtime Loyalists—

those "who have always adhered to the King's government"—were not as numerous as he had hoped. Ignoring indications of lukewarm support for the British, Clinton instead took as a hopeful sign the 1,600 men who came forward to take an oath of allegiance to the Crown in the first days after the fall of Charles Town and the ease with which he established control over backcountry forts. It seemed that the British would quickly gain control of the entire colony of South Carolina.[11]

General Henry Clinton "From every information I receive, and numbers of the most violent Rebels hourly coming to offer their services, I have the strongest reasons to believe the general disposition of the People to be not only friendly to [British] Government, but forward to take up Arms in its support."

At this point, however, British officers made a series of fatal blunders that cost them any advantage they might have had in the Southern backcountry. The first blunder came at the May 29, 1780, Battle of the Waxhaws, a confrontation between a detachment of troops from General Cornwallis's army and a Continental regiment of 350 Virginia men, commanded by Colonel Abraham Buford. The Virginians were part of a contingent sent to reinforce General Lincoln, but they did not arrive in time to aid in the defense of the city. When word came of Lincoln's surrender, they began to retreat along the road between Camden and Charlotte. Governor Rutledge was traveling with them. Meanwhile, after the fall of Charles Town, General Clinton had gained intelligence of Buford's forces and dispatched his second in command, Charles Cornwallis, to chase down the retreating Continentals. Realizing that his slow-moving infantry could not travel fast enough to capture Buford, who had a head start, Cornwallis sent dragoon commander Banastre Tarleton and a detachment of 270 men after Buford. Tarleton, the son a wealthy Liverpool merchant, studied at University of Liverpool and Oxford before taking a commission in the King's Dragoon Guards. An able officer, he volunteered for service in America where he commanded a combined infantry and cavalry force known as the British Legion. Most of the British Legion were recent Scottish immigrants to America who had been recruited in the northern colonies and arrived in the South with Clinton's forces in early 1780.[12]

Setting off in pursuit of Buford and his Continentals, Tarleton marched his men 154 miles in 54 hours. Realizing that the British were gaining on the American forces, Governor Rutledge rode ahead of the army in order to avoid capture. Tarleton and his troops caught up with Buford at mid-afternoon on May 29 at the Waxhaws, a small community on the Camden–Charlotte road near the North Carolina–South Carolina border. Tarleton offered Buford terms of surrender that the American

The Weapons of the American Revolution

During the Revolutionary War, armies on both sides employed a mixed infantry-cavalry force; that is, they used mounted troops and foot soldiers. Most of the fighting in the American Revolution was done by infantry, soldiers who fought on foot with weapons they carried. Many revolutionary infantrymen, particularly militiamen, were mounted infantry who traveled from place to place on horseback (usually their personal mounts rather than horses supplied by the army), but dismounted for combat. Revolutionary War infantrymen on both sides used two types of weapons. Most carried smoothbore, muzzle-loading, flintlock muskets which had a bayonet on the end that could remain fixed while being loaded and fired. Well-trained troops using muskets could fire three shots a minute. Muskets could be loaded quickly, but they had limited accuracy. Their range was about 50 yards. The most common form of musket in the Revolutionary War was the "Brown Bess," which fired a four-ounce lead ball. Ammunition came pre-packaged in paper cartridges loaded with "ball and buck" (gunpowder and a lead ball); militia men often made their own cartridges.

American militia troops—Loyalist and Whig alike—sometimes carried the long-barreled rifle which was commonly used for hunting on the frontier. This firearm was sometimes called the Pennsylvania rifle, Kentucky rifle, or simply the long rifle. Like the musket, the rifle was muzzle-loading and flintlock-ignited. However, unlike the musket with its smooth bore (interior barrel), the rifle barrel was grooved. This innovation caused the bullet to spin when it left the gun, giving the rifle greater range and accuracy than the musket. The long rifle could hit a target up to 200 yards away. However, it was much slower to load because the ammunition had to be wrapped in a lubricated cloth and rammed down the barrel. It was also impossible to mount a fixed bayonet on a rifle, making it less versatile in close combat.

Cavalry troops were mounted men who fought from their horses. They carried sabers and pistols or carbines, a short rifle or musket well-suited for firing from horseback. Cavalrymen conducted reconnaissance, scouting enemy positions and territory. In battle, their role was to charge enemy infantry forces, hacking at them with sabers and running them down with horses. They also chased retreating troops. Many revolutionary cavalry troops were referred to as dragoons; dragoons were a versatile all-purpose cavalry unit.

Units on both sides possessed small artillery pieces, commonly called cannons. These smoothbore weapons were quite large and had to be pulled by horses. They were capable of firing at considerable distances, and they fired roundshot (solid iron balls) and grapeshot (small balls fired in a cluster that spread to create a wide path of destruction). Artillery field pieces were designated by the size of shot they were able to fire; most commonly the armies of the Revolutionary War used three-pounders and six-pounders, that is, guns that fired three pound or six pound projectiles.

general refused. What followed became known throughout the back-country as a massacre. Having sent his cannons and supplies ahead toward Charlotte, Buford formed his men for battle without artillery support. Tarleton advanced half his men and charged the American center, keeping half in reserve. Buford ordered his men to fire on the advancing British troops in one mass volley. The terrified American soldiers only had time to get off one shot that failed to stop the advance of the cavalrymen. At this point, Buford offered the white flag which Tarleton, having been thrown from his horse, apparently did not see. Receiving no orders to the contrary, British Legion continued fighting in spite of the gesture of surrender. Buford mounted his horse and escaped, leaving his troops to face a bloodbath. Perhaps believing that their commander had been wounded, the British continued attacking, hacking fallen men with sabers. Buford's physician, Robert Brownfield, reported, "For fifteen minutes after every man was prostrate they [the British] went over the ground plunging their bayonets into every one that exhibited any signs of life." The American casualty rate was staggering: 75 percent of troops were killed, wounded, or captured. One hundred and fifty were too badly wounded to travel. The British suffered only five dead and 15 wounded. In spite of Tarleton's provisions for humane treatment of wounded prisoners, the Patriots labeled him a beast, nicknaming his "Bloody Ban." The "massacre" of surrendering troops at the Waxhaws was a terrible blow to the Continentals, but it was also a public relations asset. Whigs used the story of "Tarleton's Quarter" to rouse patriotic sentiment in backcountry folk. David Wallace, the pre-eminent nineteenth-century historian of South Carolina, said the Battle of the Waxhaws "turned Tarleton's victory into a British disaster because it planted in the hearts of thousands who had accepted a renewed British rule as inevitable the invincible determination to expel a power which could be guilty of such cruelty." Recent historians believe that tactical mistakes by Buford and confusion on the battlefield played a greater role in creating the

> Robert Brownfield, "For fifteen minutes after every man was prostrate they [the British] went over the ground plunging their bayonets into every one that exhibited any signs of life."

slaughter than on any calculated brutality by Tarleton. Historian John Ferling, in his magisterial history of the Revolutionary War, argues that Tarleton was not bloodthirsty, but acknowledges that the British leader had a record of failing to control his men after battle.[13]

The battle of the Waxhaws raised backcountry ire at the British. So did the second British blunder: tolerance of brutality against civilians committed both by British occupation forces and by Loyalist militia.

Most of this violence was directed against Whigs (or suspected Whigs) and their families. Robert Gray, a Loyalist himself, said that "the abuse of the British army in taking the peoples [sic] Horses, Cattle, & provisions . . . disgusted the inhabitants." Scots-Irish Presbyterians, whose churches were labeled "sedition shops," became particular targets of British and Tory hostilities. Individual Whig leaders were also targeted. For example, Tarleton's troops torched Thomas Sumter's home on May 28, inspiring Sumter to begin recruiting Patriot forces in backcountry. Sumter, a militia commander during the early years of the war, had been captured at Charles Town and paroled to his plantation, where he announced his intention to retire from the fighting for good. After the British destroyed his home, however, he resumed fighting on behalf of the Whigs. Sumter became a symbol of the victims of British and Loyalist violence, and he would become a powerful Whig militia commander, leading a series of successful raids against British supply lines and participating in many key backcountry battles.[14]

The Battle of the Waxhaws and the toleration of violence against civilians created considerable distrust of the British among backcountry residents. The final British blunder came in early June 1780, when General Henry Clinton revoked the terms of the surrender he had offered at Charles Town. On June 1, he issued orders promising clemency to all Whigs who would reaffirm their allegiance to the king but not those still in arms on the Whig side or those who had shed Loyalist blood. Then on June 3, he issued a new proclamation that placed new conditions on militiamen who wanted to remain free: all paroled American prisoners must swear an oath of allegiance to the Crown *and* agree to take up arms for the British if they were asked to do so. Men who had returned to their homes intending to maintain a position of neutrality were outraged.[15]

The revocation of the terms of surrender, the massacre at the Waxhaws, and violence against backcountry civilians and Whigs, especially attacks on Presbyterian ministers and churches—combined to infuriate many previously neutral backcountry settlers. In the summer of 1780, the ranks of Whig militia units swelled, and these irregular troops inflicted heavy military and psychological damage on the British cause. Much of the backcountry fighting took the form of guerilla attacks by small bands of Whig and Loyalist militiamen. Many brutal attacks targeted women and children. Old animosities from the days of the Regulator Movement often fueled intense fighting between Whigs and Loyalists, and the backcountry people chose sides based as much on their economic interests as their ideological positions. In his community study of the Waxhaws, historian Peter N. Moore found that Waxhaws residents who were recent immigrants were slower to join the Revolutionary War effort than the native born. Most recent immigrants did not join the Whig cause until after the summer of 1780s in the wake of British and Loyalist atrocities in the backcountry. Those who enlisted after 1780 also had less property. He concludes that many people, those who had little to gain from taking sides, tried to stay out of the fray until they feared that neutrality was no longer an option. He also observed that the smallest landholders in the Waxhaws became Loyalists. In other words, the wealthier a man, the more likely he would join the Whig cause early on; less wealthy people remained loyal to the Crown or sided with the Whigs only after they feared becoming targets of violence.[16]

BRUTAL FIGHTING IN THE BACKCOUNTRY: JUNE 1780

During the late summer of 1780, a series of small, but important battles in the backcountry testified to a renewed spirit of resistance among backcountry Whigs, and these clashes paved the way for the British retreat from the Carolinas and Cornwallis's surrender at Yorktown. In June, however, things seemed bleak for the Whigs. Shortly after the fall of Charles Town and the launch of campaigns in the backcountry, General Clinton decamped for New York, leaving his second in command at the head of the British army in the South. Lord Cornwallis was an outstanding field commander, forceful and fearless in battle. For years, the relationship between Clinton and Cornwallis had been tense because of critical remarks Cornwallis had allegedly made about Clinton early in the war. The strained relationship had worsened during the Charles Town campaign, deteriorating to the point that Cornwallis refused to consult on plans for the siege forcing Clinton to proceed without advice of a close aide. In spite of the tensions between the two (or perhaps because of them), Clinton was eager to leave the South, so he quickly turned the southern command over to Cornwallis.[17]

Cornwallis set up his headquarters at Camden in June 1780 and started establishing outposts along the northern frontier of the backcountry—at Rocky Mount, Hanging Rock, and Cheraw. He planned to use these garrisons as Loyalist recruiting posts. In a measure further calculated to entice people to the British side, he announced that the British Army would purchase supplies from Loyalists but confiscate them from Whigs. Cornwallis boasted a force of about 6,400 men, including six Loyalist regiments. The new British commander, like his superior officer, believed it was going to be an easy victory. He wrote "everything [is] wearing the face of tranquility and submission." Even as the ranks of Whig militias grew, Loyalists joined the British units in droves in the early days of summer, especially in the Ninety Six District. At least 1,500 Loyalist troops mobilized in the first two months after the fall of Charles Town. Runaway slaves also flocked to British lines on the assurance they would be granted freedom in return for their service. By mid-June, amid these promising signs, Cornwallis left Lord Rawdon in command at Camden and returned to Charles Town.[18]

For its part, the Continental Army scrambled to regroup in the aftermath of the disaster at Charles Town. In June, 1780, Congress appointed General Horatio Gates as the new commander of the Continental Army in the South. The British-born Gates was a veteran of the French and Indian War. In 1769, after retiring from His Majesty's service with the rank of major, Gates and his wife immigrated to Virginia, a place that offered opportunities to a man of his humble beginnings. When the Revolutionary War broke out, Gates visited Mount Vernon and offered his services to General Washington. After service as adjutant general (basically an administrative post), Gates was promoted to Major General and given a field command. He gained fame as the commander of American forces at the Battle of Saratoga. In his book, *The Road to Guilford Courthouse*, Revolutionary War historian John Buchanan says of Gates, "He was . . . a man of modest abilities, but he thought otherwise."[19]

From the beginning, Gates was dissatisfied with the conditions of his southern assignment. He was given only about 1,400 men, leading him to complain that he had been given "an army without strength . . ." He had no artillery and only 50 cavalry men; supplies were so scarce that most of his men were on half rations. As he and his troops marched south, Gates was able to obtain some supplies and troops from the governors of Virginia and North Carolina; Governor Thomas Jefferson of Virginia sent war matériel and 2,500 militia men, and Gates found about 4,000 men waiting for him in North Carolina, three-fourths of them militia. He nonetheless complained that his army was too small and ill-equipped to be effective, a complaint that make his later decisions at Camden particularly difficult to fathom.[20]

As Gates made his halting way south in the summer of 1780, the slaughter in the backcountry escalated. Throughout the summer, small bands of Patriot and Loyalist militia fighters engaged in guerilla attacks against each other and against civilian sympathizers. Colonial South Carolinians called this type of fighting partisan warfare. Partisan leaders on both sides shared many similar characteristics. They were usually first or second generation Americans who had received little formal education. Most had been Indian fighters; in fact, many had served side-by-side in the campaign against the Cherokee in 1776. Most partisan fighters were under the age of 40 and lived in frontier settlements. Many of the Whig guerillas were motivated by a desire to retaliate for Loyalist attacks on civilians. Others were furious at Clinton's revocation of the terms of parole, which would require them to serve in His Majesty's Army. Still others believed an American victory would bring about political change that would relieve them of lowcountry domination. Partisans on both sides acted to defend home and family. For example, Whig James Williams of the Ninety Six District wrote to his son to say that he had been "obliged to take the field in defense of my rights and liberties, and that of my children." Some had baser motives including settling personal scores. More than a few were interested in plunder. Between the personal nature of many of the attacks and the fact that guerillas did not always have the discipline of regular army troops, partisan fighting was particularly vicious. To make matters worse, guerillas did not possess the resources to hold or care for prisoners, so they usually killed them. Partisan fighters lived a hardscrabble life, facing the constant threat of surprise attack and forced to supply themselves with weapons, ammunition, horses, and even food. Many scholars have characterized Revolutionary War militia as untrained, but this is an inaccurate assessment. While they may not have been as well-trained in conventional tactics as regular army troops, particularly English troops, they did train. Many had served in pre-war militia units and had received limited training in the use of weapons and parade ground drills on a regular basis. In addition, in the summer of 1780, Sumter's men and many other militia units trained for the kind of hit-and-run tactics that would need to win the backcountry conflict.[21]

All over the backcountry in June 1780, British officials and Loyalist volunteers ordered residents to assemble to sign oaths of allegiance. For example, Cornwallis ordered neutral people in the Waxhaws to take up arms for the Crown or surrender their arms and horses. Their only other option, they were told, was execution. These actions set off wave after wave of partisan conflict. When the British established an outpost near the Dutch Fork settlement on the Broad River and summoned local residents to take the oath of allegiance, Loyalists in the area saw the action as permission to plunder the plantations of men who announced that they would not sign while Cornwallis looked the other way, taking the position that he could not "defend every man's house from being plundered." Whig Richard Winn recruited about 100 militia volunteers to retaliate for the Loyalist attacks. Winn's troops surrounded and attacked a crowd gathered at Mobley's Meetinghouse to sign oaths. In retribution, Loyalists ransacked Winn's plantation and burned his house to the ground. Loyalists in modern Chester County set up camp at Alexander's Old Field and ordered backcountry residents to assemble and declare their allegiance to King

George III. Whig volunteers led by Captain John McClure surrounded Alexander's Old Field on the appointed day and took aim at the Loyalists supervising the signing of oaths of allegiance, killing four and wounding two others. In North Carolina, Loyalist officer John Moore began assembling a Loyalist regiment of over 1,000 men near Ramsour's Mill. Four hundred Whig militia men attacked and drove Moore's regiment from the field in a bloody battle on June 20, 1780. In the aftermath, so many Loyalists were driven from their homes that Loyalist organizing in that part of North Carolina was permanently crippled. While both sides suffered in these attacks, there is no doubt that the attacks from irregular Whig troops inflicted heavy military and psychological damage on the British cause.[22]

Partisan attacks and counterattacks were taking place all over the backcountry nearly simultaneously, and Whig militia units were gradually becoming better organized. In early June three Whig militia commanders met in what is now Union County, South Carolina, to decide on a plan of action. The men included Colonel John Thomas, Sr., commander of Spartan Regiment; Colonel Thomas Brandon, commander of Fairforest Regiment, and Colonel James Lisle, commander of Dutch Fork Regiment from the forks of the Enoree and Tyger Rivers in modern-day Newberry County. All three men had served in the Snow Campaign of 1775. Brandon and Lisle had also participated in Williamson's campaign against the Cherokee in 1776 and the abortive Whig Florida campaign. Thomas, Lisle, and Brandon decided to join their units at an operations base on Fairforest Creek, between today's cities of Spartanburg and Union. From here they were able to launch raids in much of the New Acquisition District.[23] By late June, Thomas Sumter had established a militia camp at Tuckasegee Ford on the Catawba River in North Carolina. From here, he recruited a large band of militiamen.[24]

People on both sides committed brutal atrocities. Whigs seized and massacred fourteen Loyalist militiamen who had been taken prisoner when the Whigs took Fort Orangeburg. A band of Loyalists tortured the wife of a Whig militia captain named McKoy with thumbscrews in an attempt to get her to reveal information about her husband and his men. The attacks and counterattacks could go on indefinitely. Infuriated at attacks by Whig guerilla leader Francis Marion and his men, Cornwallis ordered one Loyalist militia leader, a Lieutenant Fulker, to move the wives of Marion's men 20 miles inland to prevent the wives from passing intelligence about British and Loyalist movements to their husbands. One of the wives was ill with smallpox, and she died after being moved. The Whigs later retaliated, capturing Fulker, stripping him of his clothes, and hanging him.[25]

As these examples, suggest, life was terrifying for the women and children caught in the cross-fire of backcountry warfare. They became convenient targets for partisan bands on both sides. In 1777, even before the height of backcountry conflict, Whig militiaman William Gipson found his widowed mother after she had been "tied up and whipped by the Tories" who also burned her house and destroyed all her property. A Loyalist witness testified that the daughters of outspoken Loyalist Flora McDonald were abused by Whigs who put "swords into their bosoms, split down their silk dresses . . . and strip[ped] them of their clothing." Families were often left to fend for themselves when husbands were imprisoned, wounded, or killed as a result of the fighting. Ann Christenbury, the wife of a North Carolina Whig militiaman taken prisoner at the Battle of Camden, successfully petitioned the North Carolina legislature for tax relief because her husband's imprisonment "renders it exceedingly inconvenient to your Petitioner to pay Her Taxes for the present Year together with the charge of Five small Children."[26]

Slaves often became pawns in the backcountry fighting. Some of the slaves freed by invading British troops served the enemy as backcountry guides. Other runaway slaves served in support roles as laborers and cooks. Many paid a high price for betting on the British. One black guide who was captured by Whigs near Monck's Corners was executed and his head was left on

> Loyalist witness: Whigs put "swords into their bosoms, split down their silk dresses . . . and strip[ped] them of their clothing."

a post as a warning to other blacks who might have contemplated siding with the Crown. Other escaped slaves became guerilla raiders and foragers. The British armed blacks not only because they were available manpower, but also because they were a powerful psychological weapon against Whigs. Tarleton employed "armed Negroes" to terrorize white plantation mistresses whose homes he raided. [27]

Slaves also became a kind of currency for both the Whigs and the British. The British rewarded Loyalists with grants of slaves. For example, Major James Weymss of the British army gave William Henry Mills of Cheraw 100 slaves in 1780, almost twice as many as he had lost in a Patriot raid a year earlier. The Whigs offered slaves as a recruiting bonus. Both Thomas Sumter and Andrew Pickens promised men who joined state regiments a slave bonus, an enticing offer to backcountry men ambitious to accumulate slaves. Sumter and Pickens intended to take these slaves from enemy plantations, but they found a shortage of slaves to distribute. In 1781, Sumter reported that the area around the Broad River had been plundered of slaves and horses. Royal Governor Wright of Georgia complained that a rebel band had carried away his slaves, likely to distribute to soldiers as rewards for their service. The British also stole slaves. In 1781, a Savannah merchant complained that British raiders from Florida frequently crossed the colony's Southern border to steal slaves. Thousands more ran away to British lines.[28]

Historian John Ferling says that Cornwallis tried to strike a balance between "the velvet glove and iron fist" in his efforts to pacify the backcountry. The British general announced that he would punish troops who abused civilians, but he also announced that parole violators would be hanged and dispatched Major James Wemyss and Major Patrick Ferguson with Loyalist troops to crush resistance in the backcountry. As June wore on, Cornwallis continued to believe he had the upper hand in the backcountry. On June 30, he wrote to General Clinton, "The submission of General Williamson at Ninety-Six . . . and the dispersion of a party of rebels, who had assembled at an iron work on the north-west border of the province . . . put an end to all resistance in South Carolina."[29]

THE BATTLE OF HUCK'S DEFEAT

The very action that Cornwallis cited as the end of resistance—the dispersion of a militia unit gathered at Hill Ironworks, was in fact one of several touchstones for resistance that Cornwallis set in motion earlier in June, when he dispatched Captain Christian Huck to recruit Loyalists in backcountry. Huck, a German immigrant to America, had been a successful lawyer in Pennsylvania when the war broke out. Because he professed Loyalist sentiments, Whigs confiscated his Philadelphia property. He sought retribution by raising a company of Loyalist volunteers to the British Army in 1778. Huck and his cavalry unit were soon attached to Tarleton's British Legion. They participated in the siege of Charles Town. Huck, known as the "Swearing Captain" because of his coarse language, was full of vitriol and rough around the edges. He particularly hated Scots-Irish Presbyterians.[30]

Huck and his detachment of Tarleton's dreaded British Legion sowed terror in many backcountry districts. The "Swearing Captain" made speeches that Presbyterians found blasphemous. Huck's troops harassed and attacked women and children. On June 11, Huck and his men plundered the home of Janet Strong, a widow who lived near Fishing Creek. Her family was known to be ardently Whig, and both sons were enlisted in Whig militia units. One story says that Huck's men came upon young William Strong in the barn reading his Bible. They shot him and began hacking his body to pieces with their swords. According to this account, Janet Strong threw herself on her son's body to prevent further desecration of his corpse. Another account says the British tracked William Strong and his brother down as they fled through a cornfield, killing one and wounding the other. The same day as the attack on the Strongs, Huck and his men plundered the home of Reverend John Simpson of Fishing Creek before torching it. Simpson's pregnant wife fled the house with four children, a set of teaspoons, some books, and enough feathers for one feather bed. She gave birth four weeks later. Some accounts suggest that Huck burned the Fishing Creek Presbyterian Church as well. Then on June 17, Huck and his men attacked the well-defended iron works belonging to William Hill. Hill's Ironworks provided important supplies to the Patriots, but it was also headquarters to a popular militia unit commanded by Hill. In this attack, Huck and his men took a few Whigs prisoner and destroyed the ironworks.[31]

Assaults like these struck fear in the hearts of Whig throughout the backcountry, but they also catalyzed a new wave of resistance to British occupation. In mid-July 1780, as Huck rampaged through the Catawba River Valley in modern-day York county, Whig militia leaders went into hiding. Huck responded by tormenting their families. At the home of William Adair, Huck's men seized the family's property, including Mary Adair's shoe buckles, rings, and neckerchief. Huck told her that they intended to hang her husband and warned her that if she wanted her sons to live, she should persuade them to abandon the American cause. When Huck arrived at Captain John McClure's homestead on July 11 and found Mary McClure harboring two Whigs, he ordered that the men would be hanged the next day. Mary McClure protested, and one of Huck's men struck her with the flat of his sword. One of McClure's daughters carried word of this attack to the nearby militia camp commanded by Thomas Sumter. Later that same day, Huck and his men arrived at the home of Colonel William Bratton. Finding him gone, they demanded that his wife Martha reveal his location; when she refused, a Loyalist militiaman in Huck's force held a reaping hook to her throat in an attempt to make her betray her husband. Only the intervention of another Loyalist officer saved her from violence.[32]

After leaving the Bratton's home, Huck and his troops moved to the plantation of James Williamson, a half-mile away, on the south fork of Fishing Creek near modern York, South Carolina. The Williamson men, like Bratton, McClure, and Adair, served in Sumter's militia. Huck and his force of 115 men (including 35 British Legion dragoons, 20 provincial soldiers from New York, and 60 Loyalist militiamen) locked the Whig prisoners they had recently captured in the Williamson's corn crib and set up camp for the night. Huck and the officers slept in the house while the rank and file bedded down in tents erected in an open field or near the road. Cornwallis later reported that, "Captain Huck, encouraged by meeting with no opposition, encamped in an unguarded manner . . ." Meanwhile Martha Bratton had dispatched a slave named Watt to locate her husband and inform him of Huck's location. Watt found Bratton camped on Fishing Creek. Another messenger, a local crippled man named Joseph Kerr, arrived at Bratton's camp later that evening and sketched a map of the layout of Huck's camp. Using the intelligence provided by Watt and Kerr, Colonel Bratton and Captain John McClure planned their attack.[33]

Bratton and McClure took over 100 volunteers from Sumter's camp; once they neared the Williamson plantation, several other partisan bands joined them. Accounts of the number of Whigs who participated in the attack vary, but it was somewhere between 140 and 250 men. At daybreak on July 12, the Whig militia surprised Huck's sleeping men. In a brief battle, Captain Huck and the dragoons resisted until Huck was shot from his

> General Cornwallis: "Captain Huck, encouraged by meeting with no opposition, encamped in an unguarded manner . . . "

horse at which point most of the rank and file panicked and ran. One Whig participant in the battle, Captain Edward Lacey, reported that many of the Loyalist militia fled into the woods where Patriots tracked them down and killed them. Perhaps as many as 85 percent of the British troops were killed, wounded, or captured in a battle that lasted only minutes. The Americans suffered the loss of one man and the wounding of another. While the size and strategic importance of the battle was negligible, the victory at Williamson's Plantation was of enormous importance for Whig morale. Less than two weeks after Cornwallis had boasted that the backcountry was under British control, a Whig militia force had surprised and routed a force that included members of the feared British Legion. As Colonel William Hill put it,

> it was the first check the enemy had received after the fall of Charles Town; and was of greater consequence to the American cause than can be well supposed from an affair of small a magnitude as it had the tendency to inspire the Americans with courage & fortitude & to teach them that the enemy was not invincible.[34]

THE FIRST BATTLE OF CEDAR SPRINGS

The same day as the Battle of Huck's Defeat (sometimes called the Battle of Williamson's Plantation), the Patriots struck another blow, this one at the Whig militia camp at Cedar Springs near modern-day Spartanburg. John Thomas, Sr., commander of the Spartan Regiment, had taken British protection after the fall of Charles Town but when the general parole of Patriot militia was revoked, he took up arms for the Whigs again. The British arrested Thomas for his activities on behalf of backcountry Patriots and jailed him at Ninety Six where he fell ill. While visiting her husband at Ninety Six, Jane Black Thomas overheard some women talking about a plan to attack the Spartan Regiment in their camp at Cedar Springs where her son, John Thomas, Jr., had succeeded his father as commander of the 60-man Spartan Regiment. On July 13, 1780, Jane Thomas traveled roughly 60 miles on horseback to warn the Whig forces. That night, the young Colonel Thomas and his men left their fires burning after dark and melted into the woods around the campsite. When the British and Loyalist forces arrived—about 150 of them—the Patriots burst out of the woods and surrounded the British. In a short fight that left several British troops dead, the Whigs forced the British to retreat.[35]

This engagement, known as the first Battle of Cedar Springs, and the Battle of Huck's Defeat not only inspired the Patriots but also demoralized many backcountry Loyalists and would-be Loyalists. As the British garrison commander at Ninety Six put it, "They [the Whigs] have terrified our friends." In the late summer and fall of 1780, emboldened Patriots initiated skirmishes all over the South Carolina backcountry, thwarting Cornwallis's hope to secure South Carolina and move into North Carolina by the end of the year. Historian Walter Edgar says that between Huck's Defeat on July 12 and Kings Mountain on October 7, Patriot militia engaged the enemy 22 times, 17 of them in the backcountry. Each skirmish served to boost Whig support. Moreover, the Americans were able to minimize their losses and maximize those of the British in most of the battles. Because it was difficult for the British to replenish their ranks after battle, manpower quickly became a major concern for the British.[36]

Supplies were also a continuing challenge for Cornwallis. He purchased some from Loyalists and confiscated some from Whigs. He also devised a system to raise or manufacture supplies on confiscated lowcountry plantations run by slaves deserted by their masters (and thus not eligible for freedom). In spite of these efforts, the British often ran short on supplies. They shipped goods to the backcountry by river or on wagon trains. Wagons proved especially vulnerable to attack by bands of Patriot guerillas.

The constant need for supplies meant that Cornwallis had to devote some of his limited manpower to seizing supplies from Whigs and securing his own supply trains. For example, in August Thomas Sumter's men captured 50 wagons and 250 prisoners when they attacked a supply train headed from Ninety Six to the Waxhaws. Francis Marion, nicknamed the "Swamp Fox," organized guerilla fighters in the Pee Dee River basin to ambush British detachments and disrupt their communications and supply lines. Marion was well-loved by his own men and also well-respected by the enemy. Cornwallis wrote to General Clinton, "Colonel Marion had so wrought on the minds of the people, partly by the terror of his threats and cruelty of his punishments, and partly by the promise of plunder, that there was scarcely an inhabitant between the Santee and Pedee that was not in arms against us."[37]

As he struggled to supply his troops, Cornwallis also sought to quell resistance in several Whig strongholds. About the same time that he had dispatched Huck to the Catawba River Valley, Cornwallis sent a force of Loyalist militia and British regulars under Major Patrick Ferguson to pacify backcountry resistance in the region around Ninety-Six and the Enoree River. Patrick Ferguson, age 26, was a Scotsman, the son of government official and a noblewoman. After studying artillery and fortifications in London, at age 15, he had received a commission in the Royal Northern British Dragoons. Quite ordinary in appearance, he stood five feet, eight inches tall. Yet his spirit was extraordinary. In her history of the Battle of Kings Mountain, historian Wilma Dykeman described him as "a professional soldier in the best possible tradition of that word." Ferguson blended diplomacy and restraint with courage and a magnetism that inspired loyalty from his men. He was also a brilliant military mind and something of an engineer. In 1776, he designed and patented a breech loading rifle, a weapon that was faster to load than rifles loaded from the muzzle end. He organized a volunteer rifle corps that served in Northern campaigns using his innovative firearm, but that unit was disbanded after Ferguson was badly wounded at the Battle of Brandywine. In spite of having one arm that was virtually useless, Ferguson doggedly rehabilitated himself from his wounds, teaching himself to sit a horse and use a pistol with one hand. He devised a system for communicating commands by blowing a whistle during battle. In October 1779, he returned to His Majesty's service when he took command of a Provincial Corps known as the American Volunteers that served in the South. Throughout the summer of 1780, Ferguson pursued Patriot militia around the backcountry, but he succeeded only in hardening resistance.[38]

THE BATTLE OF CAMDEN

Even as Whig militia enjoyed a string of successes in backcountry skirmishes that kept the British perpetually off balance, they faced a devastating setback involving the Continental Army in the South. Ignoring warnings from his own deputies about the desperate lack of supplies in his army, in mid-July Gates began marching south in search of Cornwallis. He assured his men ample supplies of "rum and rations were on the route." Relentlessly pushing his men, Gates hoped to pick off the British by stages with a rapid advance. His first stop was to be a confrontation with Loyalist forces under Lord Rawdon near Camden. Here he also planned to seize the contents of a British storage depot. Gates's men had been on short rations for several weeks already and were thus in no condition for fast marching. They trudged through terrible heat across territory where supplies had already been picked clean and residents had fled. The men ate green corn, unripened peaches and other undigestible food that gave them diarrhea. Gates had about 3,000 men when he arrived at Camden, but many of them were too sick to be effective fighters. Meanwhile, Cornwallis had arrived the day before to reinforce Rawdon and his Loyalists with British regulars. The British outnumbered the Continentals three to two.[39]

The Battle of Camden, August 15, 1780, proved to be a disaster for the Americans. Gates's haste to engage the enemy was one blunder, being surprised by Cornwallis was another, but the biggest blunder was the way he positioned his line with his best-trained Continentals facing inexperienced Loyalist troops and his relatively inexperienced militia facing highly trained British and German regulars. He compounded the mistake by ordering his militia to charge in the face of deadly fire from British regulars. The result was a catastrophe. The militia panicked and ran when they confronted British regulars with their blazing muskets and flashing bayonets. Only the Continentals and one regiment of North Carolina militia held the field. Some accounts said that Gates tried to rally his men, but others said he, too, fled the field. Historian John Ferling says, "seeing the impossibility of continuing the battle, Gates, too, rode for safety, and did not stop riding until he reached Charlotte, sixty miles away." In Charlotte, he procured a fresh horse and rode to Hillsborough, another 120 miles away. The Battle of Camden was a calamity for the Continental Army, and General Gates was skewered in popular opinion. Nearly 1,000 Americans were killed or wounded, and another 1,000 were taken prisoner, a loss in manpower that the Southern army could ill afford, particularly on the heels of the capture of Lincoln's army at Charles Town.[40]

As the events at Camden unfolded, Whig militia continued to operate throughout the backcountry. On August 18, about 200 mounted militiamen from South Carolina, Georgia, and Tennessee left their encampment in the Spartan District intending to attack a Loyalist outpost on the Enoree River. They believed that they would find about 200 Loyalist militiamen at the garrison located at Edward Musgrove's plantation and gristmill, but as they neared their destination, they learned from a local man that the Loyalists had been joined by about 300 provincial troops. Hearing that, the Whigs decided to quickly build crude fortifications and draw the garrison into an ambush. Construction completed, on August 19, a group of roughly 25 Americans crossed the river and provoked enemy forces who gave chase; the Americans planned to lead the British directly into the line of fire from the American breastworks. The plan worked. Loyalist troops followed the small group of fleeing Whigs over the Enoree River. When the Loyalists arrived within 70 feet of the breastworks, the Whigs opened fire. In less than an hour, the Americans succeeded in routing the British, killing 60, wounding 90, and capturing 70.[41]

About this time, the Patriots at Musgrove's Mill received word of Gates's defeat at Camden. Deciding that the best course of action was to regroup, Georgia and South Carolina militiamen returned to their respective camps in those states. Many of the Whig militiamen were "Overmountain Men," volunteers from the area of western North Carolina (now Tennessee) beyond the crest of the Appalachian Mountains. The mountaineers fled to the relative safety of the North Carolina mountains, pursued by a patrol detached from Colonel Patrick Ferguson's army. Elsewhere in the backcountry, Patriot resistance continued. In the fall 1780, 150 Provincials and 250 Indians under command of Thomas "Burnfoot" Brown were besieged at Augusta by a Whig militia commanded by Elijah Clarke. They Whigs withdrew only when relief forces under Lt. John Cruger from Ninety Six arrived.[42]

Meanwhile, after Camden, General Cornwallis decided to march north along the Catawba River to Charlotte, North Carolina. He intended to proceed toward Salisbury from Charlotte. Historian Robert Stansbury Lambert says that Cornwallis hoped to provide support to North Carolina Loyalists such as John Moore, the commander whose troops were routed by Whigs at Ramsour's Mill. Cornwallis argued that in spite of the fact that "the borders do not look so peaceable as they did, an offensive war in the present circumstances of the country is far preferable to a defensive position in South Carolina." In the months that followed, he would come to see the folly in that plan.[43]

CHAPTER 5

Kings Mountain

"First Link in a Chain"

*The Battle of Kings Mountain was fought in
the style eulogized in myth: Americans in
buckskins and hunting shirts, using
Kentucky and Pennsylvania long rifles and
fighting in Indian style, destroyed a major
portion of Cornwallis's Loyalist forces on the
ridges of Kings Mountain.*
Robert W. Brown, Jr., Kings Mountain and
Cowpens: Our Victory Was Complete

*Let each one of you be your own officer, and
do the very best you can, taking every care
you can of yourselves, and availing
yourselves of every advantage that chance
may throw in your way. If in the woods,
shelter yourselves, and give them Indian
play; advance from tree to tree, pressing the
enemy and killing and disabling all you can.
Your officers will shrink from no danger—
they will be constantly with you, and the
moment the enemy give way, be on the alert,
and strictly obey orders.*
Colonel Isaac Shelby, Patriot militia
commander

In spite of the setbacks in the South Carolina backcountry, Cornwallis continued to pursue his plans to invade and pacify North Carolina. In fact, he became convinced that the only way to conquer the South was to gain control of North Carolina. On August 6, 1780, he wrote to General Henry Clinton, "It may be doubted by some whether the invasion of North Carolina may be a prudent measure, but I am convinced it is a necessary one, and that if we do not attack that province, we must give up both South Carolina and Georgia, and retire within the walls of Charlestown [sic]." Cornwallis assured his commanding officer that many North Carolina Loyalists had pledged their support to the Crown. On August 29, he again affirmed his intention to invade North Carolina in order to mobilize the Loyalists there. He wrote to Clinton,

> Our friends [in North Carolina] . . . do not seem inclined to rise until they see our army in motion. The severity of the Rebel government has so terrified and totally subdued the minds of the people, that it is very difficult to rouse them to any exertions.

In late September 1780, after the intense southern heat abated somewhat, Cornwallis occupied Charlotte, a town of 500. His force included 2,200 men, and his intention was to use Charlotte as a base from which to move against the Patriot stronghold at Salisbury.[1]

In anticipation of his invasion of North Carolina, in late August, Cornwallis had ordered Major Patrick Ferguson to cover the left flank of the main British force by moving into western North and South Carolina. Ferguson, often known by the nickname, "the Bulldog," had spent a frustrating summer chasing elusive militia bands all over the backcountry of South Carolina. On September 7, he arrived at Gilbert Town, 50 miles west of Charlotte. His force included about 1,100 men, comprised of New Jersey and New York provincials and Loyalist militia from Georgia and North Carolina. At Gilbert Town, Ferguson's troops routed a band of Patriot militia commanded by Colonel Charles McDowell.[2]

"LAY WASTE . . . WITH FIRE AND SWORD"

The presence of British forces generated intense anxiety in backcountry communities around Gilbert Town. Ferguson's troops raised the ire of local citizens by stealing cattle and supplies. The British commander soon learned there were many Whig militia units operating in the area. Fearing they might join forces to attack his troops, Ferguson set out to intimidate the militia bands into sticking close to home. To set his plan in motion,

Ferguson paroled a Patriot prisoner on September 10, 1780, and sent him to Patriot militia commander Isaac Shelby with a message: If the backcountry men "did not desist from their opposition to British arms," said Ferguson, he would "march over the mountains, hang their leaders and lay their country waste with fire and sword."[3]

The paroled prisoner, a relative of Shelby's, made his way directly to Shelby's home on the Holston River in what is now Tennessee. A surveyor, Shelby had become deeply engaged in the Revolutionary War only the previous summer when he responded to Colonel Charles McDowell's appeals to assist in the backcountry fight against Ferguson. He and his men had returned home from the victory at Musgrove's Mill in the latter part of August. They were exhausted, and most of their terms of enlistment were due to expire. They had hoped to withdraw from involvement in the war, but Ferguson's message changed their minds. In his history of Kings Mountain and Cowpens, historian Robert W. Brown, Jr. noted, "The people Ferguson was trying to intimidate were exactly the kind of people that such demonstrations of bravado failed to impress." Shelby and his ilk were fiercely independent frontiersmen who had bested Indian warriors and wild animals to carve out settlements in the Appalachian wilderness. The Patriot militia leaders who emerged in the backcountry were, in the words of Brown, "at the head of troops, not through family contacts or wealth, but through their actions as men in the communities."[4]

Alarmed by Ferguson's threats, Shelby traveled to the settlement of Jonesboro to consult with John Sevier, a popular Indian fighter and leader of the militia from the Watauga and Nolichucky settlements in what is now northeast Tennessee. According to Shelby, he and Sevier agreed to "march with all the men we could raise and attempt to surprise Ferguson by attacking him in his camp." Using Ferguson's threat as a recruiting tool, Sevier and Shelby sent out a call for volunteers from the mountains, and the two men personally pledged repayment of North Carolina tax money borrowed to outfit the expedition. On September 25, about 800 "overmountain" militia forces mustered at Sycamore Shoals near present-day Elizabethton, Tennessee. Here they were joined by 400 Virginians under the command of Colonel William Campbell. The next day, the Overmountain Men began their march southeast headed toward Quaker Meadows (today's Morganton, North Carolina) where they aimed to rendezvous with additional militia forces.[5]

While the Overmountain Men were organizing their expedition, Ferguson had moved across the North Carolina border into the upper Catawba River valley of South Carolina, intending to frighten Whigs there. Feeling fairly secure, he allowed many of his Loyalist militia to go home

John Sevier

John Sevier, a descendent of Huguenot immigrants, was born in Shenandoah County, Virginia, in 1734. When he was in his twenties, he, his wife Sarah, and their children joined a group of settlers who migrated to the Holston River valley in territory claimed by both Virginia and North Carolina. Sevier became involved in local politics and the local militia where he developed a reputation as a fierce Indian fighter.

Sevier was one of the leading militia commanders in the "overmountain" region beyond the Appalachian crest, which in 1780 led Isaac Shelby to appeal to Sevier for help in attacking Major Patrick Ferguson after Ferguson promised to "lay waste" to the Overmountain settlements. Sevier, who was often called Nolichucky Jack for the river he lived on (or just Chucky Jack), led a militia unit of more than 200 men on the long march to Kings Mountain where the Whig forces easily defeated Ferguson on October 7, 1780.

After the Revolution, North Carolina bowed to the pressure from the new US Congress and ceded the land west of the Appalachian Mountains to the US government. Congress did not immediately accept the western lands or create a government there. Sevier stepped into the power vacuum in the region. Sevier joined with other leading men in the area to found the "State of Franklin," and Sevier was elected its only governor. After several years of wrangling over the status of the territory, it became part of the newly formed Territory South of the River Ohio and eventually part of the state of Tennessee. Sevier served 12 years as governor of Tennessee and later as a member of the US House of Representatives. He died the day after his seventieth birthday while surveying the boundary between the state of Georgia and the Creek nation in modern-day Alabama.

on furlough. But on October 1, having received intelligence that Shelby's men were quickly approaching, Ferguson appealed to his furloughed men to return to camp. He also called for Loyalists in the surrounding area to help reinforce his troops. Worried about the size of the force gathering to oppose him, Ferguson ordered a retreat to Charlotte where he would meet up with Cornwallis. Three days into his march, he asked Cornwallis to send reinforcements; according to one account, this message never reached the Southern commander because Patriot scouts intercepted the courier. Ferguson also tried one last time to gain significant levels of support from locals, making a special appeal to those who had previously refused to choose sides as well as those who had leaned toward the Whig cause in the past. He issued a message to backcountry citizens on October 1, 1780, that read,

> Gentlemen:—Unless you wish to be eat up by an inundation of barbarians . . . who by their shocking cruelties and irregularities, give the best proof of their cowardice and want of discipline; I say, if you wish to be pinioned, robbed, and murdered, and see your wives and daughters, in four days, abused by the dregs of mankind—in short, if you wish or deserve to live, and bear the name of men, grasp your arms in a moment and run to camp.
>
> The Back Water men have crossed the mountains; McDowell, Hampton, Shelby, and Cleveland are at their head, so that you know what you have to depend upon. If you choose to be degraded forever and ever by a set of mongrels, say so at once, and let your women turn their backs upon you, and look out for real men to protect them.[6]

His dire warning had little effect. Few new recruits arrived.

On October 5, Cornwallis sent Ferguson a dispatch ordering him to meet Tarleton at Arness Ford on the Catawba River, but Ferguson never received the order. Early in the day on October 6, Ferguson again sent Cornwallis an appeal for reinforcements:

> I am on my march towards you, by a road leading from Cherokee Ford, north of King's Mountain. Three or four hundred good soldiers, part dragoons, would finish the business. *Something must be done soon.* This is their last push in this quarter, etc.

It is not entirely clear why, but later that day, Ferguson decided to make a stand at Kings Mountain about 20 miles from Charlotte, instead of trying to reach the safety of Cornwallis's headquarters, a day's march away. Perhaps, as historian John Ferling suggests, he believed that the natural defenses at Kings Mountain would be sufficient to hold off the Patriots till reinforcements arrived. His decision proved to be a fatal mistake since reinforcements were not on the way.[7]

The Battle of Kings Mountain is the purest example of the American Revolution in the southern backcountry as civil war. Ferguson would be the only man at the battle who was not an American. His troops consisted of about 75 Provincial Rangers, trained troops from New Jersey and New York who wore British redcoat uniforms. Most of his soldiers were Loyalist militia from the Ninety Six garrison whom Ferguson had trained; an additional 500 North Carolina militia had joined him when he left Gilbert Town. In all, he had nearly 1,100 men, most armed with Brown Bess muskets and handmade bayonets designed to fit into the muzzle of the musket.[8]

Kings Mountain is hardly a mountain. Rising only about 60 feet above the surrounding landscape, it is some 600 yards long, and the top is only about 70 feet wide at its narrowest point. In his *Atlas of South Carolina,* surveyor and architect Robert Mills said that it was "so narrow that a man standing on it may be shot from either side." Located in modern-day York County, South Carolina, Kings Mountain is part of a chain of ridges about 16 miles in length that extend on a southwesterly course along the North and South Carolina border. At the time of the battle, the hillsides of Kings Mountain were covered with old growth hardwood trees. The top of the mountain was (and still is) a treeless plateau. Because high ground has traditionally been seen as the position of strength in military action and because the bare plateau made such a convenient spot for camping, it must have seemed promising to Ferguson, as evidenced by the final message he sent Cornwallis on the evening of October 6. He wrote, "I arrived today at King's Mountain and have taken a post where I do not think I can be forced by a stronger enemy than that against us." [9]

> Patrick Ferguson: "I arrived today at King's Mountain and have taken a post where I do not think I can be forced by a stronger enemy than that against us."

THE OVERMOUNTAIN JOURNEY

Meanwhile the Whig troops marched to meet Ferguson. The Overmountain Men made slow progress at first. They had brought along a herd of cattle to supply themselves with meat, but the rugged terrain and narrow Indian trails on their route made driving cattle a laborious process. After the second day of excruciatingly slow travel, the men decided to slaughter some of the cattle and pack the meat for the trip, leaving the rest of the herd behind. As the Overmountain Men continued the march, they slogged through snow in some areas that was "shoe-mouth deep." Finally, after five days of hard going, they arrived at Quaker Meadows on the McDowell family plantation, within striking distance of Gilbert Town. Additional militia men joined them here. Only a half-day's march beyond the McDowell place, the expedition bogged down again, this time due to driving rains that forced them to stay in camp for a day and a half. On October 2, they resumed the march, that night camping north of Gilbert Town, where they expected to find Ferguson. [10]

The next morning, before breaking camp, the militia leaders called their men into a conference. North Carolina militia commander Benjamin Cleveland told the men,

Now, my brave fellows, I have come to tell you the news. The enemy is at hand, and we must [be] up and at them. Now is the time for every man of you to do his country a priceless service— such as shall lead your children to exult in the fact that their fathers were the conquerors of Ferguson. When the pinch comes, I shall be with you. But if any of you shrink from sharing in the battle and the glory, you can now have the opportunity of backing out, and leaving; and you shall have a few minutes for considering the matter.

John Sevier then spoke, repeating the offer to let anyone who wished to withdraw from the fight do so.[11]

Major Joseph McDowell of North Carolina responded with a bit of a taunt. According to nineteenth-century historian Lyman Draper, McDowell, "with a winning smile on his countenance," asked the men, "Well, my good fellows, . . . what kind of a story

> Issac Shelby: "Let each one of you be your own officer, and do the very best you can, taking every care you can of yourselves, and availing yourselves of every advantage that chance may throw in your way. If in the woods, shelter yourselves, and give them Indian play; advance from tree to tree, pressing the enemy and killing and disabling all you can."

will you, who back out, have to relate when you get home, leaving your braver comrades to fight the battle, and gain the victory?" Reportedly, no one took the commanding officers up on the offer to leave.[12]

Isaac Shelby then congratulated the men on their decision, saying,

I am heartily glad . . . to see you to a man resolve to meet and fight your country's foes. When we encounter the enemy, don't wait for the word of command. Let each one of you be your own officer, and do the very best you can.[13]

After this pep talk, the force set out to confront the British, but the Overmountain Men arrived in Gilbert Town only to find Ferguson gone. Disappointed, they tried to track his meandering trail, gathering intelligence from the locals. On October 6, the same day that Ferguson camped on Kings Mountain, the Overmountain Men arrived at the Cowpens, the designated spot for their rendezvous with additional militia units. Here they were joined by two more militia units from Georgia and South Carolina. Among the new arrivals was Joseph Kerr, the crippled man who had been such a helpful spy before the Battle of Huck's Defeat. Kerr's handicap led the enemy to discount him as a potential threat, enabling

Joseph Kerr

Joseph Kerr gained fame as the "crippled spy" for the Whigs. Born in 1750, he grew up in Mecklenburg County, North Carolina. According to one biographer, Kerr became "indignant at the ravages of the British and Tories, and actuated with a true, patriotic spirit." He volunteered his services as a spy to militia General Joseph McDowell. Kerr proved adept at using his disability as a disguise. His standard practice was to locate British or Loyalist encampments, hide his horse, and enter the camp in the guise of a crippled beggar. The enemy discounted him as a potential threat, and he was able to gather intelligence freely. Kerr's intelligence was key to Whig victories at the small skirmishes at Blackstock's Ford, the turning point fight at Huck's Defeat, and the major battle at Kings Mountain. After the war, Kerr moved to Tennessee where he died "at a good old age."[14]

him to spend time with British and Loyalist forces and gather intelligence. He had been with Ferguson earlier in the day, and reported that the British commander planned to set up camp on Kings Mountain.[15]

The men and horses who arrived at the Cowpens were exhausted after their long and difficult trek. Colonel William Hill, commander of one of the newly arrived South Carolina militia units, recalled the scene that night, "The Officers of each army then convened together, the proceedings that took place was to give Col Campbell a nominal command over the whole this was done in courtesy as he & his men had come the greatest distance & from over the mountains. It also being known that Col Tarlton with his reinforcement would in at least 2 days, join Col Ferguson. This induced the Officers to select 933 men & mounted them on their fleetest horses, leaving about an equal number of foot & horse in the camp."[16]

The Whigs spent the early evening of October 6 making preparations for battle. They slaughtered additional cattle, apparently procured locally, and cooked meals for the battle. About 9 pm, the men set out in the rain, gathering intelligence on the way. William Hill described the conditions of the march,

It proved a very dark & raining night the path being small & the woods very thick, the troop got scattered & dispersed through the woods thus wondering the whole night, that when morning appeared the rear of them was but 5 miles from the Cowpens, this caused them to march uncommonly hard which caused many of the horses to give out as but few of them were shod.[17]

Arriving near Kings Mountain, the militia leaders convened a council of war. They decided to divide their forces and surround the base of the mountain. From there, ranks two men deep would attack in unison on three sides. The Whigs captured some Loyalist pickets who revealed the general arrangement of the British camp and its limited fortifications. The pickets also told them that Ferguson was wearing a distinctive plaid hunting shirt. The Overmountain Men began to move into position. The soft rain had dampened the leaves, making it easier for the Whigs to approach without being heard, but the precipitation also made the ground boggy in places. Shelby's forces headed for the north side of the mountain, while Campbell's men headed toward the south side. To distinguish themselves from Ferguson's Loyalist troops, who were not wearing uniforms, the Patriots put pieces of paper in their hats. (For their part, Loyalists identified themselves with pine sprigs.)[18]

THE BATTLE COMMENCES

About 3pm that afternoon (at least one eyewitness account says 1pm), some of Shelby's men became mired in mud and attracted the attention of Loyalist pickets. The pickets opened fire, alerting Ferguson and his men to the presence of the Whig forces. Meanwhile, on the southwest side of Kings Mountain, a Whig soldier encountered another Loyalist picket and had to shoot him. Now Ferguson knew he was surrounded on at least two sides. Even though not all his men were in position, Campbell made the decision to proceed with the attack. Lyman Draper described it this way: "Colonel Campbell had thrown off his coat, and while leading his men to the attack, he exclaimed at the top of his voice,—'Here they are, my brave boys; *shout like h—l, and fight like devils!'* The woods immediately resounded with the shouts of the line . . ." Campbell first ordered mounted forces up the mountain to attack a fortified position, followed by men on foot. Shelby's men soon joined the attack, followed by Sevier and Cleveland's. William Hill reported that there was "very little military subordination as all that was required or expected was that every Officer & man should ascend the mountain so as to surround the enemy on all quarters . . ."[19]

The loud yells unnerved Ferguson's forces. Historian Lyman Draper reported that when Captain DePeyster, Ferguson's second-in-command,

heard these almost deafening yells—the same in kind he too well remembered hearing from Shelby's men at Musgrove's Mill—he remarked to Ferguson: 'These things are ominous—these are the

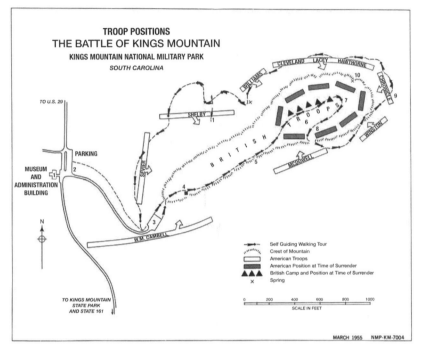

Figure 5.1 Map of the Battle of Kings Mountain

d—d [damned] yelling boys!' And when these terrific shouts
saluted Ferguson's ears, he expressed fears for the result.

    Robert Campbell, a Patriot militia man, reported that upon hearing
the war cries, "The British beat to arms and immediately formed on the
top of the mountain behind a chain of rocks that appeared impregnable
and had their wagons drawn up along their flank at the end of the
mountain by which they made a strong breastwork."[20]
    Ferguson ordered a bayonet charge that inflicted heavy casualties on
Campbell's Virginia militia, which included four free blacks and a slave.
Though the men retreated after the bayonet charge, they regrouped and
attacked again. The British launched a second and a third bayonet charge,
forcing the Virginia men to retreat each time. Each time they regrouped
and resumed the attack. Shelby later reported, "They repelled us three
times with bayonet charges; but being determined to conquer or die, we
came up a fourth time." The men used the trees and rock formations for
cover as they advanced up the mountain guerilla style. Colonel William
Hill left a vivid account of the scene:

there being a small flat of ground where he had pitched his camp
on, the sides of the mountain being very Rocky & steep as well
as a great number of fallen & standing trees so that the
Americans could attack his camp on all quarters, & their shot
went over the americans without effect . . . [H]e trusted much to
the bayonet, as a proof of this he had trained his men to that
purpose & those which he could not furnish with this weapon he
had contrived a substitute by getting the Blacksmiths to make
long knives to answer this purpose with a tang [tongue] put in a
piece of wood to fit the calibre of the gun & a button to rest on
the muzzle of the piece, In the commencement of the action he
ordered a charge on the Americans, but the ground was so rough
as before mentioned that they were not able to overtake the
americans to injure them, in this way, & when they had went a
certain distance they had orders to retreat to their camp. & then it
was that the americans had every advantage required. [sic][21]

Historian Robert W. Brown observed, "The insect-like swarming
effect of the small groups ascending the hill effectively negated Ferguson's
conventional tactics" because he could not focus his fire. Much of the
fighting became hand-to-hand. Ferguson insisted on massing his troops
in the British-style, an ineffective tactic on the wooded mountain. To
make matters worse, as Hill's description suggests, the British were over-
shooting the Americans—shooting over their heads—a common mistake
when shooting downhill. After several minutes of fierce battle, some of
Ferguson's troops began to run out of ammunition. Loyalist militiaman
Samuel Williams reported that "[N]umbers being without ammunition
gave way, which natural threw the rest of the militia into confusion."[22]

There were two women encamped with Ferguson at Kings Mountain,
Virginia Paul and Virginia Sal. Probably they were mistresses of Ferguson,
but they also provided some laundry and cooking services to the officers.
Virginia Sal was killed in the first wave of the Whig assault. Now, at the
height of the battle, Virginia Paul fled down the mountain on horseback
stopping to tell Whig forces what Ferguson was wearing and where he
was. The Whigs detained Paul and later sent her to Cornwallis's camp.[23]

Shelby and Campbell's men attained the summit first at the southwest
end of the mountaintop plateau. Ferguson led his men in a last ditch attack
of volleys followed by bayonet charges that caused the American lines to
falter but not break. As more and more Patriots reached the summit and
began to surround the Loyalists, the latter group began to panic, laying
down their arms and asking for quarter. Mounted on his white horse and
wearing his distinctive checkered shirt, using his silver whistle to signal

commands, Ferguson tried desperately to rally his men and fight his way out of the encirclement. Reportedly, he yelled that he would not yield to "such a damned banditti." The Patriots spotted his checked shirt; he was shot multiple times. His foot lodged in his stirrups as he fell from his horse and he was dragged across the mountaintop until a Loyalist managed to get his horse under control. Led by Abraham DePeyster, Ferguson's second in command, the remaining Loyalists surrendered. When DePeyster asked for quarter for his men, Whigs invoked "Tarleton's Quarter," their reference to the Waxhaws Massacre. Reports indicate that some of the men trying to surrender were killed. John Sevier's son Joseph was one soldier who continued firing at surrendering troops. He had been told, erroneously as it turned out, that his father had been killed in the fighting, and he declared, "The damned rascals have killed my father, and I'll keep loading and shooting till I kill every son of a bitch of them!" Isaac Shelby reported, "It was some time before a complete cessation of the firing, on our part, could be effected."[24]

The Whigs were elated at their important victory. They had lost fewer than 90 men to death or wounds, while they had killed or wounded 407 Loyalists and taken roughly another 700 prisoner. Most important, they had eliminated the threat of having their homes "laid waste" by Ferguson and his men. Nonetheless, the aftermath of the battle was particularly ugly. The men desecrated Ferguson's body, stripping him naked and dividing his clothing and possessions among themselves as souvenirs. A group of Patriots relieved themselves on the Scotsman's body. Finally some Loyalist officers were allowed to bury Ferguson and Virginia Sal on the mountaintop.[25]

THE AFTERMATH

Exhausted from their punishing overland march and the pitched battle, the Patriots camped that night on the ridge top with their prisoners and with the dead and dying. Wounded men cried out for help all night. Whig soldiers later recalled the horrors of that long night. Thomas Young wrote, "Awful, indeed . . . was the scene of the wounded, the dying and the dead, on the field, after the carnage of that dreadful day." His fellow soldier, Benjamin Sharp, observed, "We had . . . to encamp on the ground with the dead and wounded, and pass the night amid groans and lamentations." The son of one Kings Mountain veteran later recalled, "My father, David Witherspoon . . . used to describe the scenes of the battle-ground the night after the contest as heart-rending in the extreme— the groans of the dying, and the constant cry of 'water! water.' "[26]

The next morning, wives and children of Loyalist militia men arrived searching for their loved ones. One witness described the scene as "really distressing. The wives and children of the poor Tories came in, in great numbers. Their husbands, fathers and brothers lay dead in heaps, while others lay wounded or dying, a melancholy sight indeed!" Those who identified their dead or wounded among the fallen were allowed to remove them. The young Whig soldier, James Collins, reported,

> We proceeded to bury the dead, but it was badly done. They were thrown into convenient piles and covered with old logs, the bark of old trees, and rocks . . . the wolves became so plenty, that is was dangerous for anyone to be out at night, for several miles around. The hogs in the neighborhood gathered into the place to devour the flesh of man . . .

The Whigs further divided the spoils of battle among themselves. Then, believing that Tarleton would soon be in pursuit of the Whig forces, the Overmountain militia officers conferred and decided to gather the prisoners and march toward the Moravian settlement in North Carolina (near modern-day Winston-Salem) before Cornwallis could arrive with troops.[27]

The Whigs burned 17 baggage wagons from Ferguson's camp because taking them along would slow down the march. Then the prisoners were lined up, and the column set off overland. The march was long and arduous and provisions were scarce. One Loyalist later reported to a British newspaper,

James Collins: "We proceeded to bury the dead, but it was badly done. They were thrown into convenient piles and covered with old logs, the bark of old trees, and rocks . . . the wolves became so plenty, that is was dangerous for anyone to be out at night, for several miles around. The hogs in the neighborhood gathered into the place to devour the flesh of man . . . "

> The morning after the action we were marched sixteen miles, previous to which orders were given by the Rebel Col. Campbell . . . that should they be attacked on their march, they were to fire on, and destroy their prisoners. The party was kept marching two days without any kind of provisions.

Tempers grew short. Some prisoners escaped on the march, and others were killed trying to escape. Colonel Tarleton later wrote, "The mountaineers, it is reported, used every insult and indignity, after the action, towards the dead body of Major Ferguson, and exercised horrid cruelties on the prisoners that fell into their possession." Eventually the rank and file soldiers' treatment of the prisoners became so abusive that, on October 11, Colonel Campbell ordered, "I must request officers of all ranks in the army to endeavor to restrain the disorderly manner of slaughtering and disturbing the prisoners." One of those rank and file Whigs, Robert Campbell (unrelated to Colonel William Campbell), recalled,

> The third night after the action the officers of the Carolinas complained to Col. Campbell that there were among the prisoners a number who had, previous to the action on King's Mountain, committed cool and deliberate murder, and other enormities like atrocious, and requested him to order a Court Martial to examine into the matter; they stated that if they should escape, . . . they fear they would commit other enormities worse than they had formerly done.[28]

Either Robert Campbell's memory of the timing of the request for the court martial was incorrect or it took several days for the officers to agree to the proceeding. It was not until October 14 that the tired and ragged Whig troops decided to court-martial Loyalist troops they accused of having made attacks on women and children in the backcountry over recent months. Loyalist witnesses described these court-martials as "mock trials," and it is indeed doubtful that anything resembling the rule of law prevailed. Thirty men were convicted and ordered to be hanged. Lyman Draper, a nineteenth-century historian of the battle who interviewed veterans of the battle and made an intensive study of the written accounts, described the scene,

> Early in the evening, the trials having been brought to a conclusion, a suitable oak was selected, upon a projecting limb of which the executions were to take place. It was by the road side, near the camp, and is yet standing, known in all that region as the *Gallows Oak*. Torch-lights were procured, the condemned brought out, around whom the troops formed four deep. It was a singular and interesting night scene, the dark old woods illuminated with the wild glare of hundreds of pine-knot torches; and quite a number of the Loyalist leaders of the Carolinas about to be launched into eternity . . . According to Lieutenant Allaire's account, they died like soldiers—like martyrs, in their own and friends' estimation.[29]

The Whigs arranged a crude gallows with nooses swung over trees, and prisoners were place astride on horses that would be walked out from under them. The hanged slowly choked to death from the crude arrangement as the other prisoners were forced to look on. One Whig leader was reported to have crowed at the dangling bodies, saying, "Would to God every tree in the wilderness bore such fruit as that." Finally after nine men—six privates and three captains—were hanged, senior Patriot officials stopped the proceedings. Whig William Hill insisted that the men who were hung well deserved the punishment. He wrote,

> 9 of those who surrendered were hanged by their conquerors they were provoked to this by severity of the British who had lately hanged a great number of americans at Camden, Ninety six, Augusta & & — But a much better reason that each individual of them was guilty of crimes for which their lives were forfeited by the Laws of the State & one in particular had taken a number of Indians to a small fort on the frontiers & murdered a number of women & children the men being absent from the fort.

Loyalist Anthony Allaire disagreed with Hill's characterization of the condemned men, instead insisting that they were among the "most respectable." Whatever the hanged men may or may not have done before the Battle of Kings Mountain, historian Robert W. Brown is correct when he notes that the treatment of the Loyalist prisoners tarnished the important victory.[30]

Over the next several days, the Patriot army began to disperse. The Overmountain Men headed westward, back across the mountains. Others returned to their homes in South Carolina. Virginians and North Carolinians continued to escort the prisoners to General Gates's headquarters in Hillsborough, but so many had escaped along the way that fewer than 200 were delivered to the Continental commander.[31]

Rumors and piecemeal accounts of the defeat reached General Cornwallis in the days after the battle, but he did not received official word for several days. (Some sources say October 10 and others October 14). The defeat was an enormous blow. The Battle of Kings Mountain destroyed the left wing of General Cornwallis' army. His plans to advance further into North Carolina were ruined; without the protection Ferguson's troops provided on his left flank, he would be vulnerable to attack from Whig militia forces. Neither did he have sufficient forces to suppress raids by Whig militia in the backcountry. He also knew that the victory offered the Patriots an important psychological victory; it reinforced Whig resistance and confidence that they could win the war while further eroding

Loyalist morale. British control at the backcountry outposts at Ninety Six, Camden, and Augusta was slowly but surely deteriorating. British commanders were also losing faith in Loyalist militia forces. In November 1780, John Harris Cruger, the commander of the British garrison at Ninety Six, wrote, "I think I shall never again look to the [Loyalist] militia for the least support, and I am convinced that it is the King's troop only that can hold this country." That winter, Cornwallis would write to Clinton, "The militia of Ninety-Six, on which alone we could place the smallest dependence, are so totally disheartened by the defeat of Ferguson that of the whole district we could with difficulty assemble 100, and even those, I am convinced, would not have made the smallest resistance if we had been attacked . . ." Tarleton also recorded the psychological blow that resulted from the defeat at Kings Mountain. He wrote that the defeat communicated "depression and fear" to the "loyalists upon the borders and to the southward."[32] Later Sir Henry Clinton wrote,

> The instant I heard of Major Ferguson's defeat, I foresaw most of the consequences likely to result from it. The check so encouraged the spirit of rebellion in the Carolinas that it could never afterward be humbled. [It was] the first link in a chain of evils that followed each other in regular succession until they at last ended in the total loss of America.[33]

On October 14, Cornwallis withdrew his troops from Charlotte to Winnsborough, South Carolina to regroup. He knew that at Winnsborough, he would have access to a good road network and the ferry over the Broad River at Columbia, both important resources for his supply lines. With easy access to support from his outposts at Georgetown and Savannah on the coast and Camden and Ninety Six in the backcountry, Cornwallis believed Winnsborough provided an ideal location from which to control the backcountry throughout the coming long winter. His calculations would prove to be incorrect, but in the meantime, backcountry fighting between Whigs and Loyalists continued. In December 1780, General Greene wrote, "The Whigs and Tories pursue one another with the most relentless fury, killing and destroying each other wherever they meet." The "relentless fury" would not abate for many more months.[34]

CHAPTER 6

The Battle of Cowpens

Victory for "The Flying Army"

> *The battle [at Cowpens] marked a turning point in American fortunes. The road through the American position led symbolically, if not quite literally, to Yorktown and British surrender on 19 October 1781.*
>
> Lawrence E. Babits, *A Devil of a Whipping: The Battle of Cowpens*

> *Near the Cow-pens on Thickety Creek . . . we suffered a total defeat by some dreadful bad management.*
>
> Alexander Chesney, *Loyalist*

On October 26, 1780, when news reached George Washington of the American victory at Kings Mountain, he stated in his General Orders that the victory was "proof of the spirit and resources of the country." Indeed, resistance to the British was intensifying in the backcountry. Even General Henry Clinton, hundreds of miles away, was aware of this attitude. Earlier in the fall, he had ordered a 2,200 man British invasion force to Virginia to provide a diversion for Cornwallis's army. They arrived at Portsmouth and conducted some destructive raids against coastal residents, but after he learned of the defeat at Kings Mountain, Clinton sent these troops to Charlotte to join Cornwallis. Meanwhile, Patriot militia bands continued their hit-and-run attacks. During the fall and winter of 1780 and 1781, British supply trains and detachments in the backcountry fell victim to a series of raids from partisan bands. Thomas Sumter achieved small but important victories at Fishdam Ford in modern Chester County and at Blackstocks in modern Union County, both in South Carolina.[1]

NEW LEADERSHIP FOR THE CONTINENTAL ARMY

Kings Mountain had been a great militia victory, orchestrated by independent and self-organized volunteers who plotted their own battle plans. Nonetheless, it remained to the command structure of the Continental Army to devise a strategy for defeating Cornwallis and his southern army. General Horatio Gates, the commander of the southern branch of the Continentals, had been languishing with his army at Hillsborough, North Carolina, since his defeat at Camden. Congress had appointed Gates to command the southern branch of the Continentals without much consultation with George Washington, and they had made a disastrous choice. Tacitly acknowledging their mistake, in October 1780, Congress deferred to General Washington to name a successor to Gates. He chose General Nathanael Greene.[2]

Greene, a Rhode Island native and the scion of an old Quaker family, was largely self-educated. He rejected the Quaker insistence on pacifism, embracing a study of military science early in his adulthood. A community leader and a member of the Rhode Island General Assembly, Greene immediately volunteered his services when the Revolutionary War broke out, and he developed a reputation as a courageous and able commanding officer in early battles of the war. His abilities as a capable administrator proved invaluable when Washington put him in charge of securing supplies for the troops encamped at Valley Forge during the bleak winter of 1777–78. By 1780, Washington counted Greene as one of his most trusted lieutenants. In his history of the American victory in the Revolutionary War, historian John Ferling says Washington believed that the Southern Department needed someone who "understood the wisdom of Fabian tactics and possessed sufficient backbone to stand up to the South's civilian leaders." Washington had resorted to Fabian tactics—avoiding pitched battles in favor of wearing down the enemy in a war of attrition —throughout most of the war because he realized that the Continental Army could never muster sufficient strength to defeat the mighty British military machine in head-to-head confrontation. Greene concurred with Washington as to strategy. Greene was also a skilled diplomat, and he would prove adept in dealing with independent-minded Southern militia commanders.[3]

Before joining his army in North Carolina, General Greene appeared before Congress in Philadelphia to appeal for more money for the army. He then stopped in each state along the way making similar appeals, finally arriving in Charlotte in December. The army he found there included about 950 Continentals and 1,500 militia. The forces were plagued by a lack of supplies and a smallpox outbreak. Because British had been there first and had stripped the area of provisions, Greene realized there were few supplies in Charlotte, a situation exacerbated by poor harvests that fall. Due to inadequate clothing, food, and shelter, the troops were in a poor state of discipline. Greene immediately began to reorganize his command structure and secure supplies. He sent officers to explore the countryside and provide intelligence about locations of strategic importance. At the same time, he engaged in deft diplomacy to cultivate the powerful and popular Patriot militia commanders Thomas Sumter and Francis Marion. He knew that he needed the support of these leaders and their units, but he also had to fend off their demands for immediate offensive action. Anxious to capitalize on the momentum generated by the victory at Kings Mountain, Thomas Sumter appealed to Greene to launch an immediate attack on Cornwallis's army. Greene visited Sumter at his home where the militia commander was recuperating from wounds he had received in the fall. Greene was able to soothe Sumter by promising to consider offensive action, but privately Greene and his lieutenants believed a precipitous attack would be a bad idea. In addition to the challenges of supplies, morale, and impatient militia commanders, Greene worried that the British, little more than a day's march away at Winnsborough, might attack at any time.[4]

Assessing his situation in mid-December, 1780, Greene decided on a bold move: to reduce the number of men he had to feed in one place, he divided his army, a move generally thought to be dangerous. He sent General Daniel Morgan with 600 Continentals plus Thomas Sumter's militia to forage in the countryside west of Charlotte. Greene moved his main army to Hick's Creek, South Carolina, southeast of Charlotte near modern day Cheraw. Greene's own force now lay within easy reach of military support from General Francis Marion and his men. In South Carolina, Greene found it easier to supply his troops; he also was able to threaten British garrisons in eastern North Carolina. Most of all, he hoped that Cornwallis might chase one detachment or the other, leaving British backcountry garrisons largely undefended. Ferling calls Greene's plan "the first evidence of imaginative thinking from headquarters in the

Southern Department since the war had descended on this region two years before." In a letter written some time after Christmas 1780, Greene said,

> I am well satisfied with the movement [division of the army], for it has answered thus far all the purposes from which I intended it. It makes the most of my inferior force, for it compels my adversary to divide his, and hold him in doubt as to his own line of conduct.[5]

Meanwhile, anticipating that Cornwallis would soon reinvade North Carolina, General Clinton ordered a British invasion force commanded by the American turncoat Benedict Arnold to Virginia. The British arrived in Jamestown on January 2, 1781. Arnold's assignment was to complete the same diversionary and disruptive mission as the earlier force. He launched a devastating raid on Richmond, destroying a foundry, tobacco warehouses, and a shipyard. Then Arnold and his troops went into winter quarters at Portsmouth. He had demonstrated Virginia's vulnerability. He also discredited Governor Jefferson who had delayed calling up militia forces to defend the colony, but Arnold had not subdued the Old Dominion.[6]

Cornwallis and his men were suffering through a difficult winter in Winnsborough. Hundreds of the men fell ill as did Cornwallis himself. Terror reigned in the backcountry as Whig militia launched hit-and-run raids against Loyalists who believed they should be protected by the occupying British forces. Although Loyalist militia sometimes offered tit for tat, the Whig militia attacks had the effect of discouraging open support of the Crown. On December 9, Cornwallis wrote to his commanding officer, General Clinton, "Marion has so wrought on the minds of the people, partly by the terror of his threats and cruelty of his punishments, and partly by the promise of plunder, that there is scarcely any man between the Pee Dee and the Santee that was not in arms against us." Cornwallis ordered Colonel Banastre Tarleton to search for the notorious Marion throughout the fall and early winter, but Tarleton was unsuccessful in capturing the wily partisan known as the "Swamp Fox." After the defeat at Kings Mountain, Cornwallis encouraged the Indians in the Over-mountain districts to launch attacks on settlers, reasoning correctly that the need to protect their homes and families would prevent many of the fierce mountain fighters from returning to militia service on behalf of the Patriot cause. Cornwallis continued to plan for an invasion of North Carolina with his diminished force. On January 6, he wrote to his superior officer, General Henry Clinton,

I shall begin my march to-morrow, having been delayed a few days by a diversion made by the enemy towards Ninety Six, and propose keeping on the west of Catawba for a considerable distance. I shall then proceed to pass that river and the Yadkin. Events alone can decide the future steps.[7]

DANIEL MORGAN'S "FLYING ARMY"

Events were about to decide those future steps. Daniel Morgan and his large force of light infantry left Charlotte for the New Acquisition District on December 21, 1780, setting up a camp at a place called Grindal Shoals on the Pacolet River. Greene expected them to be a "flying army" that would force Cornwallis to divide his force in order to pursue them. Greene also hoped Morgan's troops would threaten British posts in the back-country. Daniel Morgan proved to be an inspired choice to lead Greene's parry into the backcountry. A poorly educated Virginia frontiersman who had served in the French and Indian War, Morgan had survived the administration of 499 lashes as punishment for striking a British officer. For the rest of his life, he bragged that the soldier manning the whip had miscounted and given him one lash too few. He hated the British army with a passion born of that painful experience. Later Morgan served as a rifleman with provincial forces guarding the Virginia frontier. After the battles of Lexington and Concord, the Virginia House of Burgesses selected him to form one of its new rifle companies. He distinguished himself through valorous service in the northern department of the Continental Army, including the Battle of Saratoga. In 1779, Morgan briefly retired due to severe back and leg pain, but after the disastrous defeat at Camden in 1780, he re-entered the army in the southern division. He looked the part of a soldier; he was more than six feet tall and powerfully built. He bore a scar on his cheek, a souvenir of a musket ball wound from the French and Indian War. A charismatic and determined commander, Morgan knew how to inspire loyalty from his men. One contemporary said he "reflected deeply, spoke little, and executed with keen perseverance everything he undertook."[8]

Morgan's army included Continentals, state troops, and militia. The Continentals included a light infantry force and some cavalry from the Third Continental Dragoons, led by William Washington, a cousin of the commander-in-chief. Continental infantry hailed from Maryland, Delaware, and Virginia. State troops from North and South Carolina were also part of Morgan's "flying army." State troops had not served as long as Continental Regulars, but they had received more training and had served more consistently than militia. Morgan also had two militia battalions, one from Virginia and one from North Carolina. In the field, he was joined almost daily by more militia forces from throughout the backcountry including Andrew Pickens' forces, and units from North Carolina and Georgia. Large numbers of South Carolinians would join the ranks in mid-January of 1781, many arriving as late as the night before the great battle at Cowpens. Accounts of Morgan's numbers vary. Ferling estimates that Morgan had 800–1000 men, and Morgan himself had reported a figure of 800. But subsequent research by historian Lawrence Babits indicates that Morgan likely had between 1,800 and 2,400 troops at the Battle of Cowpens, a figure that is closer to Tarleton's estimate of 2,000 Patriots. Babits reached this conclusion by careful analysis of the pension records of men who claimed to have been with Morgan at Cowpens. Babits believed that Morgan and others who estimated troop strength at only around 800 men counted only the Continental regulars in their reports.[9]

The "Flying Army" proved to be as flexible as Greene had hoped, and their presence in the backcountry kept the British off-balance and helped delay Cornwallis's plan to re-invade North Carolina. For example, on December 27, while camped at Grindal Shoals, Morgan received intelligence that a unit of Georgia Loyalists had entered the South Carolina backcountry. In response, Morgan detached General William Washington's dragoons and about 200 militia troops to intercept the Loyalists. At the Battle of Hammond's Store, the Patriots soundly defeated the Loyalist militia. Though the battle was small and of relatively little military importance, it was an enormous boost for Whig morale in the backcountry.[10]

Morgan needed all the morale boost he could find. Knowing that the British were advancing on his position, in early January he wrote to General Greene about the lack of food and livestock forage in the area around Grindal Shoals. Concerned that a hungry army would become a disgruntled one, he wrote, "Here we cannot subsist so that we have but one alternative, either retreat or move into Georgia." Morgan recognized, however, that a retreat would destroy morale among the army, civilians, and militia alike. He went on, "A retreat [would] . . . be attended with the most fatal consequences. The Spirit which now begins to pervade the people and call them into the Field will be destroyed." Greene soon replied, ordering Morgan to hold his ground, saying "Col. Tarleton is said to be on his way to pay you a visit. I doubt not that he will have a decent reception and a proper dismission." Morgan worried that his position on the Pacolet River left him vulnerable to being trapped between Cornwallis and Tarleton. Morgan also knew that the enlistments of many of the militia troops with him were due to expire, and they were likely to leave his camp. To make matters more challenging, Morgan had to manage the inflated and prickly egos of militia commanders, particularly Thomas Sumter, who ordered his men not to take orders from Morgan. Greene advised Morgan to treat Sumter with kid gloves. By mid-January, Morgan knew that Tarleton was advancing toward him, and he made his decision. He would move northward in search of more plentiful supplies and a good opportunity to set the conditions for a military confrontation.[11]

CHASING MORGAN

In response to Greene's division of his army, in early January, Cornwallis dispatched Lord Rawdon to defend the area south of Cheraw from partisan raids. He sent Tarleton to protect the British garrison at Ninety Six. Tarleton placed his force between Ninety Six and Morgan. From there, he could reinforce the outpost or move against Daniel Morgan. Cornwallis ordered that

> Charles Cornwallis: "Push [Morgan] to the utmost."

once Ninety Six was secure, Tarleton was to "push [Morgan] to the utmost." Tarleton was directed to stay west of the Broad River and to make sure that Morgan's men also stayed west of it until they were driven from South Carolina. Meanwhile Tarleton was camped at Bush River Plantation, about 20 miles west of the Brierly's Ferry crossing of the Broad River, gathering supplies and preparing to advance on Morgan.[12]

Throughout this period, Morgan and Tarleton were both engaged in intelligence gathering, and each had a good idea of where the enemy was encamped and of their relative troops strengths. Ironically, Morgan and his men camped on land owned by Alexander Chesney, the Loyalist prisoner from Kings Mountain who had managed to escape and return home. Chesney would end up fighting with the British at the Battle of Cowpens. Although the main camp was at Grindal Shoals, detachments camped at other locations nearby. Some of the militia units foraged near the Broad River. On January 8, as the first step of beginning to move his army and evade Tarleton, Morgan ordered the militia forces camped at Grindal Shoals to move across the Pacolet River.[13]

Tarleton began to move on January 11, marching his men almost due north. He was soon joined by Alexander Chesney, who was to serve as his guide to the Pacolet River area. Chesney's aid was invaluable since he knew all the roads and the river crossings that stood between Tarleton and his quarry. Those river crossings posed a particular challenge to the British troops. It had rained heavily in the backcountry that January, and rain-swollen rivers slowed Tarleton's advance. He was forced to spend a great deal of time finding usable fords, many of which were guarded by detachments of Morgan's troops. Tarleton's spies informed him that Morgan's force was growing every day as militia arrived, adding to the British commander's sense of urgency and his frustration at his slow advance.[14]

On January 14, Tarleton and his men crossed the Enoree and Tyger Rivers and then turned northwest in the general direction of Grindal Shoals. Andrew Pickens' militia forces positioned themselves between Tarleton and Morgan's main force. They would soon be driven back to Morgan's camp. Tarleton led about 1,100 men—regulars, provincials, and Loyalist spies from the local area–on this advance. His force included the famed British Legion, made up 250 cavalry and another 200 light infantrymen, a troop of Light Dragoons (mounted infantry troops), a battery of the Royal Artillery with two three-pounder cannons, an additional company of light infantry, the 71st Regiment, also known as Fraser's Highlanders, and Loyalist forces. His troops coped with bitter cold and unrelenting rain that made travel slow and delayed reinforcements from reaching Tarleton. Once he reached the area around Grindal Shoals, he also had difficulty supplying his troops because the area had been picked clean by Morgan's forces. If the horrible travel conditions and meager rations were not enough to undermine the morale of the rank and file, Tarleton made things worse by bringing along a train of wagons carrying luxury goods for his officers.[15]

The same day that Tarleton crossed the Enoree and Tyger Rivers, Morgan positioned troops to block all the fords over the Pacolet in the nearby area and then he retreated north toward the Broad. Militia continued to arrive to reinforce him. Morgan's withdrawal was strategic; he wanted to force Tarleton into territory picked clean of supplies and he wanted to lead him further away from Cornwallis and potential reinforcements. He also wanted Tarleton to believe that the Americans were retreating. Tarleton had his own strategic objectives. On the night of January 15, British troops ostentatiously made camp on one side of the Pacolet River, making sure that Patriots scouts saw them. After dark, leaving their fires burning, Tarleton found an unguarded ford and he and his men crossed the Pacolet River only six miles from Morgan.[16]

PREPARING FOR BATTLE

Now the chase was on in earnest. Morgan spent January 16 setting a furious pace along the Green River Road, heading in the direction of the

Cowpens. He was also conducting reconnaissance with the assistance of a local man, Captain Dennis Trammell. While many of his men assumed he was retreating, he was actually choosing the ground where he wanted to fight. By mid-afternoon, he had made his decision: he and his troops would wait for Tarleton at the Cowpens.[17]

The Cowpens was a well-known location to backcountry residents, and it had served as a mustering point for troops several times during the Revolution, most recently before the Battle of Kings Mountain. The Cowpens was located at a crossroads; cattle drovers bringing cattle from the western mountains to Charles Town often used it as a resting place for their herds on the long trek to the coast. A number of spots in South Carolina were known as "cowpens." This one, northeast of modern-day Spartanburg, consisted of a wide meadow dotted with trees, but no undergrowth. Morgan intended to exploit the topography of the site for his advantage. A swamp on the east and a ravine and creek on the west sides of the field would make it difficult for Tarleton's dragoons to outflank the Americans. There were points of high ground and also some low spots—swales—where troops could be concealed. With the Broad River at their backs, it would be difficult for American militia troops to flee if they panicked in the heat of battle.[18]

That evening, Morgan developed his battle plan, and then he briefed his officers. Morgan decided that he would position a unit of Carolina and Georgia militia out front. These rifleman would be the first to engage the enemy. Their instructions were to hold their fire until the enemy drew within a few yards, then to hit Tarleton's first line with a blast of rifle fire. After a few volleys, militiamen were to retreat to the second Patriot line, 150 yards back. The second line, also a militia line under command of Pickens, was to fire three times, aiming for officers, then to retreat and reform behind a third line under Lt. Col. John Eager Howard with his force of Continentals. William Washington's cavalry would be concealed behind a small knoll just to the rear of this third line where they would wait for the right moment to surprise Tarleton's troops. Morgan aimed to make Tarleton believe that the militia were retreating in terror as they had done at previous battles. As the British army advanced deeper and deeper onto the battlefield, they would be drawn into a trap in which they could be outflanked by American infantry and cavalry troops. The most difficult part of the plan was the planned orderly fallback, hard to achieve under the best of circumstances, and exceedingly difficult to execute while under fire. If panic took hold, retreat could easily become rout. Morgan knew that most of these militiamen had been in battle before and that they were skilled marksmen, and by placing them at the front of his lines and ordering them to retreat, he harnessed their survival instincts

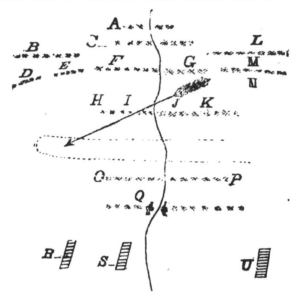

BATTLE OF THE COWPENS.

FIRST VIEW OF THE TWO ARMIES FORMED FOR ACTION.

References to the Plate.

A.—American Main Guard.
B.—Triplet's command.
C.—The Continentals.
L.—Pickens' command.

The commencement of the battle.

D.—Triplet's.
E.—Beaty's.
F and G.—Colonel Howard's.
M and N.—Pickens, with Anderson and Brandon.
H, I, J, K.—Georgia and Carolina riflemen, under Cunningham, Mc-
   Dowal, Samuel Hammond and Donnolly.

Valley or ravine.

O and P.—British advance, under Inman and Price.
Q.—British line of battle with artillery.
R—British horse,—reserve.
S.—McArthur, 71st regiment—reserve.
U.—Tarleton's cavalry.
34

Figure 6.1 American Troop Formation at the Battle of Cowpens

to his plan. Morgan believed that it was important that every man on the field should know the battle plan so that he would understand and execute the master plan. Morgan also ordered that each soldier should keep 24 rounds of ammunition in his own pack. In his definitive history of the battle, historian Lawrence Babits says, "By stipulating the number of bullets a man carried, Morgan knew how long a unit could keep firing and when it should be ordered to the rear before running out of ammunition."[19]

South Carolina militiaman Thomas Young later recalled that the troops "received with great joy" the news that Morgan planned to fight. He said, "[We] arrived at . . . Cowpens about sun-down, and were then told that there we should meet the enemy . . . [M]any a hearty curse had been vented against Gen. Morgan during that day's march, for retreating . . ." Cattle had been driven to the Cowpens that day; that evening, they were butchered and the men fed. Thomas Young praised Morgan's actions on the evening of January 16.

> It was upon this occasion that I was more perfectly convinced of
> Gen. Morgans's [sic] qualifications to command militia . . .
> He went among the volunteers, helped them to fix their swords,
> joked with them about their sweet-hearts, told them to keep in
> good spirits, and the day would be ours. And long after I laid
> down, he was going among the soldiers encouraging them.

Morgan urged his men to get a good night's rest, though Young said of his commander, "I don't believe he slept a wink that night!"[20]

That night, Tarleton's men camped at the Grindal Shoals site recently abandoned by Morgan's troops. Loyalist scouts fanned out over the area, securing information about Morgan's position. While the rank and file attempted to get some sleep, Tarleton did his own planning. Believing that Morgan was retreating, Tarleton wanted to prevent his adversary from crossing the Broad River because he might be able to connect with reinforcements if he did so. As a result, Tarleton decided to get an early start in an attempt to overtake Morgan before he reached the river. At 2am on January 17, the British commander had his men

Thomas Young, "It was upon this occasion that I was more perfectly convinced of Gen. Morgans's [sic] qualifications to command militia . . . He went among the volunteers, helped them to fix their swords, joked with them about their sweet-hearts, told them to keep in good spirits, and the day would be ours. And long after I laid down, he was going among the soldiers encouraging them."

awakened. He did not allow them to make a hot meal before departing, meaning that many of the men would become weakened by hunger as the night wore on. By 3am, they were marching in darkness over rugged, muddy terrain, fording knee-deep streams in the icy night. Tarleton wrote that the ground was "broken and much intersected by creeks and ravines, the march of the British troops during the darkness was exceedingly slow, on account of the time employed in examining the front and flanks as they proceeded." In the wee hours of January 17, the exhausted and hungry British troops marched twelve miles in the dark to meet Morgan. Dragoons took the lead as they traveled the last few miles up the Green River Road, a major backcountry thoroughfare. [21]

THE BATTLE OF COWPENS

Military historian Lawrence E. Babits conducted the definitive study of the Battle of Cowpens. By comparing and analyzing dozens of eyewitness accounts, exploring the terrain, and even recreating the battle with the help of Revolutionary War re-enactors, Babits reconstructed the events of January 17, 1781. While this account relies on the work of several historians, the main credit goes to Babits.

Morgan's scouts had kept him apprised of Tarleton's progress, and he did not rouse his men until he received word that the British troops were about an hour's march away. The last report came that "one hour before daylight . . . they had advanced within five miles of our camp." General Morgan sent out an advance patrol of mounted men who were charged with ascertaining Tarleton's location. When these men encountered the British advance guard a mile from the Cowpens, they wheeled their horses and sped back to camp, but not before two of them were captured. It was from these two American prisoners that Tarleton learned that Morgan was forming battle lines at the Cowpens. Morgan moved his men into position before sunrise, which came about 7:36 a.m. The morning was cold, cloudy, and exceptionally humid. Expert riflemen formed the skirmish line in the damp morning light.[22]

According to Babits, in the dim light of dawn as Tarleton was interrogating the American prisoners, the British dragoons came under fire from Patriot skirmishers as much as two miles in front of Morgan's main line. One of the American riflemen, James Caldwell, reported that it was easy for the skirmishers to hide behind large trees to avoid British musket fire, but that the dragoons pursued skirmishers into the woods and hacked them with broad swords. The skirmishers succeeded in slowing the British advance by forcing them to guard against ambush along the road.[23]

Just before dawn, Tarleton recalled, "the commanding officer in front reported that the American troops were halted and forming." He rode forward to inspect the American position. Patriot militia man James Collins recalled the scene: "About sunrise . . . the enemy came in full view. The sight, to me at least, seemed somewhat imposing; they halted for a short time. We look'd at each other for considerable time." Morgan had placed his skirmishers at the southern end of the battlefield, facing Tarleton's approach, and Tarleton could see them, but he could not see the Continentals massed further away on the field, concealed by their position in the swale, the low ground at the center of the field. Before advancing, Tarleton consulted with Alexander Chesney and others about the terrain Morgan had chosen. By Tarleton's account, he was assured that "the woods were open and free of swamps" and that the Broad River, six miles to Morgan's left flank, then curved around behind his rear, cutting off any easy escape. Apparently the little clumps of militia men did not faze Tarleton. Writing of himself in the third person, Tarleton said, "Lieutenant-colonel Tarleton having attained a position, which he certainly might deem advantageous, on account of the vulnerable situation of the enemy," began to organize his troops for battle.[24]

In spite of the fact that his infantry line had not yet caught up with the head of the column, Tarleton sent fifty dragoons ahead to engage first line of militia, intending that they would learn more about how the Americans were positioned and report back to him. From past experience, he expected the militia to run without putting up much resistance in the face of advancing dragoons with deadly swords. But this time the militia did not flee; instead, when the dragoons had advanced to within about 50 yards, the Americans opened fire. The Americans' right flank was positioned on a bit of rising ground behind a small stream; the soggy ground in front of them helped protect them from British troops who deployed largely against the center and left flank. As the Americans fired, 15 of the legendary cavalrymen fell from their horses, and the rest retreated back to the British line. Babits says that "casualties inflicted by the skirmishers were probably minor, but they played a key role in wearing down the British in terms of physical stamina and mental desire to win. . . . " Most of all, because they did not immediately retreat, an action that would have enabled the dragoons to scout the rest of the American line; Babits argues that the skirmishers denied Tarleton information on the American position and strength. In his memoir, Tarleton himself claims to have had an accurate understanding of Morgan's troop positions, but the subsequent unfolding of the battle suggests that Tarleton's clear picture was formed after the fact.[25]

As the dragoons advanced and then fell back, Tarleton's infantry reached his position. Now the British commander formed the light infantry and the Legion infantry to attack the American left. He also ordered his artillerymen to fire three-pounders at the American lines, but Babits argues that the cannon had little impact on the battle. While the British advanced, Morgan circulated among the rank and file, encouraging them, and ordering them "don't touch a trigger until you see the whites of their eyes." The second American militia line withheld their fire until the British infantry advanced within "thirty or forty paces," then opened fire. The British line sagged as many men fell, but they regrouped and kept coming, firing their first volley. They were climbing a slight incline and overshot their targets. Moreover, one unit of British infantry lagged behind due to confusion in the ranks. The blaze of gunfire devastated the British foot soldiers who made two ineffectual attempts to charge the American lines. After at least two militia volleys, which took out a good two-thirds of the British infantry officers, the militia fell back behind the Continental lines as planned, pursued by British dragoons on the left flank. The mounted soldiers hacked at the retreating Americans with swords, inflicting injuries on some and inspiring others to fight back fiercely. William Washington's cavalry, heretofore undetected by the British because they had been concealed near a band of trees, now rode forward to relieve the militia, charging the British dragoons. The militia was able to reform on the urging of General Morgan who rode in front of them waving his sword and shouting, "Form, form, my brave fellows! Given them one more fire and the day is ours. Old Morgan was never beaten."[26]

The British infantry continued to advance, taking the militia withdrawal as a sign that the battle was nearly won. Until the British had topped the ridge in front of the militia, they had not even seen the Continental main line. Throughout the militia fight, Continental officers kept the troops of the main line in good order, waiting their turn at the engagement. As the militia slipped behind the Continental lines, one participant reported, "The Enemy Seeing us Standing in such Good Order Halted for Some time to dress their line . . . The[y] then advanced On boldly." Two battalions of British infantry now faced three battalions of Continentals. The Continentals opened fire. As a Virginia private named Richard Swearington put it, "the Regulars came up and began to Pour it into them nicely." The fighting was intense as both sides held their ground. Tarleton recalled,

> As the contest between the British infantry in the front line and
> continentals seemed equally balanced, neither retreating,
> Lieutenant-colonel Tarleton thought the advance of the 71st into

The Double Envelopment at Cowpens

Several aspects of Daniel Morgan's strategy at the Battle of Cowpens contributed to the "combat shock" that historian Lawrence Babits identifies as the cause of the British defeat, but double envelopment was perhaps the most effective. This military maneuver—in which the defending army waits until the opponent has advanced towards the center of its lines and then simultaneously attacks the attacking opponent's flanks in a pincer-like motion—was extremely effective at Cowpens. When the attacking army faces a double envelopment by definition, it is forced to face the enemy on all four sides. In short, the attacking army is encircled.

While a double envelopment would seem the obvious tactic for any battle, it is difficult to achieve. One of the first military thinkers to propose that such a maneuver would be possible was the Chinese general Sun Tzu in *The Art of War*. In 216 B.C., the Carthagenian general Hannibal successfully executed a double envelopment at the Battle of Cannae, in a case still taught in military academies around the world.

Morgan's plan to use successive lines of his militia who withdrew after getting a few shots off certainly left Tarleton's forces off guard. Consecutive lines of British troops attacked and drove back Morgan's men, only to encounter another, stronger line. Based on past experience with Whig militia, attacking British troops assumed that the withdrawal of the first two lines signified a full blown American retreat. The British advanced headlong into the final line of American troops. This third line, as it turned out, was not a militia unit, but a rank of disciplined regulars. As Morgan had anticipated, Tarleton's 71st Highlanders were ordered to flank the American right. Continental General John Eager Howard spotted their intentions and ordered the Virginia militiamen on the American right to turn and face the British troops. At first, disaster threatened: the Virginians misunderstood Howard's order. In the intense noise of battle, militia commanders and men believed they had been commanded to withdraw.

When the exhausted British troops, who had marched double time all night on empty stomachs, saw the American withdrawal, they believed that victory was imminent. The Highlanders charged in a disorganized fashion. Morgan ordered the withdrawing militia to face about and fire a volley. The militia made an about-face and fired at a range of less than 30 yards. The British line faltered, halted, and then as Howard organized his Continentals to launch a bayonet charge, many of Tarleton's troops turned tail to run. As Howard's men rushed forward, General William Washington's cavalry came around from behind the American left to hit the British on their right flank and rear. Pickens' militia circled behind American troops and charged the British from the left and rear. Now the fleeing British troops were surrounded. The shock was too much for the exhausted British troops. Hundreds dropped their weapons and surrendered in spite of Tarleton's orders that they face about and fight.

line, and a movement of the cavalry in reserve to threaten the
enemy's right flank, would put a victorious period to the action.

Tarleton sent his cavalry against the American flanks, where they unleashed
deadly swords against Patriot forces.[27]

Then a fateful moment—a misunderstood order—almost cost the
Americans the battle. General John Eager Howard, commander of the
bulk of the Continental main line, ordered a withdrawal of a portion of
his troops; the rest of his men were confused, thinking he had ordered
an all-out retreat, and they too began to withdraw. The British also believed the Americans were retreating. As the Americans withdrew—perhaps as much as 80 yards, say Babits—Morgan again rode among the men and gave orders for the men to wheel

> Thomas Young reported that the "British broke, and throwing down their guns and cartouch boxes, made for the wagon road, and did the prettiest sort of running."

about. The American line turned and fired on the storming British troops.
One American reported that "The ground was instantly covered with the
bodies of the killed and wounded, and a total rout ensued." Now General

Figure 6.2 William Ranney's *The Battle of Cowpens*

Howard ordered the Americans to make a bayonet charge. They were joined by the skirmishers and militia men and by William Washington's cavalry. American Thomas Young reported that the "British broke, and throwing down their guns and cartouch [sic] boxes, made for the wagon road, and did the prettiest sort of running." Tarleton rode about trying to rally his men but they ignored him, until he finally ordered a retreat. After a final man-to-man confrontation between Tarleton and William Washington, using swords and pistols, Tarleton fled on horseback. Washington's men gave chase for 24 miles, but Tarleton managed to escape.[28]

Loyalist Alexander Chesney described the battle this way:

> I overtook them [Tarleton's forces] before 10 o'clock near the Cow-pens on Thickety Creek where we suffered a total defeat by some dreadful bad management. The Americans were posted behind a rivulet with Rifle-men as a front line and Cavalry in the

William Ranney's The Battle of Cowpens

In the first decades after American independence, American writers and artists engaged in the national project of defining and celebrating an American national identity. Artists spotlighted a heroic American past through portraits of Revolutionary War heroes and history paintings. History painting is an artistic genre that depicts a particular moment in the narrative of the past. Among the best-known practitioners of this genre were Emanuel Leutze (*Washington Crossing the Delaware*), John Trumbull (*The Declaration of Independence*), and William Ranney. Ranney was born in Connecticut and studied art in New York. He was a veteran of the war for Texas independence; his experiences there would influence his choice of subject matter for the rest of his career. He painted at least three versions of a work entitled *Marion Crossing the Pee Dee*.

Ranney's painting *The Battle of Cowpens* (1845) depicts an incident in the battle described in John Marshall's biography of George Washington. Marshall reported that in the final tense moments of the battle, General William Washington (a relative of George Washington's), the commander of charging Continental cavalry forces, was about to be cut down by a sword wielded by one of Tarleton's dreaded dragoons. According to Marshall, an African American man, "a waiter, too small to wield a sword," saved William Washington's life "by wounding the officer with a ball from a pistol." The "waiter" was probably William Ball, Washington's orderly. Historians have documented at least 15 African Americans who fought at the Battle of Cowpens; that figure does not include the body servants of officers such as Ball. Today, Ranney's painting depicting the episode hangs in the South Carolina State House.

> rear so as to make a third line; Col Tarleton charged at the head
> of his Regiment of Cavalry called the British Legion which was
> filled up from the prisoners taken at the battle of Camden; the
> Cavalry supported by a detachment of the 71st Reg' . . . broke
> the Riflemen without difficulty, but the prisoners on seeing their
> own Reg' opposed to them in the rear would not proceed against
> it and broke: the remainder charged but were repulsed this gave
> time to the front line to rally and form in the rear of their Cavalry
> which immediately charged and broke the 71st (then
> unsupported) making many prisoners: the rout was almost total.
> I was with Tarleton in the charge who behaved bravely but
> imprudently the consequence was his force dispersed in all
> directions the guns and many prisoners fell into the hands of the
> Americans.[29]

Chesney's statement offers one clue as to why some troops on the British side surrendered easily. Some of Tarleton's troops were Americans who had surrendered at the Battle of Camden the previous August. Cornwallis offered the prisoners a choice: they could join the British army or they could face imprisonment. Several chose military service, but when they found themselves face-to-face with other Americans in a battle that the British seemed to be losing, these men decided to switch sides again. They threw down their arms and surrendered to the Americans. This episode vividly illustrates the contingent nature of the loyalties of many of the Americans.

Chesney's statement also hints at another remarkable fact about the Battle of Cowpens: the speed with which it unfolded. Historian Lawrence Babits has worked with re-enactors who were well-schooled in the details of the battle to try to recreate the sequence of combat. In his book *A Devil of a Whipping*, Babits argues that actual combat from the time the infantry advanced until Tarleton's dragoons fled, lasted fewer than forty minutes. Since that book was published, Babits has done additional analysis and has led additional re-enactments, and he now concludes that the battle may have been as short as twenty minutes.[30]

As the fighting ended, "four new activities began: plundering, treatment of the wounded, pursuit and prisoner collection." Militiamen proceeded to loot the packs and equipment the British left behind on the field, finding a wealth of riches including clothing. They took shoes from some of the wounded. Patriots also confiscated horses, 35 baggage wagons, two field pieces, ammunition, cash, and even the swords of some of the officers. Once they finished gathering the spoils, many of the militia forces left Morgan and his army behind.[31]

Morgan assigned to the remaining militia forces the job of protecting the wounded and searching for stragglers from Tarleton's force. Only about 250 of Tarleton's men escaped while more than 800 were taken prisoner. (Morgan reported 600, but that did not include the badly wounded left behind at the Cowpens.) Morgan assigned forces commanded by William Washington to escort the prisoners north. Fearing that Cornwallis was pursuing him, Morgan and his Continentals also headed north, camping at the Island Ford crossing of the Broad River on the night of January 17.[32]

Morgan's fears were well-founded. Cornwallis had obtained intelligence on January 16 that Morgan was retreating northwest and decided that Morgan was no longer a threat to the British army or to the garrison at Ninety Six. Cornwallis headed northeast hoping to find Greene, but took his time, waiting for additional troops to catch up with him. On January 17, he received initial reports about the disaster at Cowpens. Tarleton reported in on January 18, and Cornwallis was furious at his news. An American prisoner in Cornwallis's camp reported that, as Tarleton delivered an account of the battle, his commanding officer pressed the tip of his sword into the ground and leaned on it so hard that the blade snapped in two. Cornwallis would write to Lord Rawdon that the defeat had "almost broke my heart." Once more, his Lordship's plans to invade and pacify North Carolina and his ambition to destroy Greene's army had been thwarted. He had lost one-fourth of his army. Determined to recapture the troops that had been taken prisoner, on January 18, he made plans to pursue Morgan.[33]

For his part, Greene was pleased with the victory, but not optimistic about the long-term outcome of the war. He wrote to a member of Congress, "Our prospects are gloomy notwithstanding these flashes of success." Although none of the participants was yet convinced, the war was racing toward its climax.[34]

CHAPTER 7

Denouement

*The crucial battles were primarily small
engagements . . . Because the conflict in the
South was fundamentally a struggle for the
allegiance of the rank-and-file of the colonies'
white population, these battles were often
fought between neighbors. It was a civil war,
with all the pain and agony that such a
political catastrophe brings upon a people.*
Dan L. Morrill, Southern Campaigns
of the American Revolution

*[In] an American campaign, everything is
terrible, the face of the country, the climate,
the enemy . . . A vast inhospitable desart,
unsafe and treacherous . . . where victories
are not decisive, but defeats are ruinous. [sic]*
British Brigadier-General Charles O'Hara

Cornwallis found his prospects much reduced after the battle of
Cowpens. Before the battle, his total force had consisted of 3,200 to
3,300 men; after Cowpens, he had 2,550 troops. Worst of all, he had lost
most of his fast-moving, well-trained light infantry. Nonetheless, he did
not abandon his plan to invade North Carolina, writing to General Clinton
on January 18, "Nothing but the most absolute necessity shall induce me
to give up the important objective of this Winter's campaign." Once again
Cornwallis changed course, marching after Morgan in hopes of preventing
Morgan's branch of the Continental army from reuniting with Greene's

main force. Cornwallis feared that if he didn't take action, backcountry Loyalists would lose heart and abandon the British cause. He also had two other objectives in mind: recapturing the prisoners from his army and cutting off the Whigs' flow of supplies from the north into the Carolinas. He waited 36 hours to begin his pursuit so that additional troops could catch up with him.

> General Cornwallis: "Nothing but the most absolute necessity shall induce me to give up the important objective of this Winter's campaign."

The delay put him hopelessly behind Morgan. Due to the loss of his cavalry, he also had little intelligence on where Morgan had gone. Assuming that his enemy would remain west of the Broad River, Cornwallis started northwest, but Morgan had crossed the river and was headed northeast toward Hillsborough.[1]

THE PURSUIT

Two days into his march, Cornwallis finally gained reliable information on Morgan's route. He altered his course. Only when he reached Ramsour's Mill, North Carolina, five days into his march, did Cornwallis get intelligence that he was 20 miles behind Morgan. Cornwallis ordered his men to discard all non-essential items in order to help them move more quickly. Luxury items such as china, alcohol, extra clothing, silver, and beds were set ablaze in a magnificent bonfire. A British officer wrote, "Lord Cornwallis set the example by burning all his wagons, and destroying the greatest part of his baggage." Historian Dan L. Morrill says that destroying the baggage was a grave mistake because Cornwallis found himself in territory that the Patriots had already picked clean of supplies. His men would suffer meager and unappetizing rations on the arduous march ahead. One of Cornwallis's senior officers, Brigadier-General Charles O'Hara summed up the state of affairs, "In this situation, without Baggage, necessaries, or Provisions of any sort for the officer or soldier, in the most barren inhospitable part of North America, . . . it was resolved to follow Greene's army to the end of the World."[2]

Believing that Cornwallis outnumbered him three to one now that most of the Whig militia had departed, Morgan was determined to avoid a fight. He managed to cross the Catawba River ahead of Cornwallis. Fortuitously, a torrential rainstorm raised the river to flood stage, preventing Cornwallis from crossing for nearly 60 hours. Morgan took advantage of the weather delay to rest his exhausted troops. "The Old Waggoner" himself was ailing. He wrote to Greene, "I grow worse every hour. I can't ride out of walk [faster than a walk]" due to intense joint pain. Meanwhile, General Greene had been in winter camp between Charlotte and Cheraw. When he heard about the victory at Cowpens, Greene sent his main army to Salisbury under the command of General Isaac Huger while he personally set out to join Morgan and his men. He hoped to rejoin the two branches of the American army at Salisbury. Greene finally caught up with Morgan at Beattie's Ford on the Catawba River south of Charlotte.[3]

In his history of the Southern campaigns of the American Revolution, military historian Dan Morrill has observed,

> From the very outset of assuming command in the South, Greene had envisioned his army as being a highly mobile force, one that could move easily from place to place and thereby deny victory to the more sedentary redcoats . . . To survive, he would have to outmaneuver Cornwallis while the entire southern army was in full retreat.

Morrill adds that a skillful and orderly withdrawal is one of the most valuable and professional tactics an army can use. One of Cornwallis's senior officers, Brigadier-General Charles O'Hara confirmed the effectiveness of this strategy when he wrote, "It is a fact beyond a doubt that their own Numbers are not materially reduced, for in all our victories, where we are said to have cut them to pieces, they very wisely never staid long enough to expose themselves to these desperate extremities." [sic] At times, British frustrations with their inability to subdue the elusive American troops reached epic proportions.[4]

With Cornwallis on the other side of the Catawba River, thwarted from an attack by only a raging river, Greene again decided that the orderly withdrawal was his best course of action. Disappointed that the North Carolina militia had not turned out in force in response to the threat posed by Cornwallis's invasion, on January 31 when the water levels began to fall, Greene ordered a resumption of Morgan's retreat. Even as he ordered his troops to withdraw in front of Cornwallis, however, he was making careful contingency plans. He ordered a detachment led by Edward Carrington to begin gathering boats on the Dan River in case a mass river crossing might prove necessary. He wrote to General Isaac Huger explaining his decision, "It is necessary that we should take every possible precaution. But I am not without hopes of ruining Lord Cornwallis . . ." He hoped that rejoining his divided army would provide him with a force strong enough to make a stand against Cornwallis on carefully chosen ground. The Americans marched eastward toward the Dan River, which marked the North Carolina-Virginia border. Greene appointed a force of 800 militia to serve as his rear guard. They were to watch the fords and delay a British crossing as long as possible.[5]

THE RACE TO THE DAN

Cornwallis's troops crossed the Catawba River in icy, chest high water, under fire from Greene's rear guard. Then the British general pressed on with his pursuit. Having burned his baggage wagons, Cornwallis had a large supply of unencumbered horses, so he mounted his men two to a horse. Riding, the British were able to move through the thick mud at the speed of light infantry, enabling them to nearly catch up with Morgan and Greene again at the Yadkin River on February 3. Once more, a flood-swollen river prevented Cornwallis from crossing to attack the Americans who were camped on the opposite shore within sight. The Americans then marched 47 miles in two days, reuniting with the rest of Greene's southern army near Guilford Courthouse. Cornwallis was not far behind, having finally crossed the Yadkin River on February 9 near the North Carolina town of Salem (now Winston-Salem). He was only 25 miles from Greene's position at Guilford Courthouse.[6]

The arrival of both armies sent panic through the countryside in central North Carolina. Thousands became refugees, packing up their valuables and trying to get out of the path of the advancing armies. Patriot militia man James Collins recalled, "Scouting parties of both sides were scouring the countryside in every direction." As a result, families hid all their valuables, including food supplies, and men hid out in the woods to avoid being forced into service by either side.[7]

Civilians were not the only ones who suffered. The march was grueling for the men of both armies. General Morgan was so ill with sciatica and hemorrhoids that he could not sit on his horse. Greene discharged him on February 10 and sent him home to Virginia. Of his officer, Greene wrote, "Great generals are scarce—there are few Morgans to be found." For the men who remained, the steady rain and the resulting mud made every day's march an endurance test. One American described it, "every step being up to our knees in mud, it raining on us all the way." The Continentals were in terrible shape. Many wore uniforms that were in tatters, and some were barefoot. British soldiers, unaccustomed to living under such harsh conditions, also faced a punishing endurance test. One British soldier complained,

> Sometimes we had turnips served out for food when we came
> to a turnip field; or arriving at a field of corn, we . . . ground
> our Indian corn for bread; when we could get no Indian corn,
> we were compelled to eat liver as a substitute for bread,
> with our lean beef.[8]

With the British hot on their heels, the Americans continued their withdrawal. Greene's goal was to cross the Dan River so that he would have easy access to his Virginia supply bases. The subsequent march from Guilford Courthouse to the Dan River has been called "the race to the Dan." For his part, Cornwallis believed that Greene would be searching for a shallow river ford on the upper part of the Dan River, near Cornwallis's own position at Salem. The British general focused on guarding those upper crossings, intending to intercept the Americans and wage battle before Greene could cross the Dan. Cornwallis's intelligence operation was becoming less effective by the day; he did not know that Greene had ordered General Edward Carrington to assemble a fleet of boats to facilitate a river crossing in the deeper waters downstream. As the Americans marched toward the river, light infantry troops served as a rear guard, again delaying the British.[9]

Late in the day on February 14, Greene arrived at the Dan River and used the fleet collected by Carrington to ferry wagons, troops, and horses into Virginia in a matter of a few hours. The British did not arrive until the next morning. Having no boats, Cornwallis was again thwarted by a swollen river, unable to cross at the deep fords on the lower part of the river. Greene's successful march to the Dan River and the orderly crossing were remarkable logistical and strategic triumphs. In his book, *The Road to Guilford Courthouse*, historian John Buchanan noted, "Cornwallis had driven his army forty miles in thirty-one hours, but the Americans had done it in twenty." Banastre Tarleton would later call the American retreat "judiciously designed and vigorously executed."[10]

THE BATTLE OF GUILFORD COURTHOUSE

The British force was exhausted from the long march with inadequate rations. Cornwallis was now nearly 250 miles from his nearest supply base at Camden. In hostile territory picked clean of supplies, he was also moving somewhat blindly, receiving little intelligence on the American position or on the status of the army he left behind in the South Carolina backcountry. He would later write, "The immense extent of this country, cut with numberless rivers and creeks, and the total want of internal navigation . . . will make it very difficult to reduce the province to obedience by a direct attack on it." Cornwallis decided to give his men time to rest before crossing into Virginia where he believed he would face powerful military opposition from Greene's force, heavily augmented by Virginia militia. The British commander set up camp at the backwoods town of Hillsborough, North Carolina, about 50 miles south of the Dan. Food was so scarce that the British were forced to slaughter and consume some of their draft horses, and Cornwallis sent a detachment of men to seize food from the locals. He also issued a call for Loyalist militia forces to join his cause.[11]

The Americans, on the other hand, were enjoying ample supplies in Virginia. Greene debated his options. He was loath to leave Cornwallis to settle in at Hillsborough where he could arouse Loyalist militia forces again; he set out to harass the British at every turn. He dispatched Andrew Pickens to gather militia forces whose mission was to hound British forces with hit-and-run attacks. After a few days of rest, on February 19, Greene sent cavalry forces under the command of Light Horse Harry Lee (the father of Confederate general Robert E. Lee) back across the river into North Carolina. They were charged with collecting intelligence and joining Pickens's militia forces in harassing the British. Lee's cavalry was able to decimate a force of 400 Loyalist troops who had assembled not far from Hillsborough. The Loyalists mistook the green-coated Americans for Tarleton's dragoons and thus failed to mount a defense until it was too late. News of the massacre, often called Pyle's Massacre after the commander of the Loyalist unit, chilled Cornwallis's efforts to recruit Loyalist militia.[12]

Meanwhile, militia recruits steadily made their way to Greene's camp. On February 22, the American general and the main body of his troops re-crossed the Dan. In North Carolina, he was joined by Overmountain men and North Carolina state troops. By March 11, his troop strength had swelled to 4,400 men, nearly half of whom were Continentals or former Continentals turned Virginia militia. In short, he had a seasoned force nearly twice the size of his adversary's. Greene recognized that the iron was hot, and it was time to strike. He wanted to achieve a major British defeat in hopes of driving Cornwallis and his troops from the Carolina piedmont. As Morgan had done at Cowpens, Greene wanted to choose the ground on which he was going to fight. He chose a site near Guilford Courthouse.[13]

The site he chose was huge, almost a mile and a half long and nearly that wide. A road, flanked first by hills, then a meadow, then dense forest, led through the site. The terrain of the forest floor was uneven; Greene believed that the uneven footing and the heavy stand of trees would provide his army an advantage by preventing the British from keeping their formations intact and mounting massed bayonet charges. Greene had little confidence in the courage or discipline of militia troops. He was concerned about bayonet charges because militia troops were notoriously afraid of bayonets. Nonetheless, he needed to make good use of militia forces at this battle. Trying to replicate the brilliant tactics that Morgan had used at the Battle of Cowpens, Greene deployed his troops in three lines. He placed his unseasoned militia forces in the front of his line with instructions to fire two shots and retreat. More seasoned militia and state troops formed a second line. The final line of hardened Continentals was placed about 500 yards behind the second line. Unlike Morgan, Greene did not keep units in reserve.[14]

On March 14, Cornwallis obtained intelligence that Greene had taken up the position near the hamlet of Guilford Courthouse. Knowing that his hungry and poorly clad men could not remain in the field much longer, Cornwallis marched toward Greene's position. In the hours before the battle, Greene, like Morgan, visited the men, stirring up their battle spirit. Learning of the enemy's approach at about 4 am on March 15, Greene sent Light Horse Harry Lee and his cavalry forces forward to scout the British position. Lee was able to charge and capture a small British forward force, but then he was beaten back by a larger cavalry force led by Tarleton. Lee beat a swift retreat back to Greene's lines where he reported that his commander should prepare for imminent combat.[15]

Around noon, the first column of British soldiers advanced on Greene's assembled troops. Cornwallis spent half an hour or more forming his lines as each side lobbed artillery shells ineffectually at each other. Historian John Ferling describes what followed as "two hours of mayhem." Some of the militiamen in Greene's front line panicked and fired too soon, while the British troops were still mostly out of range 100 yards away. Greene reported that many of the militia retreated "without firing at all." Most, however, held their fire until the British advanced to 50 yards and then fired with deadly effect, creating large gaps in the British lines. The British charged but found that the Americans had retreated swiftly back through the woods after their second volley, just as Greene had planned. As the British advanced on the second American line, the fighting dissolved into chaos. As Greene had planned, the Americans used the trees for cover, but the British were not completely confused by forested terrain that disrupted their orderly ranks. Historian John Ferling noted, "Redcoats advanced in some places, and in some places were beaten back." On some sectors of the battlefield, the British were able to mount bayonet charges. An hour and a half into the battle, the British left was showing signs of weakness. Ferling argues that an American charge, like that mounted by

William Washington's cavalry and John Eager Howard's light infantry at Cowpens, might have turned the tide of the battle, but Greene never ordered such an attack. At this point, Cornwallis ordered a massive wave of artillery fire that took out Redcoats as well as Americans. The fighting petered out, and British officers were able to regroup their survivors. At this point, Greene ordered a withdrawal, leaving the field to the British. Greene later wrote that the "Enemy got the ground ... but we the victory." Most military historians agree with his assessment. Cornwallis had lost 550 men, twice as many as the Americans, and fully 27 percent of his army. As for the Americans, their army was intact, and they were able to retreat in order to fight again another day.[16]

Greene had miscalculated in emulating Morgan's battle plan; neither the terrain nor the circumstances were the same as Morgan had enjoyed at Cowpens. For one thing, his militia troops were neither as experienced nor or as fierce as the backcountry men who fought at Cowpens. The heavy woods, traversed by gullies and rocks, proved to be less advantageous than he had hoped; as historian John Buchanan, one of the leading historians of the Battle of Guilford Courthouse, put it, "The firefights at the second line should have ended forever the myth that British regulars could not adapt to woods fighting. The dogged Britons kept slugging away." Moreover, at the crucial moment, Greene did not boldly order an attack on the fraying British right. John Ferling says that Greene's caution may very well have been advisable. And John Buchanan notes that while "Greene was neither a first-rate tactician nor a charismatic battle commander[, h]e was a cool strategist of the first order and always had uppermost in his mind that he could not, he must not, lose the army."[17]

In the wake of Guilford Courthouse, Cornwallis marched eastward, hoping to find that supplies had arrived for him on the Cape Fear River. One British officer reported, "This whole Country is so totally destitute of subsistence, that forage is not nearer than nine miles, and the Soldiers have been two days without bread." After pursuing Cornwallis briefly, Greene withdrew what was left of his army, turning back toward South Carolina. He seemed drained from the "race to the Dan" and the subsequent battle at Guilford's Courthouse. John Ferling says that for a time, Greene's "private correspondence took on the tone of one broken by unendurable stress and the brutal realities of which he had been a part." The American commander did recover, however, and redoubled his efforts on behalf of the Continental Army. As he explained in a letter to George Washington, Greene was "determined to carry the war immediately into South Carolina." His aim was to pick off British garrisons one by one.[18]

BACKCOUNTRY FIGHTING—1781

A major element of Greene's strategy was to use the hit-and-run militia units commanded by Francis Marion, Andrew Pickens, and Thomas Sumter to cripple the British army by disrupting their supply lines. The backcountry commanders succeeded brilliantly in this effort, helped along by the fact that Loyalists were deserting Tory militia units in droves. Nonetheless, scattered pockets of Loyalist resistance remained, especially around Cheraw and along the North Carolina–South Carolina border. In April, Greene was defeated by a British force at Hobkirk's Hill near Camden, but again, the victory was a pyrrhic one for the British who sustained heavy casualties. Believing that the garrison at Camden would be nearly impossible to supply because of backcountry militia attacks, the British abandoned the post in the wake of the Battle of Hobkirk's Hill. Meanwhile, in the early months of 1781, Patriot militia forces were picking off British garrisons at Fort Watson, Fort Motte, Georgetown, and Monck's Corner. In May and June, American militia forces retook British garrisons in and around Augusta, Georgia.[19]

From May 22 to June 19, 1781, Green laid siege to the British garrison at Ninety Six. Ninety Six, site of the first major backcountry battle of the war in 1775, had been occupied by the British after the fall of Charles Town. It was the most important of the backcountry strategic posts that Clinton and Cornwallis had secured in the summer of 1780. Situated in a community of ardent Loyalists and located at the intersection of several major backcountry roads, Cornwallis believed that the garrison at Ninety Six was essential to securing his backcountry supply chain. After the defeat at Cowpens, Cornwallis worried that Loyalist support would fade. In early February 1781, he wrote to Lieutenant-Colonel Francis Rawdon, the commander of all British forces remaining in South Carolina, "Our friends must be so disheartened by the misfortune of the 17th, that you will get but little good from them. You know the importance of Ninety-Six: let that place be your constant care."[20]

Rawdon did recognize the importance of Ninety Six, and he and his officers had worked hard to strengthen defenses there. Under the direction of an outstanding Loyalist officer from New York, Colonel John Harris Cruger, and chief engineer Lieutenant Harry Haldane, the British had designed and installed extensive fortifications including an earthenworks redoubt shaped like an eight-point star. A series of fraise (pointed sticks) were embedded in the walls of the Star Redoubt to prevent the enemy from climbing it. The base of the fort was surrounded by a dry ditch that would impede advancing troops, and an abatis, an obstacle constructed of felled trees with sharpened branches facing the approach to the fortified position. Ninety Six was a formidable target.[21]

After he withdrew British forces from Camden, Lord Rawdon sent multiple letters to Cruger, instructing him to withdraw from Ninety Six and march to Charles Town. Cruger never received these orders, however, because militia men serving under Andrew Pickens seized the British couriers time after time. Greene hoped to take Ninety Six before Cruger could evacuate so that Rawdon would not be able to use the troops there as reinforcements at Georgetown or Charles Town. Greene arrived at Ninety Six on May 22 with fewer than 600 men. He was accompanied by Thaddeus Kosciusko, an exceptionally competent Continental Army engineer. Upon arrival, Greene was astonished at the strength of the fortifications there, marveling to the Marquis de Lafayette that "the fortifications are so strong and the garrison so large and so well furnished that our success is very doubtful."[22]

Greene decided to attack the Star Redoubt by digging a series of parallels, embanked trenches that zigzagged toward the fortress, providing cover for advancing troops. His intention was to move troops close enough to tunnel under the abatis and a wall of the Star Redoubt so that he could demolish the obstacles with gunpowder and give his men access to the redoubt. On the first pass, he began the parallels only seventy yards from the Star Redoubt. Cruger mounted his cannons on top of the redoubt and rained artillery fire down on the laborers digging the trenches. He then sent a small detachment of men to charge the laborers with bayonets. The small Continental detachment was slaughtered, and Greene was forced to begin again, this time starting the parallels a safer 400 yards from the fort and covering the laborers with artillery and rifle fire.[23]

Digging trenches was slow work, and the siege wore on for weeks. On June 10, Greene learned that reinforcements from Charles Town under the command of Lord Rawdon were marching west to Ninety Six. In spite of attempts by Patriot militia to harass and delay Rawdon's forces, on June 17, Greene received word that Rawdon's arrival was imminent. In spite of the fact that his attack trenches were not complete, Greene gave the orders for a final assault on the Star Redoubt the next day. In spite of withering Continental artillery fire and a valiant charge by infantry troops, Greene was unable to take the fort and halted the assault. American casualties were fewer than 200 killed, wounded, or missing. British casualties were fewer than 100. On June 19, Greene lifted the siege and marched his troops east. Rawdon arrived with reinforcements two days later, but he quickly decided that he could not guarantee a secure supply line between Ninety Six and Charles Town. Rawdon ordered that the garrison be abandoned. Once again, Greene had failed to win the battle, but he had achieved his objective. The British troops left the area in July, accompanied by Loyalist families from the area who sought their protection.[24]

Loyalist families who demanded protection from the British posed a challenge for the army bureaucrats in Charles Town. By mid-1781, the officers there were devoting increasing amounts of time and money to aiding Loyalist refugees displaced by backcountry fighting. They received specific allowances, provisions, and payments of small sums in cases of financial emergency. For example, Margaret Reynolds, a widow from Ninety Six, was employed as a nurse in the Charles Town military hospital and received occasional special payments from the British Army. In spite of this British assistance, Loyalist families faced often crippling financial hardships as a result of their support of the Crown.[25]

If Loyalists faced an uncertain future, southern Indians paid an even higher price for their efforts on behalf of the British. In the summer of 1781, the Cherokee launched a new round of attacks in the backcountry in an effort to aid the British by distracting Patriot militia troops. As a result of the attacks, militia from the Overmountain region felt compelled to stay home for defensive duty and did not march to assist Greene's efforts. Troops under Isaac Shelby defeated the Cherokee in late July, causing a rift among the Cherokee themselves: Indians who wanted to keep fighting were at odds with those who were willing to sign a peace treaty with the Whigs. Bands of Cherokee continued to launch sporadic attacks on the frontier. The Creeks, too, attacked whites in the Georgia backcountry. After another round of Cherokee attacks in early 1782, Andrew Pickens launched yet another devastating counter-offensive. As a result of defeat by his forces, in the fall of 1782, they signed a peace treaty surrendering all their land claims south of the Savannah River and east of the Chattahoochee River.[26]

Meanwhile fighting between Patriots and the British continued. The last major backcountry engagement of the war took place in September 1781 at Eutaw Springs, south of the Santee River in modern-day Orangeburg County, South Carolina. Here Greene's Continentals and state troops commanded by Francis Marion and Thomas Sumter clashed with British regulars and provincials commanded by Colonel Alexander Stewart. The Americans overran the British position but then fell to plundering the British camp. Seizing stores of British liquor, the Americans got drunk, allowing Stewart time to regroup and counter-attack. After heavy casualties on both sides, the British withdrew to Charles Town.[27]

THE SURRENDER AT YORKTOWN

In the meantime, after parting with Greene in the wake of the Battle of Guilford Courthouse, Cornwallis had holed up at the British garrison in Wilmington, North Carolina. In mid-April, determining that Virginia was a better target for an offensive campaign than South Carolina with its "numberless rivers and creeks" and that he could accomplish nothing further in the Carolinas, he marched his troops north. Clinton would later claim that Cornwallis took this action in direct violation of Clinton's orders to protect Charles Town and to avoid offensive actions that might endanger that city. In fact, Clinton's first orders upon placing Cornwallis in command of the British army in the South had been "to secure the South and recover North Carolina." Cornwallis steadfastly believed that he had to cut off Virginia's supply lines to the Carolinas before he could quell backcountry resistance and maintained that he had not violated orders by moving into Virginia.[28]

Cornwallis arrived in Virginia in early May where he was able to unite with British forces at Petersburg. Additional troops soon arrived from New York, leaving Cornwallis in command of about 7,000 men. The British commander pursued Continental forces under the Marquis de Lafayette, and several small skirmishes ensued throughout the summer. The British general also set out to find a suitable naval base for British forces. Ultimately he settled on establishing a naval base at Yorktown, situated on a peninsula between the James and York Rivers. Perched on a bluff over the York, Yorktown afforded a clear view of a narrow stretch of river, making it a formidable spot from which to guard the water approach to the Virginia coast. By late summer 1781, Cornwallis found himself encamped at Yorktown while his commanding officer, Henry Clinton, dithered over whether to pursue an all-out offensive in New York or to leave some troops in Virginia. Ultimately Clinton left Cornwallis's entire force in Virginia. It was a fateful mistake. While Clinton vacillated, George Washington decided to move his troops southward. By late September, American troops were in control of York Neck, the narrow isthmus of land that linked Yorktown to the rest of Virginia. Cornwallis and his army were now trapped, with Continental forces preventing his escape by land, while French warships off the coast blocked reinforcements or evacuation by sea. After a long and devastating siege, on October 19, Cornwallis surrendered his army to George Washington. One Patriot officer wrote of the occasion, "This is to us a most glorious day, but to the English one of bitter chagrin and disappointment." That "glorious day" came just over one year after the Battle of Kings Mountain formed the "first link in a chain" that set the British on the course to defeat.[29]

William "Bloody Bill" Cunningham

"Bloody Bill" Cunningham, a Loyalist from the Ninety Six District, became known for committing atrocities against Whigs, but "Bloody Bill" only became a bloodthirsty Tory after considerable provocation. Born in Ireland, Cunningham owned about 200 acres on the Saluda River. When war broke out in 1775, he initially took the Whig side. He participated in the Whig raid on Fort Charlotte and the Cherokee Campaign of 1776. Apparently he had a dispute with Whigs over the terms of his enlistment, and he returned home to his farm. At some point, he tracked down and killed a Whig who had killed his lame epileptic brother and injured his father, but he did not join a Loyalist militia until the British army gained control of backcountry in 1780. At that point, William Cunningham enlisted in the regiment formed by Patrick Cunningham, a distant kinsman.

After the British garrison at Ninety Six was evacuated in the summer of 1781, Cunningham assembled a band of about 60 Loyalists who conducted a series of raids against Whig targets. That fall, South Carolina Governor John Rutledge ordered the wives and children of Loyalists in the British service be sent to the British Lines near Charles Town. "Bloody Bill" and his men swore vengeance on anyone who participated in executing the order. In November, he and some of his men cornered 30 Whigs at dawn. Some reports said that most of the Whigs were drunk. The Loyalists hacked the Whigs, including a teenage boy, to death with swords. Only two men escaped with their lives. The episode was known as the "Bloody Scout." Also in November 1781, in the Spartan District, Cunningham and his force attacked the home of Whig militia commander Captain Andrew Barry and skirmished with Barry's unit. In another episode north of the Saluda River, one of Cunningham's men came upon a small party of Whigs at the residence of Colonel Joseph Hayes. The Loyalist demanded that Hayes surrender, but the Whig commander refused. A Whig shot one of Cunningham's men. Cunningham came on the scene moments later and ordered an assault on Hayes's house. The Loyalists laid siege to the residence, set it afire, and then killed Hayes and his men as they fled the fire and asked for quarter. When asked why he murdered Hayes, Cunningham replied that the dead man had mistreated Tory women and children.

Cunningham like many other leading Loyalists, left the United States after the Revolution. He was reported to have died of old age at his home in the West Indies.

The war had not officially ended, though the siege of Yorktown would mark the last major engagement by Continentals and British regulars. Skirmishes continued in the Carolina backcountry as militia

> A Patriot officer: "This is to us a most glorious day, but to the English one of bitter chagrin and disappointment."

forces under Pickens, Marion, and Sumter continued to harass Loyalists and Loyalists retaliated. In 1782, Greene reported that Georgia and the Carolinas "are still torn to pieces by little parties of disaffected who elude all search and conceal themselves in the thickets and swamps . . . and issue forth from these hidden recesses committing the most horrid Murders and plunder and lay waste the country." The last South Carolina battle was fought at Johns Island on November 14, 1782. The British army departed Charles Town in December. The Treaty of Paris, signed in September 1783, marked the formal end of the war and the British recognition of American independence.[30]

THE FATE OF THE LOYALISTS

Animosities between Patriots and Loyalists continued long after the Revolution, in part because the victors were determined to punish the Loyalists whom they regarded as traitors. For example, in January 1782, the South Carolina general assembly convened in Jacksonborough on the Edisto River and took up issue of how to identify and punish Loyalists. An initial act identified 238 "rank Tories" whose estates were to be confiscated while the Tories themselves were to be banished from the state. Another act identified 47 whose estates would be hit with a fine equaling 12 percent of the appraised value. An amnesty act provided for pardon of others if they paid a fine of ten percent of the value of their estates. Over the next four years, about two-thirds of these punishments were reduced, and only a small fraction of the estimated 12,000 to 15,000 who aided the British received any legal punishment at all. Still, life could not have been pleasant for most Loyalists as they tried to rebuild their lives surrounded by hostile neighbors. Thousands of Loyalists left the United States, most bound for Canada or England. Some took temporary refuge in Florida. Others changed their names and moved to the American frontier where they could start over.[31]

Other Loyalists faced extralegal punishment. For example, one of Bloody Bill Cunningham's lieutenants, a man named Love, was arrested and held in jail at Ninety Six until November 1784 when a local judge released him on the grounds that he was immune to prosecution under the terms of the Treaty of Paris. The families of some of the Whigs that he or others of Cunningham's men had killed seized Love outside the courthouse. When he pleaded for his life on the grounds that no one should be executed without a fair trial, the Whigs told him that "he should have thought of that when he was slaughtering their kinsman." The Whigs hanged him from a tree near the courthouse.[32]

One example of the devastation wrought on entire Loyalist families was the case of the Henderson family of Long Canes, South Carolina, a backcountry family who paid a particularly heavy toll for loyalty to the Crown. The Henderson men had thrown themselves into the King's cause. Two sons were killed in service to a Loyalist militia. A son-in-law was "hanged by the rebels." Mrs. Henderson, her husband, her widowed daughter Agnes, and two grandchildren fled to Charles Town and the protection of the British Army. There her husband and daughter died leaving her to support her grandchildren.[33]

The fate of the Loyalists also reveals the ambiguous legal position of women of the time. Many of those who petitioned for legislative restoration of their property were Loyalist women. Because women were not granted a political voice, they themselves were not considered loyalists; their husbands were. Yet, they also became casualties of confiscation and banishment; they, too, were victims of the "calamities of war." Many petitioned state legislatures to restore their trusteeships, dower rights, and marriage settlements lost to confiscation. In South Carolina about 65 of these cases came before the legislature. Only eight were granted total relief from confiscation, but many received at least a partial restoration of property. The arguments women used to get their property restored tell us much about their ambiguous legal position and about the variety of ways that women saw themselves. Some women claimed that they had been helpless to change husbands' political views. Petition after petition noted that women found themselves in "a calamitous condition" or facing "great misfortune." After all, custom decreed that women had to depend on men for support. By taking away the husband's property, it left married women and their children without the support to which they were entitled. A few claimed to be Patriots themselves in spite of their husbands' Loyalist views. Mary Rowand of South Carolina admitted that her husband was a Loyalist, but maintained that she herself was "descended from Ancestors whose Industry and Valour Contributed greatly to the prosperity of [South Carolina]." [sic] Another South Carolinian, Florence Cook, insisted in her petition to the legislature that she had always been a "Sincere friend to her Country," in spite of her husband's Loyalist sentiments. Jane Spurgin of North Carolina told legislators in that state that she had "always behaved herself as a good Citizen" and that she found it "hard to be deprived of the Common rights of other Citizens." In professing herself entitled to the rights of other citizens, Jane Spurgin was asserting an independent political identity. Unfortunately, the North Carolina legislature did not agree with her; they denied her petition for a restoration of property.[34]

MORE HUMAN COSTS

The Loyalists were not the only people who suffered in the aftermath of the war. Much of the interior of South Carolina had been desolated by the fighting. Portions of the towns of Camden and Ninety Six had been destroyed. Homes and barns had been burned or abandoned. Herds of livestock had been stolen and killed to feed armies on the move and stocks of grain had also been depleted. Those who owned slaves also faced losses. Georgia's black population dropped by two-thirds during the war. South Carolina lost five to six thousand blacks not including the slaves carried away by banished Loyalists. Some estimates suggest that as many as 10,000 blacks left the colony.[35]

The slaves who had obtained their freedom by siding with the British faced an uncertain future. When Cornwallis marched into Virginia, black Loyalists went with him. Many tried to run away to offer their services to the French when the impending British defeat became apparent. As British troops at Yorktown ran short of food, Cornwallis ordered smallpox-infected blacks driven from his camp. A Hessian officer wrote, "We had used them to good advantage and set them free, and now, with fear and trembling, they had to face the reward of their cruel masters." General Washington had those runaway slaves seized and returned to their owners. Other runaways hid out in the Great Dismal Swamp of Virginia and North Carolina trying to evade capture. St. Augustine was a temporary home for many Loyalists fleeing the colony, and many took their slaves with them. The black population there swelled. Some black maroon settlements in Georgia and the Carolinas survived for some time, and many African Americans apparently found refuge with native Americans. Some set sail with the departing British. Those who left South Carolina for New York stood a far better chance of maintaining their freedom; they would eventually be resettled in Canada. However, most departing British ships were bound for the West Indies where blacks on board were likely to be re-enslaved. Historian Gary Nash says that 2,960 African-Americans on board a ship that left Charles Town bound for Jamaica and St. Lucia were scheduled to be returned to slavery.[36]

In the final analysis, the war in the South was a essentially a civil war, and as historian Dan L. Morrill has put it, the backcountry war inflicted "all the pain and agony that such a political catastrophe brings upon a people." It was that bitter backcountry war that led to American victory, however. Dozens of small frontier battles led to two huge ones: at Kings Mountain and Cowpens. Those battles were the beginning of the end of the pain and suffering of backcountry southerners.[37]

Documents

Colonel William Hill on the Battle of Huck's Defeat

*W*illiam Hill, a resident of the New Acquisition District in the South Carolina
backcountry, operated an ironworks. A committed Whig who hosted a Whig
militia on his property, Hill became the target of British ire in 1780. Captain
Christian Huck, the Provincial leader sent to quell Whig resistance in the New
Acquisition District, burned Hill's Ironworks. Hill was among the Whig militia
who participated in the Battle of Huck's Defeat, and he offers an eyewitness account
of Huck's depredations and his defeat on July 12, 1780.

[A] certain captain Hook[1] with a company of Horse and about 500
Tories came to the Iron works,[2] destroyed all the property they
could not carry away. Burned the forge furnace, grist and saw
mills together with all other buildings even to the negro huts, &
bore away about 90 negroes . . .

After we had been some time at this camp [on the Pacolet River]
. . . we were informed by our friends, that Capt. Hook, the same
that had a few weeks before destroyed the Iron works, had sent
to most of the houses in the settlement, to notify the aged men,
the young being in Camp, to meet him at a certain place, that he
desired to make terms with them, & that he would put them in the
King's peace. [A]ccordingly they met him, he undertook to
harrangue them, on the certainty of his majesty reducing all the
Colonies to obedience, . . . saying that God almighty had become
a Rebel, but if there were 20 Gods on that side, they would all be
conquered . . . Whilst he was employed in this impious blasphemy
he had his officers & men taking all the horses fit for his purpose,

so that many of the aged men had to walk many miles home afoot. This ill behaviour of the enemy made an impression on the minds of the most serious men in this little band and raised their courage under the belief that they would be made instruments in the hand of Heaven to punish this enemy for his wickedness and blasphemy, and no doubt, the recent injuries that many of their families received from the said Hook and his party had an effect to stimulate this little band to a proper courage The number of the Americans was 133 and many of them without arms. Cap[tai]n. Hook had about 100 horses & Col. Ferguson, at this time commander of the Tory Militia, had about 300 men: they were encamped in a Lane [with] a strong fence on each side, the Horse[s] picketed in the inside of a field next to the lane, with their furniture [saddles] on, the officers in a mansion house in the field, in which was a number of women,[3] which the said Hook had brought there, and at the moment the action commenced, he was then flourishing his sword over the head[s] of these unfortunate women & threatening them with death if they would not get their husbands & sons to come in. [M]arching all night, we made the attack about the break of day. The plan was to attack both ends of the Lane at the same time, but unfortunately the party sent to make the attack on the east end of the lane met with some embarrassments, by fences, brush, briars &c. that they could not get to the end of the lane until the firing commenced at the west end The probability is that if that party had made good their march in time very few of them w[oul]d have escaped. However Cap. Hook was killed, and also Col. Forguson of the Tory Militia, Hook's [Lieutenant], was wounded & died afterwards; considerable number of privates [were killed], the number not known, as there were many of their carcasses found in the woods some days after. This happened about the 10th of July 1780[4] at Williamsons Plantation in York District, and it was the first check the enemy had received after the fall of Charleston; and was of greater consequence to the American cause than can be well supposed from an affair of small a magnitude as it had the tendency to inspire the Americans with courage & fortitude & to teach them that the enemy was not invincible.

Backcountry Women in the War

Inevitably, backcountry women were drawn into the conflict. Most backcountry women did not record their exploits in the Revolutionary War, but in 1848, American writer Elizabeth F. Ellet published the stories of many of these women in a two-volume work entitled Women of the American Revolution. *(A third volume was published in 1850.) To research her subjects, Ellet sought out unpublished material and interviewed descendants of the women. She did not tell the stories of Loyalist women. Excerpts from Ellet's accounts of the experiences of several backcountry women are included below. Even as she celebrates the courage and boldness of these women, Ellet emphasizes their femininity by focusing on their devotion to family and their roles as the wives and mothers of Patriots.*

JANE BLACK THOMAS AND HER NEIGHBORS

THE state of popular feeling after the occupation of Charleston by the British, and during the efforts made to establish an undisputed control over the State, might be in some measure illustrated by the life of Mrs. Thomas, were there materials for a full narrative of incidents in which she and her neighbors bore an active or passive part. It is in wild and stirring times that such spirits are nurtured, and arise in their strength. She was another of the patriotic females in whose breast glowed such ardent patriotism, that no personal hazard could deter from service, wherever service could be rendered. She was a native of Chester County, Pennsylvania, and the sister of the Reverend John Black, of Carlisle, the first president of Dickinson College. She was married about 1740, to John Thomas, supposed to be a native of Wales, who had been brought up in the same county. Some ten or fifteen years after his marriage, Mr. Thomas removed to South Carolina. His residence for some time was upon Fishing

Creek in Chester District. About the year 1762, he removed to what is now called Spartanburg District, and settled upon Fairforest Creek, a few miles above the spot where the line dividing that district from Union crosses the stream. Mrs. Thomas was much beloved and respected in that neighborhood. She was one of the first members of the Presbyterian congregation organized about that time, and known as Fairforest church, of which she continued a zealous and efficient member as long as she resided within its bounds.

For many years previous to the commencement of the Revolutionary war, Mr. Thomas was a magistrate and a captain of militia. Before hostilities began, he resigned both these commissions. When Colonel Fletcher [probably Fletchall] refused to accept a commission under the authority of the province of South Carolina, an election was held, and John Thomas was chosen Colonel of the Spartan regiment. The proximity of this regiment to the frontier imposed a large share of active service on the soldiers belonging to it, and devolved great responsibilities upon its commander. Colonel Thomas led out his quota of men to repel the Indians in 1776, and shared the privations and dangers connected with the expedition under General Williamson into the heart of the Indian territory, in the autumn of that year. When that campaign terminated, and the Indians sued for peace, the protection of a long line of the frontier was intrusted [sic] to him. With diligence, fidelity and zeal did he perform this duty; and retained his command till after the fall of Charleston.

As soon as the news of the surrender of that city reached the borders of the State, measures were concerted by Colonels Thomas, Brandon and Lyles, for the concentration of their forces with a view to protect the country. Their schemes were frustrated by the devices of Colonel Fletcher, who still remained in the neighborhood. Having discovered their intentions, he gave notice to some British troops recently marched into the vicinity, and to a body of tory cavalry thirty miles distant. These were brought together, and surprised the force collected by Brandon at the point designated, before the others had time to arrive. Within a short time after this event, almost every whig between the Broad and Saluda rivers was compelled to abandon the country or accept British protection. Numbers of them fled to North Carolina. Colonel Thomas, then advanced in life, with some others in like defenceless [sic] circumstances, took protection. By this course, they hoped to secure permission to remain unmolested with their families; but in this supposition they were lamentably mistaken. It was not long before Colonel Thomas was arrested, and sent to prison at Ninety Six. Thence he was conveyed to Charleston, where he remained in durance till near the close of the war.

One of the congenial co-operators in these plans of the British commander [to suppress backcountry resistance], was Colonel Ferguson. He encouraged the loyalists to take arms, and led them to desolate the homes of their neighbors. About the last of June he came into that part of the country where the family of Colonel Thomas lived, and caused great distress by the pillage and devastation of the bands of tories who hung around his camp. The whigs were robbed of their negroes, horses, cattle, clothing, bedding, and every article of property of sufficient value to take away. These depredations were frequent, the expeditions for plunder being sometimes weekly; and were continued as long as the tories could venture to show their faces. In this state of things, while whole families suffered, female courage and fortitude were called into active exercise; and Mrs. Thomas showed herself a bright example of boldness, spirit and determination.

While her husband was a prisoner at Ninety-Six, she paid a visit to him and her two sons, who were his companions in rigorous captivity. By chance she overheard a conversation between some tory women, the purport of which deeply interested her. One said to the others: "To-morrow night the loyalists intend to surprise the rebels at Cedar Spring." The heart of Mrs. Thomas was thrilled with alarm at this intelligence. The Cedar Spring was within a few miles of her house; the whigs were posted there, and among them were some of her own children.

Her resolution was taken at once; for there was no time to be lost. She determined to apprise them of the enemy's intention, before the blow could be struck. Bidding a hasty adieu to her husband and sons, she was upon the road as quickly as possible; rode the intervening distance of nearly sixty miles the next day, and arrived in time to bring information to her sons and friends of the impending danger. The moment they knew what was to be expected, a brief consultation was held; and measures were immediately taken for defence. [sic] The soldiers withdrew a short distance from their camp-fires, which were prepared to burn as brightly as possible. The men selected suitable positions in the surrounding woods.

Their preparations were just completed, when they heard in the distance, amid the silence of night, the cautious advance of the foe. The scene was one which imagination, far better than the pen of the chronicler, can depict. Slowly and warily, and with tread as noiseless as possible, the enemy advanced; till they were already within the glare of the blazing fires, and safely, as it seemed, on the verge of their anticipated work of destruction. No sound betrayed alarm; they supposed the intended victims wrapped in heavy slumbers; they heard but the crackling of the flames, and the hoarse murmur of the wind as it swept through the pine trees.

The assailants gave the signal for the onset, and rushed towards the fires—eager for indiscriminate slaughter. Suddenly the flashes and shrill reports of rifles revealed the hidden champions of liberty. The enemy, to their consternation, found themselves assailed in the rear by the party they had expected to strike unawares. Thrown into confusion by this unexpected reception, defeat, overwhelming defeat, was the consequence to the loyalists. They were about one hundred and fifty strong, while the whigs numbered only about sixty. The victory thus easily achieved they owed to the spirit and courage of a woman! Such were the matrons of that day.

Not merely upon this occasion was Mrs. Thomas active in conveying intelligence to her friends, and in arousing the spirit of Independence among its advocates. She did, as well as suffered much, during the period of devastation and lawless rapine. One instance of her firmness is well remembered. Early in the war Governor Rutledge sent a quantity of arms and ammunition to the house of Colonel Thomas, to be in readiness for any emergency that might arise on the frontier. These munitions were under a guard of twenty-five men; and the house was prepared to resist assault. Colonel Thomas received information that a large party of tories, under the command of Colonel More of North Carolina, was advancing to attack him. He and his guard deemed it inexpedient to risk an encounter with a force so much superior to their own; and they therefore retired, carrying off as much ammunition as possible. Josiah Culbertson, a son-in-law of Colonel Thomas, who was with the little garrison, would not go with the others, but remained in the house. Besides him and a youth, the only inmates were women. The tories advanced, and took up their station; but the treasure was not to be yielded to their demand. Their call for admittance was answered by an order to leave the premises; and their fire was received without much injury by the logs of the house. The fire was quickly returned from the upper story, and proved much more effectual than that of the assailants. The old-fashioned "batten door," strongly barricaded, resisted their efforts to demolish it. Meanwhile Culbertson continued to fire, the guns being loaded as fast as he discharged them, by the ready hands of Mrs. Thomas and her daughters, aided by her son William; and this spirited resistance soon convinced the enemy that further effort was useless. Believing that many men were concealed in the house, and apprehending a sally, their retreat was made as rapidly as their wounds would permit. After waiting a prudent time, and reconnoitering as well as she could from her position above, Mrs. Thomas descended the stairs, and opened the doors. When her husband made his appearance, and knew how gallantly the plunderers had been repulsed, his joy was only equaled by admiration of his wife's heroism. The powder thus preserved constituted the principal supply for Sumter's army in the battles at Rocky Mount and Hanging Rock.

Mrs. Thomas was the mother of nine children; and her sons and sons-in-law were active in the American service. John, the eldest son, rose during the war from the rank of captain till he succeeded his father in the command of the Spartan regiment. This he commanded at the battle of the Cowpens, and elsewhere. He was with Sumter in several of his most important engagements. Robert, another son, was killed in Roebuck's defeat. Abram, who was wounded at Ninety-Six and taken prisoner, died in the enemy's hands. William, the youth who had assisted in defending his home on the occasion mentioned, took part in other actions. Thus Mrs. Thomas was liable to some share of the enmity exhibited by the royalists towards another matron, against whom the charge, "She has seven sons in the rebel army," was an excuse for depredations on her property. If she had but four sons, she had sons-in-law who were likewise brave and zealous in the cause. Martha, one of the daughters, married Josiah Culbertson, who was the most effective scout in the country. He fought the Indians single-handed and in the army; was in nearly every important battle; and killed a number of celebrated tories in casual encounter. He seems to have been a special favorite with Colonel Isaac Shelby, in whose regiment he served in the battle at Musgrove's Mill, King's Mountain, and elsewhere. To this officer his daring spirit and deadly aim with the rifle, especially commended him; and he was employed by Shelby in the execution of some important trusts. He received a captain's commission towards the close of the war.

Ann was the wife of Joseph McJunkin, who entered the service of his country as a private, at the age of twenty, and rose to the rank of major before the close of 1780. He was in most of the battles before March, 1781, and contributed much to the success of those fought at Hanging Rock, Musgrove's Mill, Blackstock's Ford, and the Cowpens. This brave and faithful officer died in 1840 . . .

Jane, the third daughter, married Captain Joseph McCool; and Letitia was the wife of Major James Lusk. Both these were brave and efficient patriots; but the scenes of their exploits, and the success that attended them, are now remembered but in tradition. Of how many who deserve the tribute of their country's gratitude, is history silent! Every member of this family, it will thus be seen, had a personal interest in the cause of the country.

Not only was Mrs. Thomas distinguished for her indomitable perseverance where principle and right were concerned, and for her ardent spirit of patriotism, but for eminent piety, discretion, and industry. Her daughters exhibited the same loveliness of character, with the uncommon beauty of person which they inherited from her. All accounts represent Mrs. Culbertson as a woman of great beauty; and her sister Ann is said to have been little inferior to her in personal appearance. Mrs. Thomas herself was rather below the ordinary stature, with black eyes and hair, rounded and pleasing features, fair complexion, and countenance sprightly and expressive.

Soon after the close of the war, Colonel Thomas removed into Greenville district, where he and his wife resided till their death. But few of their descendants remain in the section of country where their parents lived, being scattered over the regions of the far West.

A few anecdotes of other women in the region where Mrs. Thomas lived during the war, are of interest as showing the state of the times. Isabella Sims, the wife of Captain Charles Sims, resided on Tyger River, . . . When she heard of . . . [a nearby Whig defeat], she went up and devoted herself for several days to nursing the wounded soldiers. Daniel McJunkin shared her maternal care, and recovered to render substantial service afterwards.

On another occasion, having heard the noise of battle during the afternoon and night, she went up early in the morning to Leighton's. A scout consisting of eight whigs had been surrounded by a very large body of tories. Some of the scouts made their escape by charging through the line; four defended themselves in the house till after dark, when they surrendered. Mrs. Sims, on her arrival, found that John Jolly, a whig officer who belonged to the vicinity, had been shot in attempting to escape. She sent for his wife, and made the necessary arrangements for his decent burial. Sarah, his widow, was left with five children; and for a time had great difficulty in procuring a subsistence. Her house was visited almost weekly by plundering parties, and robbed of food and clothing. At one time one of the robbers remained after the others had gone; and to an order to depart returned a refusal, with abusive and profane language. The exasperated mother seized a stick, with which she broke his arm, and drove him from the premises.

Not long after the death of Jolly, the famous Cunningham [William "Bloody Bill" Cunningham], a tory colonel who acted a prominent part in the partisan warfare of Laurens, Newberry, and Edgefield districts, came with a squadron of cavalry to the house of Captain Sims, who was gone for safety to North Carolina. Calling Mrs. Sims to the door, Cunningham ordered her to quit the place in three days; saying if he found the family there on his return, he would shut them in the house and burn it over them. Mrs. Sims fled with her family across the country to the house of a friendly old man; and remained there till her husband came and took them to York District, and thence to Virginia.

The wife of Major Samuel Otterson, a distinguished patriot, who lived also on Tyger River, chanced to know the place where a barrel of powder was concealed in the woods close at hand. She received intelligence one night that a party of tories would come for the treasure the next morning. Resolved that it should not fall into their hands, she prepared a train immediately, and blew up the powder. In the morning came the enemy, and on their demand for it, were told by Mrs. Otterson what she had done. They refused to believe her, but cut off her dress at the waist, and drove her before them to show the place of deposit. The evidence of its fate was conclusive, when they reached the spot.

Other instances of female intrepidity are rife in popular memory. Miss Nancy Jackson, who lived in the Irish settlement near Fairforest Creek, kicked a tory down the steps as he was descending loaded with plunder. In a great rage he threatened to send the Hessian troops there next day; which obliged her to take refuge with an acquaintance several miles distant. On one occasion the house of Samuel McJunkin, a stout patriot, but too old for the battle-field, was visited by a party under the noted Colonel Patrick Moore. They stayed all night; and when about to depart, stripped the house of bed-clothes and wearing apparel. The last article taken was a bed-quilt, which one Bill Haynesworth placed upon his horse. Jane, Mr. McJunkin's daughter, seized it, and a struggle ensued. The soldiers amused themselves by exclaiming, "Well done, woman!"—"Well done, Bill!" For once the colonel's feelings of gallantry predominated; and he swore if Jane could take the quilt from the man, she should have it. Presently in the contest, Bill's feet slipped from under him, and he lay panting on the ground. Jane placed one foot upon his breast and wrested the quilt from his grasp.

Dicey Langston

THE portion of South Carolina near the frontier, watered by the Pacolet, the Tyger, and the Ennoree [Rivers], comprising Spartanburg and Union Districts, witnessed many deeds of violence and blood, and many bold achievements of the hardy partisans. It could also boast its full complement of women whose aid in various ways was of essential service to the patriots. So prevalent was loyalism in the darkest of those days, so bitter was the animosity felt towards the whigs, and so eager the determination to root them from the soil, that the very recklessness of hate gave frequent opportunities for the betrayal of the plans of their enemies. Often were the boastings of those who plotted some midnight surprise, or some enterprise that promised rare pillage—uttered in the hearing of weak and despised women—unexpectedly turned into wonder at the secret agency that had disconcerted them, or execrations upon their own folly. The tradition of the country teems with accounts of female enterprise in this kind of service, very few instances of which were recorded in the military journals.

The patriots were frequently indebted for important information to one young girl, fifteen or sixteen years old at the commencement of the war. This was Dicey, the daughter of Solomon Langston of Laurens District. He was in principle a stout liberty man, but incapacitated by age and infirmities from taking any active part in the contest. His son was a devoted patriot, and was ever found in the field where his services were most needed. He had his home in the neighborhood, and could easily receive secret intelligence from his sister, who was always on the alert. Living surrounded by loyalists, some of whom were her own relatives, Miss Langston found it easy to make herself acquainted with their movements and plans, and failed not to avail herself of every opportunity to do so, and immediately to communicate what she learned to the whigs on the other side of the Ennoree River. At length suspicion of the active aid she rendered was excited among the tory neighbors. Mr. Langston was informed that he would be held responsible thenceforward, with his property, for the conduct of his daughter. The young girl was reproved severely, and commanded to desist from her patriotic treachery. For a time she obeyed the parental injunction; but having heard by accident that a company of loyalists, who on account of their ruthless cruelty had been commonly called the "Bloody Scout," intent on their work of death, were about to visit the "Elder settlement" where her brother and some friends were living, she determined at all hazards to warn them of the intended expedition. She had none in whom to confide; but was obliged to leave her home alone, by stealth, and at the dead hour of night. Many miles were to be traversed, and the road lay through woods, and crossed marshes and creeks, where the conveniences of bridges and foot-logs were wanting. She walked rapidly on, heedless of slight difficulties; but her heart almost failed her when she came to the banks of the Tyger—a deep and rapid stream, which there was no possibility of crossing except by wading through the ford. This she knew to be deep at ordinary times, and it had doubtless been rendered more dangerous by the rains that had lately fallen. But the thought of personal danger weighed not with her, in comparison to the duty she owed her friends and country. Her momentary hesitation was but the shrinking of nature from peril encountered in darkness and alone, when the imagination conjures up a thousand appalling ideas, each more startling than the worst reality. Her strong heart battled against these, and she resolved to accomplish her purpose, or perish in the attempt. She entered the water; but when in the middle of the ford, became bewildered, and knew not which direction to take. The hoarse rush of the waters, which were up to her neck—the blackness of the night—the utter solitude around her—the uncertainty lest the next step should ingulph [engulf] her past help, confused her; and losing in a degree her self-possession, she wandered for some time in the channel without knowing whither to turn her steps. But the energy of a resolute will, under the care of Providence, sustained her. Having with difficulty reached the other side, she lost no time in hastening to her brother, informed him and his friends of the preparations made to surprise and destroy them, and urged him to send his men instantly in different directions to arouse and warn the neighborhood. The soldiers had just returned from a fatiguing excursion, and complained that they were faint from want of food. The noble girl, not satisfied with what she had done at such risk to herself, was ready to help them still further by providing refreshment immediately. Though wearied, wet, and shivering with cold, she at once set about her preparations. A few boards were taken from the roof of the house, a fire was kindled with them, and in a few minutes a hoe-cake, partly baked, was broken into pieces, and 'thrust into the shot pouches of the men. Thus provisioned, the little company hastened to give the alarm to their neighbors, and did so in time for all to make their escape. The next day, when the "scout" visited the place, they found no living enemy on whom to wreak their vengeance.

At a later period of the war, the father of Miss Langston incurred the displeasure of the loyalists in consequence of the active services of his sons in their country's cause. They were known to have imbibed their principles from him; and he was marked out as an object of summary vengeance. A party came to his house with the desperate design of putting to death all the men of the family. The sons were absent; but the feeble old man, selected by their relentless hate as a victim, was in their power. He could not escape or resist; and he scorned to implore their mercy. One of the company drew a pistol, and deliberately leveled [sic] it at the breast of Lansgton. Suddenly a wild shriek was heard; and his young daughter sprang between her aged parent and the fatal weapon. The brutal soldier roughly ordered her to get out of the way, or the contents of the pistol would be instantly lodged in her own heart. She heeded not the threat, which was but too likely to be fulfilled the next moment. Clasping her arms tightly round the old man's neck, she declared that her own body should first receive the ball aimed at his heart! There are few human beings, even of the most depraved, entirely insensible to all noble and generous impulses. On this occasion the conduct of the daughter, so fearless, so determined to shield her father's life by the sacrifice of her own, touched the heart even of a member of the "Bloody Scout."

Langston was spared; and the party left the house filled with admiration at the filial affection and devotion they had witnessed.

. . .

After the war was ended, Miss Langston married Thomas Springfield, of Greenville, South Carolina. She died in Greenville District, a few years since. Of her numerous descendants then living, thirty-two were sons and grandsons capable of bearing arms, and ready at any time to do so in the maintenance of that liberty which was so dear to the youthful heart of their ancestor.

Katharine Steel

THIS heroine was of a stamp rarely seen or described in recent times. It needed a primitive country, as well as unusual hardships and perils, to develop such lofty, yet unambitious heroism, such sagacity mingled with homely simplicity, such a spirit of patience, constancy and self-sacrifice, without an aspiration for praise, or a thought of reward.

. . .

Katharine Fisher was a native of Pennsylvania. When about twenty years old she was married to Thomas Steel, of the same State. Both belonged to the race called the Pennsylvania Irish, so many of whom emigrated to Carolina about the middle of the century. Katharine had this destination in view at the time of her marriage, and being of a mirthful disposition, as well as romantic and fond of adventure, she looked upon it as quite a matter of frolic to lead the life of a pioneer on the borders of the wilderness. The young pair made their removal to South Carolina some time in 1745 . . .

It was not long before the young wife began to understand what was to be the life of pioneers. She was too lighthearted, however, to be discouraged by hardships, and with the good humor which is the best philosophy, endeavored to find food for merriment in the various inconveniences they had to encounter. She spared not her own strength, not shrinking from her share of labor in the field or the woods; she also learned in a short time the use of the rifle, and became an excellent shot.

[Other families settled nearby.] These families visited each other, going up and down the creek in canoes. In time, it became necessary to unite in their defence [sic] against the hostile Indians—the Cherokees giving them much trouble. The place owned by Mr. Steel was fortified as a block-house, to which the inhabitants could betake themselves when danger threatened. These block-houses were scattered over the country at convenient distances for the unprotected settlers . . . While the men were out fighting the Cherokees, or engaged in providing for the defence and maintenance of their families, the women were in the habit of resorting on any alarm to this place of refuge. Mrs. Steel was chief and ruler among them, not merely by her right of ownership, or her superior firmness and courage, but by virtue of her hearty kindness and good humor. She was acknowledged master of the Fort, and was called familiarly, "Katy of the Fort." Possessing great influence, she could at once calm the fears of the women who had quitted their homes at the dead hours of night to flee thither; they felt in fact a sense of security in her presence. She taught the young girls the use of the rifle, a useful accomplishment in those days, when no one knew what hour she might be compelled to wield that deadly weapon, relying on her skill in its use to save herself or her children from the hands of bloody savages. For weeks together the females would occupy the fort in the absence of their husbands or fathers. Their place of public worship, the attendance on which was never willingly neglected, was the Waxhaw meeting-house, in after years the scene of so much suffering and such disinterested benevolence.

. . .

[Steel's husband died, and when the revolutionary war began, her sons became ardent Patriots.] At the time of the alarm, Mrs. Steel was engaged in combing the captain's hair. He boasted a remarkably fine head of hair; it was very long and of raven blackness, and was usually worn tied in a queue behind. John's important services to the whig cause, employing him almost night and day, had of late left him little leisure for attention to his locks; they had been long uncombed, and probably showed very plainly the neglect they had experienced. The personal appearance of her son was a matter of pride to the matron, only less than her delight in his gallant conduct; she loved to see him look well, for he was a fairer image of herself. With her features he inherited her high qualities of mind and heart; he regarded her with reverence as well as affection, and never once in his life had disobeyed her. She had instilled into him the principles which guided herself; she had breathed into him her own romantic and unconquerable spirit . . .

[W]hile thus occupied, they heard the sharp crack of the rifle, followed immediately by Lockart's warning shouts, and the screams of the young girls who had been stationed in the field. In a moment after, several guns were fired in quick succession, and the girls were seen running towards the house, while the two divisions of the enemy, at no great distance behind them, could be perceived advancing through the standing corn. Not an instant was to be lost; yet such was the effect of sudden surprise on the brave men who, only two days before, had been taken unawares on Fishing

Creek, that they seemed utterly at a loss what to do. Mrs. Steel alone retained perfect self-possession. Starting up, she called to the men, "You must fight!" but directly after, seeing the confusion, that prevailed, she shouted an order for them to "clear themselves" as fast as possible. She urged her son to mount his horse at once, and save the public papers in his charge, while she pulled down the bars to let out him and his men. John was quick in all his movements, and it may easily be conceived that no time was now wasted. First in the saddle, he spurred his noble horse towards the bars, which he cleared at a bound—his mother having had no time yet to let them down—and galloped off. He was followed by James Harbinson, and the greater number of his men, for whom Mrs. Steel removed the bars as fast as she could; several, however, were slower in getting off, and paid the penalty of their delay, being now exposed to the fire of the advancing tories. About fifty guns were discharged at the bars, and two of the whigs—William Anderson and James Barber—fell dead from their horses, bearing Mrs. Steel under them to the ground. Another received wounds of which he expired in a few days, and three others, also severely wounded, succeeded in making their way to the house of McFadden, one of the neighbors. Robert McFadden, who could not get his horse, in leaping the bars had part of his foot shot off; Samuel McCance, riding at full speed up the lane, received a shot in the hip, and John Lockart's hunting-shirt filling with the wind as he rode, was riddled through and through with bullets that missed his body. Capt. Steel, determined to cut his way through the assailants, rode foremost up the lane at full speed, his long hair, unfastened, streaming in the wind, his rifle in one hand, held high above his head in defiance of the foe. He was closely followed by those of his company who had escaped. The tories made no attempt to stop them; but startled by the fury of their onset on their own party, gave way precipitately and scattered from the road, though they might have overpowered them by numbers; nor were they able to rally till the fugitives were beyond their reach. The whigs who were taken prisoners were carried to Camden; one or two died in the gaol [jail] there, while others languished for seven months, suffering incredible cruelties.

How was it meanwhile with the matron, as she struggled to release herself from the weight of the dead bodies, rising from the ground covered with the blood of the slain, her dress pierced in different places with bullet holes! Her first thought was for "John and the papers." When she heard they were safe, she burst into an exclamation of thankfulness, and as she was fortunately unhurt, turned her attention to the relief of others. The tories, meanwhile, enraged at their disappointment, and ascribing their failure to the energetic aid of Mrs. Steel, with one accord turned their course to her house. This they burned to the ground, and destroyed her property of every description, wherever they could find anything belonging to her. This vindictive outrage was the strongest testimony they could give of their estimate of the importance of her services to her friends.

. . .

It was no trifling part of woman's mission to reconcile the discordant elements left by the disorganizing ravages of civil war, and to build up a new and promising state of society. Mrs. Steel showed no less of the truly heroic in her character in her labors after the establishment of peace, than in the darkest hour of the actual struggle. Her days were ended at the old fort in 1785.

Elizabeth F. Ellett, *Women of the American Revolution,* vol. 1, fifth edn (New York: Baker & Scribner, 1848), 250–66, 284–91, available online at http://books.google.com/books?pg=PA308&id=BTYEAAAAYAAJ#v=onepage&q&f=false

Elizabeth F. Ellett, *Women of the American Revolution,* vol. 3 (New York: Baker & Scribner, 1850), 83–117, available online at http://books.google.com/books?pg=PA118&id=f_t_IScv4z0C#v=onepage&q&f=false

An Account of the Overmountain March and Battle of Kings Mountain

By An Unknown Member of Campbell's Regiment

*W*e do not know who authored this account. His account varies from most reports in a couple of respects. He says the Overmountain Men commenced their march on September 27, but the official report of the battle says the march began on September 26. He says that Ferguson was shot three times while most accounts say he was shot at least seven times.

On hearing of a large body of British and Tories assembled in North Carolina, under the command of Col. Ferguson, and threatening to visit Holston river, on the 22d of September, 1780, two hundred and fifty of the militia of Washington County, Virginia, were ordered out under the command of Col. William Campbell; and rendezvoused on Watauga, where they were joined by three hundred and fifty men from the western part of North Carolina [now East Tennessee] under the command of Col. [John] Sevier and Col. Isaac Shelby, together with a party of one hundred and fifty men, under the command of Col. Charles McDowell, who had been driven over the mountains by Col. Ferguson. While we were yet at the place of rendezvous, Col. Arthur Campbell, believing that there was not a sufficient force to successfully engage with the enemy, ordered out, and came on with two hundred more of the Washington militia, and joined us at Watauga. Col. Arthur Campbell returned home to take care of the frontiers, which were left bare of men, and were in danger of being attacked by the Indians, who were near neighbors.

A council was held to select a commander, and it was unanimously given to Col. William Campbell. We began our march from Watauga on the 27th of September, with nine hundred and fifty men. With a very bad road, we were four days in passing the mountains, when we arrived at the settlements of North Carolina; and the next day we were joined by Col. Cleveland, from Wilkes County, and Maj. Winston, from Surry, with four hundred men. From there we proceeded on, living mostly on parched corn. We left four hundred footmen [infantrymen] behind, not being able to keep up with the horse, and the fifth of October, joined Col. Williams, and some Georgia troops, being about three hundred and fifty. From Col. Williams' camp [near Gilbert Town], we set out about dark, and traveled all that night, expecting to attack the enemy about break of day; but Col. Ferguson sometime before, hearing of our coming, retreated, and took an advantageous position at a place called King's Mountain, where the enemy thought they were very safely posted, and sent to Cornwallis for a re-inforcement. But Col. Campbell proceeded so precipitately on his march, that we came on them with surprise, on the 7th of October, the sun being about an hour and a half high.

Col. Campbell ordered Col. Williams and Col. Cleveland to the left, and Col. Shelby for a reserve, and attacked on the right himself, making the first onset; but the action soon became general—Col. Williams and Col. Cleveland acting with great bravery on the left. Col. Ferguson ordered a charge to be made on the Virginia regiment, which forced some of them to retreat a short distance; but they were rallied again, but the enemy fell so fast that they were obliged to retire to the top of the mountain. Col. Shelby with the reserve came up, and in about half an hour the enemy was surrounded.

Too much cannot be said in praise of our brave commander, who exerted himself, animating the men to victory. We advanced on the enemy, and broke their lines; but they were rallied three times by Col. Ferguson, but to no effect; our men pressing so close on them on every side, at length that active British officer, losing all hopes of victory, thought with some others to break through our lines and get off; but fell in the attempt, Col. Ferguson having two balls through his body, and one through his head. The enemy then soon surrendered. The action lasted an hour and five minutes. The enemy had about two hundred and thirty dead on the ground, and a number wounded. We lost some brave officers, and about thirty-five lay dead on the ground. The enemy mostly over-shot us, as we marched up the mountain. It was dark again [by the time] we got the prisoners under guard. Cornwallis had sent Tarleton with four hundred dragoons to re-inforce Col. Ferguson, but hearing of his retreat, returned.

Excerpted from Lyman C. Draper, *King's Mountain and Its Heroes: History of the Battle of King's Mountain, October 7th, 1780, and the Events Which Led to It* (Cincinnati: P.G. Thomson, 1881): 529–30.

Official Report of the Battle of Kings Mountain

*This report from Isaac Shelby, William Campbell, and Benjamin Cleveland
was published in the* Virginia Gazette *on November 18, 1780 and in the*
Massachusetts Spy *on November 30, 1780.*

*A state of the proceedings of the Western Army, from the 22nd of September,
1780, to the reduction of Major Ferguson, and the army under his command.*

On receiving intelligence that Major Ferguson had advanced as high
up as Gilbert Town, in Rutherford County, and threatened to cross the
mountains to the western waters, Col. William Campbell, with four
hundred men from Washington County, Virginia, Col. Isaac Shelby, with
two hundred and forty from Sullivan County of North Carolina, and
Lieut.-Col. John Sevier, with two hundred and forty men, of Washington
County, assembled at Watauga, on the 25th of September, where they
were joined by Col. Charles McDowell, with one hundred and sixty men
from the Counties of Burke and Rutherford [North Carolina], who had
fled before the enemy to the western waters.

We began our march on the 26th, and on the 30th we were joined
by Col. Cleveland, on the Catawba river, with three hundred and fifty
men, from the Counties of Wilkes and Surry [North Carolina]. No one
officer having properly a right to command in chief, on the 1st of October,
we dispatched an express to Maj. Gen. Gates, informing him of our
situation, and requesting him to send a general officer to take the command of the whole. In the meantime Col. Campbell was chosen to act as
commandant till such general officer should arrive. We marched to the
Cowpens, on Broad river, in South Carolina, where we were joined
by Col. James Williams, with four hundred men, on the evening of
the 6th of October, who informed us, that the enemy lay encamped

somewhere near the Cherokee Ford, of Broad river, about thirty miles distant from us.

By a council of the principal officers, it was then thought advisable to pursue the enemy that night with nine hundred of the best horsemen, and leave the weak horses and footmen to follow as fast as possible. We began our march with nine hundred of the best men, about eight o'clock the same evening; and, marching all night, came up with the enemy about three o'clock p. m. of the 7th [of October], who lay encamped on the top of King's Mountain, twelve miles north of the Cherokee Ford, in the confidence that they could not be forced from so advantageous a post. Previous to the attack, on the march, the following disposition was made: Col. Shelby's regiment formed a column in the center, on the left; Col. Campbell's regiment, another on the right; with part of Col. Cleveland's regiment, headed in front by Major Winston, and Col. Sevier's regiment, formed a large column on the right wing. The other part of Cleveland's regiment, headed by Col. Cleveland himself, and Col. Williams' regiment, composed the left wing. In this order we advanced, and got within a quarter of a mile of the enemy before we were discovered.

Col. Shelby's and Col. Campbell's regiments began the attack, and kept up a fire on the enemy, while the right and left wings were advancing to surround them, which was done in about five minutes, and the fire became general all around. The engagement lasted an hour and five minutes, the greater part of which time, a heavy and incessant fire was kept up on both sides. Our men in some parts, where the regulars fought, were obliged to give way a small distance, two or three times; but rallied and returned with additional ardor to the attack. The troops upon the right having gained the summit of the eminence, obliged the enemy to retreat along the top of the ridge to where Col. Cleveland commanded, and were there stopped by his brave men. A flag was immediately hoisted by Capt. DePeyster, the commanding officer (Maj. Ferguson having been killed a little before), for a surrender. Our fire immediately ceased, and the enemy laid down their arms, the greatest part of them charged, and surrendered themselves to us prisoners at discretion.

It appears from their own provision returns for that day, found in their camp, that their whole force consisted of eleven hundred and twenty five men; out of which they sustained the following loss: Of the regulars, one Major, one Captain, two Sergeants, and fifteen privates killed; thirty-five privates wounded, left on the ground, not able to march; two Captains, four Lieutenants, three Ensigns, one Surgeon, five Sergeants, three Corporals, one Drummer, and forty-nine privates taken prisoners. Loss of the Tories—two Colonels, three Captains, and two hundred and one privates killed; one Major, and one hundred and twenty-seven privates wounded, and left on the ground, not able to march; one Colonel, twelve Captains, eleven Lieutenants, two Ensigns, one QuarterMaster, one Adjutant, two Commissaries, eighteen Sergeants, and six hundred privates taken prisoners. Total loss of the enemy, eleven hundred and five men at King's Mountain.

Given under our hands at camp,
WILLIAM CAMPBELL,
ISAAC SHELBY,
BENJ. CLEVELAND.

The losses on our side were—one Colonel, one Major, one Captain, two Lieutenants, Four Ensigns, nineteen privates killed—total, twenty eight killed; one Major, three Captains, three Lieutenants, and fifty-five privates wounded—total, sixty-two wounded. Published by order of Congress,

CHARLES THOMSON, SECRETARY.

Excerpted from Lyman Copeland Draper, *King's Mountain and Its Heroes: History of the Battle of King's Mountain, October 7th, 1780, and the Events Which Led to It* (Cincinnati: P.G. Thomson, 1881), 522–5.

Lieutenant Anthony Allaire's Account of the Battle of Kings Mountain and its Aftermath

*A*nthony Allaire was a New York-born Loyalist. He joined the Loyal American Volunteers, a provincial unit of the British army, and he came south with Colonel Patrick Ferguson when the unit was assigned to the southern campaign. He kept a diary from March through November of 1780, and the excerpt below describes the movements of Ferguson's army in the two weeks before the Battle of Kings Mountain as well as the battle itself and its aftermath. Ferguson was taken prisoner and marched to North Carolina where he was released in a prisoner of war exchange. After the war, he settled in New Brunswick, Canada.

Saturday, [September] 23d. Got in motion at nine o'clock in the morning; marched three miles to Gilbert Town; took up our ground on a height about half a mile from the town. This town contains one dwelling house, one barn, a blacksmith's shop, and some out-houses.

. . .

Monday, 25th, and Tuesday, 26th. Lay at Gilbert Town; nothing extra.

Wednesday, 27th. Got in motion at five o'clock in the morning, and marched three miles to Rucker's Mill, and halted.

Thursday, 28th. Got in motion at five o'clock in the morning; marched seven miles to Mountain creek, forded it, although very difficult, continued on about a mile farther to Twitty's Ford of Broad river, and took up our ground on its banks. At six o'clock in the evening got in motion, forded the river; marched two miles to McDaniel's Ford of Green river; forded it, and marched two miles farther; halted on the road; lay on our arms till four o'clock the next morning.

Friday, 29th. We then, at that early hour, moved on three miles to one James Step's plantation, and halted. This man has been very unfortunate in his family; his wife, who is a very decent woman, was caught by the Indians about a twelvemonth past. They scalped and tomahawked her several times in the head, treated the infant she had in her arms in a most inhuman and savage manner. They mashed its head in such a manner that its recovery is truly astonishing; but what this poor, unhappy woman seems most to regret is the loss of her oldest son, whom the savages took, and she now remains in a state of uncertainty, not having heard from him since.

Saturday, 30th. Lay at James Step's with an expectation of intercepting Col. Clarke on his return to the mountains; but he was prudent enough to take another route.

Sunday, October 1st. Got in motion at five o'clock in the morning, and marched twelve miles to Denard's Ford of Broad river, and took up our old ground where we lay the 8th September.

Monday, 2d. Got in motion at four o'clock in the afternoon; forded Broad river; marched four miles; formed in line of action and lay on our arms. This night I had nothing but the canopy of heaven to cover me.

Tuesday, 3d. Got in motion at four o'clock in the morning; marched six miles to Camp's Ford of Second Broad river, forded it and continued on six miles to one Armstrong's plantation, on the banks of Sandy Run. Halted to refresh; at four o'clock got in motion; forded Sandy Run; marched seven miles to Buffalo creek; forded it; marched a mile farther and halted near one Tate's plantation. John West came in camp, who is a hundred and one years of age; is amazingly strong in every sense.

Friday, 6th. Got in motion at four o'clock in the morning, and marched sixteen miles to Little King's Mountain, where we took up our ground.

Saturday, 7th. About two o'clock in the afternoon twenty-five hundred Rebels, under the command of Brig.-Gen. Williams, and ten Colonels, attacked us. Maj. Ferguson had eight hundred men. The action continued an hour and five minutes; but their numbers enabled them to surround us. The North Carolina regiment seeing this, and numbers being out of ammunition, gave way, which naturally threw the rest of the militia into confusion. Our poor little detachment, which consisted of only seventy men when we marched to the field of action, were all killed and wounded but twenty; and those brave fellows were soon crowded as close as possible by the militia. Capt. DePeyster, on whom the command devolved, saw it impossible to form six men together; thought it necessary to surrender to save the lives of the brave men who were left. We lost in this action, Maj. Ferguson, of the Seventy-first regiment, a man much attached to his King and country-, well informed in the art of war; he was brave and humane, and an agreeable companion; in short, he was universally esteemed in the army, and I have every reason to regret his unhappy fate. We had eighteen men killed on the spot; Capt. Ryerson and thirty-two privates wounded of Maj. Ferguson's detachment; Lieut. McGinnis, of Allen's regiment of Skinner's Brigade, killed. Taken prisoners, Two Captains, four Lieutenants, three Ensigns, and one Surgeon, and fifty-four sergeants rank and file, including the mounted men under the command of Lieut. Taylor. Of the militia, one hundred were killed, including officers; wounded, ninety; taken prisoners, about six hundred. Our baggage all taken, of course. Rebels lost Brig.-Gen. Williams, one hundred and thirty-five, including officers, killed; wounded, equal to ours.

Sunday, 8th. They [the rebels] thought it necessary to move us sixteen miles, to one Waldron's plantation, where they halted.

Monday, 9th. Moved two miles and a half to Bullock creek; forded it, and halted on the banks.

Tuesday, 10th. Moved twenty miles and halted in the woods.

Wednesday, 11th. Moved at eight o'clock in the morning; marched twelve miles to Col. Walker's, and halted.

Thursday, 12th. Those villains divided our baggage, although they had promised on their word we should have it all.

Friday, 13th. Moved six miles to Bickerstaffs plantation. In the evening their liberality extended so far as to send five old shirts to nine of us, as a change of linen—other things in like proportion.

Saturday, 14th. Twelve field officers were chosen to try the militia prisoners —particularly those who had the most influence in the country. They condemed [sic] thirty—in the evening they began to execute Lieut.-Col. Mills, Capt. Wilson, Capt. Chitwood, and six others, who unfortunately fell a sacrifice to their infamous mock jury. Mills, Wilson, and Chitwood died like Romans—the others were reprieved.

Excerpted from Lyman C. Draper, *King's Mountain and Its Heroes: History of the Battle of King's Mountain, October 7th, 1780, and the Events Which Led to It* (Cincinnati: P.G. Thomson, 1881): 484–515.

Alexander Chesney Describes the Battle of Kings Mountain

*A*lexander Chesney was a backcountry South Carolina Loyalist. At the outset *of the war, he served as a guide for Loyalist refugees fleeing the state. He was captured by Whigs and held prisoner, but released after several days when he promised to serve in the Whig militia. Chesney participated in the campaign against the Cherokee in 1776. After the fall of Charles Town, Chesney rejoined the Loyalist forces, he was serving with Colonel Patrick Ferguson at the Battle of Kings Mountain. Taken prisoner after the battle, he ultimately escaped and returned home.*

Col. Ferguson having resumed the command and finding himself pretty strong he marched us to the North Carolina line and encamped. A dissatisfaction prevailed at this moment amongst the Militia founded on general Clinton's hand-bill which required every man having but three children, and every single man to do six months duty out of their province when required. [T]his appeared like compulsion, instead of acting voluntarily as they conceived they were doing, and they were in consequence ready to give up the cause. [B]ut owing to the exertions of their officers a great part of which I attribute to myself, the tumult was happily appeased . . . At this period the North Carolina men joined us fast. Our spies returned from beyond the mountains [October] with intelligence that the rebels were embodying rapidly . . . Our spies from Holsteen[1] as well as some left at the Gap of the Mountains[2] brought us word that the Rebel force amounted to 3000 men; on which we retreated along the North side of Broadriver and sent the waggons [sic] along the South-side as far as Cherokeeford, where they joined us we marched to King's Mountain and there encamped with a view of approaching Lord Cornwallis' Army and receiving support; by Col. Ferguson's orders I sent expresses to the Militia Officers to join us here; but we were attacked before any support arrived by 1500 picked men from Gilbert's-town under the command of Col[s]. Cleveland, Selby [Shelby] and Campbell,[3] all of whom were armed with Rifles, well-mounted and of course could move with the utmost celerity [quickness]; so rapid was their attack that I was in the act of dismounting to report that all was quiet and the pickets on the alert when we heard their firing about half a mile off; I immediately paraded the men and posted the officers, during this short interval I received a wound which however did not prevent my doing duty; and on going towards my horse I found he had been killed by the first discharge. [October 7, 1780].

Kings Mountain from its height would have enabled us to oppose a superior force with advantage, had it not been covered with wood which sheltered the Americans and enabled them to fight in the favorite manner; in fact after driving in our piquets [pickets] they were able to advance in three divisions under separate leaders to the crest of the hill in perfect safety until they took post and opened an irregular but destructive fire from behind trees and other cover: Col Cleaveland's was first perceived and repulsed by a charge made by Col. Ferguson: Col. Selly's [Shelby's] next and met a similar fate being driven down the hill; last the detachment under Col. Campbell and by desire of Col. Ferguson I presented a new front which opposed it with success; by this time the Americans who had been repulsed had regained their former stations and sheltered behind trees poured in an irregular destructive fire; in this manner the engagement was maintained near an hour, the mountaniers [mountaineers] flying whenever there was danger of being charged by the Bayonet, and returning again so soon as the British detachment had faced about to repel another of their parties. Col. Ferguson was at last recognized by his gallantry although wearing a hunting shirt[4] and fell pierced by seven balls at the moment he had killed the American Col. Williams[5] with his left hand; (the right being useless)[6] I had just rallied the troops a second time by Ferguson's orders when Capt. De Peyster[7] succeeded to the command but soon after gave up and sent out a flag of truce, but as the Americans resumed their fire afterwards ours was also renewed under the supposition that they would give no quarter; and a dreadful havoc took place until the flag was sent out a second time, then the work of destruction ceased; the Americans surrounded us with double lines, and we grounded arms with the loss of one third our numbers.

I had been wounded by the first fire but was so much occupied that I scarcely felt it until the action was over. We passed the night on the spot where we surrendered amidst the dead and groans of the dying who had not surgical aid, or water to quench their thirst; Early next morning we marched at a rapid pace towards Gilbert's town between double lines of mounted Americans; the officers in the rear and obliged to carry two muskets each which was my fate although wounded and stripped of my shoes and silver buckles in an inclement season without covering or provisions untill Monday night when an ear of Indian corn was served to each; at Gilbert's town a mock tryal [trial] was held and 24 sentenced to death, 10 of whom suffered before the approach of Tarlton's force obliged them to move towards the Yadkin [River] cutting and striking us by the road in a savage manner Col. Cleveland then offered to enlarge me on condition that I would teach his Regiment for one month the exercise practised by Col. Ferguson which I refused, although he swore I should suffer death for it at the Moravian town; luckily his threat was not put to the test as I had the good fortune to make my escape one evening when close to that place; in the hurry to get off I took the wrong road and did not discover my error until I found I was close to the Moravian town:[8] I then retraced my steps until close to the pickets I had left and taking a fresh departure I crossed the Yadkin river before morning, proceeded through the woods toward home, John Weedyman one of my company had supplied me with a pair of shoes, which were of great use on this occasion, but as he remained a prisoner I never had an opportunity of making him a return.

The first night I slept in the woods, next day I was supported by haws grapes &c as I could find them in the woods: The second or third day in pushing through the woods to get to a ford I heard a noise of some people (whom I knew to be Americans by white paper in their hats) on which I lay down and was so close to them that I could have touched one of their horses in passing; fortunately I was not observed, and soon after crossed the Creek after them: I then made for the Mountains in order to be guided by the Appalachian range and get over the rivers with greater facility. After crossing Broad-river I met one Heron who had been with me in King's Mountain and who had with some others taken flight early in the action, putting white papers in their hats, by which disgraceful stratagem[9] they got through the American lines: I passed a night at Heron's house and one before at another man's on whom I could depend, from both I took some provisions all the other nights I slept out; I do not remember the number exactly, but must have been nearly a fortnight. I reached home on the 31st October I found the Americans had left me little. My wife had a son on the 20th whom I named William which was all the christening he had.

James P. Collins on the Battle of Cowpens

*J*ames P. Collins enlisted in a Whig militia unit under the command of Colonel John Moffitt in 1780, not long after the fall of Charles Town. He fought at the Battles of Huck's Defeat and Kings Mountain as well as at Cowpens. His autobiography was published in 1859, and this account is extracted from that work.

About sunrise on the 17th January, 1781, the enemy came in full view. The sight, to me at least, seemed somewhat imposing; they halted for a short time, and then advanced rapidly, as if certain of victory. The militia under Pickins and Moffit, was posted on the right of the regulars some distance in advance, while Washington's cavalry was stationed in the rear. We gave the enemy one fire; when they charged us with their bayonets; we gave way and retreated for our horses, Tarleton's cavalry pursued us; ("now," thought I, "my hide is in the loft;") just as we got to our horses, they overtook us and began to make a few hacks at some, however, without doing much injury. They, in their haste, had pretty much scattered, perhaps, thinking they could have another Fishing creek frolic, but in a few moments, Col. Washington's cavalry was among them, like a whirlwind, and the poor fellows began to keel from their horses, without being able to remount. The shock was so sudden and violent, they could not stand it, and immediately betook themselves to flight; there was not time to rally, and they appeared to be as hard to stop as a drove of wild Choctaw steers, going to a Pennsylvania market. In a few moments the clashing of swords was out of hearing and quickly out of sight; by this time, both lines of the infantry were warmly engaged and we being relieved from the pursuit of the enemy began to rally and prepare to redeem our credit, when Morgan rode up in front, and waving his sword, cried out, "form, form, my brave fellows! Give them one more fire and the day is ours. Old Morgan was never beaten." We then advanced briskly, and gained the right flank of the enemy, and they being hard pressed in front by Howard, and falling very fast, could not stand it long. They began to throw down their arms, and surrender themselves prisoners of war. The whole army, except Tarleton and his horsemen, fell into the hands of Morgan, together with all the baggage. After the fight was over, the sight was truly melancholy. The dead on the side of the British, exceeded the number killed at the battle of King's Mountain, being if I recollect aright, three hundred or upwards. The loss, on the side of the Americans, was only fifteen or sixteen, and a few slightly wounded. This day, I fired my little rifle five times, whether with any effect or not, I do not know. Next day after receiving some small share of the plunder, and taking care to get as much powder as we could, we (the militia) were disbanded and returned to our old haunts, where we obtained a few day's rest.

Source: James P. Collins, *Autobiography of a Revolutionary Soldier,* edited by John M. Roberts (New York: Arno Press, 1979 reprint of 1859 edition), 56–8.

Daniel Morgan to Nathanael Greene—Report of the Battle of Cowpens

In this official report to his commanding officer, General Morgan is careful to give credit for the victory at Cowpens to his men and to "the justice of our cause."

CAMP ON CAIN CREEK ON PEDEE, January 19th, 1781

DEAR SIR—The troops I have the honor to command have gained a complete victory over a detachment from the British Army commanded by Lieut.-Col. Tarleton. It happened on the 17th inst[ant], about sunrise, at a place called the Cowpens, near Pacolet River. On the 14th, having received intelligence that the British Army were in motion, and that their movements clearly indicated the intention of dislodging me, I abandoned my encampment at Glendale Ford, and on the 16th, in the evening, took possession of a post about seven miles from Chroke on Broad River. My former position subjected me at once to the operations of Lord Cornwallis and Colonel Tarleton, and in case of a defeat my retreat might easily have been cut off. My situation at Cowpens enabled me to improve any advantage that I might gain and to provide better for my security should I be unfortunate. These reasons induced me to take this post, notwithstanding it had the appearance of a retreat. On the evening of the 16th, the enemy occupied the ground we had removed from in the morning. One hour before daylight one of my scouts informed me that they had advanced within five miles of our camp. On this information the necessary dispositions were made. From the activity of the troops we were soon prepared to receive them. The light infantry commanded by Lt.-Col. Howard, and the Virginia Militia under Major Triplett, were formed on a rising ground. The Third Regiment of Dragoons, consisting of about 80 men, under command of Lt. Col. Washington, were so posted in the rear as not to be injured by the enemy's fire, and yet to be able to charge them should an occasion offer; the Volunteers from North Carolina, South Carolina and Georgia under the command of Col. Pickens were posted to guard the flanks. Major McDowal [McDowell] of the North Carolina Volunteers, were posted on the right flank in front of the line 150 yards. Major Cunningham of the Georgia Volunteers, on the left, at the same distance in front, Colonels Brannon and Thomas, of the South Carolina Volunteers, on the right of Major McDowal, and Colonels Hays and McCall of the same corps to the left of Major Cunningham. Capts. Tate and Buchanan, with the Augusta Riflemen, were to support the right of the line. The enemy drew up in one line four hundred yards in front of our advanced corps. The first battalion of the 71st Regiment was opposed to our right, the 7th to our left, the Legion Infantry to our centre, and two companies of the light troops, 100 each, on our flanks. In their front they moved two pieces of artillery, and Lieut. Col. Tarleton, with 280 cavalry, was posted in the rear of the line. The disposition being thus made, small parties of riflemen were detached to skirmish with the enemy, on which the whole line advanced with the greatest impetuosity, shouting as they advanced. Majors McDowal and Cunningham gave them a heavy and galling fire, and retreated to the regiments intended for their support; the whole of Col. Pickens' command then kept up a fire by regiments, retreating agreeable to orders. When the enemy advanced on our lines they received a well directed and incessant fire, but their numbers being superior to ours they gained our flanks, which obliged us to change our position. We retired, in good order, about fifty paces, formed and advanced on the enemy and gave them a brisk fire, which threw them into disorder. Lieut.Col. Howard observing this gave orders for the line to charge bayonets, which was done with such address that the enemy fled with the utmost precipitation. Lieut.Col. Washington, discovering that the cavalry were cutting down our riflemen on the left, charged them with such firmness as obliged them to retire in confusion. The enemy were entirely routed, and the pursuit continued upwards of twenty miles. Our loss was inconsiderable, not having more than twelve killed and sixty wounded. The enemy's loss was 10 commissioned officers and over 100 rank and file killed and 200, wounded, 29 commissioned officers and about 500 privates prisoners which fell into our hands with two pieces of artillery, two standards [flags], 800 muskets, one travelling forge, thirty-five baggage wagons, seventy negroes and upwards of 100 dragoon horses, with all their musick. They destroyed most of the baggage which was immense. Although our success was complete we fought only 800 men and were opposed by upwards of one thousand chosen British Troops. Such was the inferiority of our numbers that our success must be attributed, under

God, to the justice of our cause and the bravery of our Troops. My wishes would induce me to mention the name of every private centinel [sic] in the Corps. In justice to the brave and good conduct of the officers, I have taken the liberty to enclose you a list of their names from a conviction that you will be pleased to introduce such characters to the world. Major Giles, my aid de camp, and Captain Brooks, acting as Brigade Major, deserves to have my thanks for their assistance and behavior on this occasion. The Baron de Glabuck, who accompanies Major Giles with these despatches, [sic] behaved in such manner as to merit your attention.

I am sir, Your obedient servant,

DAN MORGAN.

Source: Myers, Theodorus Bailey. *Cowpens Papers, Being Correspondence of General Morgan and the Prominent Actors.* Charleston: News and Courier Book Press, 1881. Available online at http://books.google.com/books ?id=jF4SAAAAYAAJ&pg=PA47&lpg=PA55&ots=fk7QTLggmw&dq= theodorus+myers+cowpens+papers&output=text#c_top

Alexander Chesney describes the Battle of Cowpens

*W*hen *Loyalist Alexander Chesney heard of Tarleton's expedition into the backcountry in pursuit of Daniel Morgan, he assembled a militia company, and offered his services to the British general. He describes the Battle of Cowpens.*

. . . I heard that Col. Tarlton [sic] had defeated Sumpter [sic] at Black-stocks fort on Tyger-river on [hearing] which I raised a company with great difficulty and joined a strong party at Col. Williams'[1] house on Little-river where there was a strong party under General Cunningham.[2] [Major] Frost . . . directed me to assemble my company of Militia and join him at an appointed place on the Enoree. When I came to that place the Americans under Captn then Major Roebuck[3] in possession of it who immediately disarmed and marched us off. It was a great blunder in Major Frost to alter the place of meeting: however he did his best to remedy it; he pursued and overtook us about 12 miles higher up and having attacked Roebuck's party where they were advantageously posted at a house. [P]oor Frost was killed the rest retreated. Roebuck who was acquainted with me formerly: paroled me to Ninety-six where I was exchanged for Captain Clerk, a son to Col Clerk who had been taken after the attack on Augusta in Georgia.[4] I was then sent to garrison the goal [jail] of NinetySix [December, 1780,] which I fortified and had the command of the Militia stationed there . . . where I continued until Tarleton came into Ninety-Six district to go in quest of General Morgan [January, 1781,] and sent to the garrison for guides acquainted with Morgan's situation which was then convenient to my house on Pacholet.[5] I joined Col Tarleton and marched to Fair-forest. [H]aving failed to get intelligence of Morgan's situation he sent me out [January 16,] to endeavour [sic] to do so and to make the mills grind for the Army: when I reached Pacholet-river [Pacolet] I swam my horse over a private ford not likely to be guarded, leaving the man behind me to go on more quietly & reconnoiter [sic] the same. I found the fires burning but no one there,[6] on which I rode to my father's who said Morgan was gone to the Old-fields[7] about an hour before; my wife said the same and that they had used or destroyed my crop & took away almost every thing.[8] I immediately returned to Col Tarleton and found he had marched towards the Old fields. I overtook them before 10 o'clock near the Cow-pens on Thickety Creek where we suffered a total defeat by some dreadful bad management. The Americans were posted behind a rivulet with Rifle-men as a front line and Cavarly in the rear so as to make a third line; Col Tarleton charged at the head of his Regiment of Cavalry called the British Legion which was filled up from the prisoners taken at the battle of Camden;[9] the Cavalry supported by a detachment of the 71st Reg'[t] under Major McArthur broke the Riflemen without difficulty,[10] but the prisoners on seeing their own Reg'[t] opposed to them in the rear would not proceed against it and broke: the remainder charged but were repulsed this gave time to the front line to rally and form in the rear of their Cavalry which immediately charged and broke the 71st (then unsupported) making many prisoners: the rout was almost total. I was with Tarleton in the charge who behaved bravely but imprudently the consequence was his force dispersed in all directions the guns and many prisoners fell into the hands of the Americans.

The men being dispersed I desired them to meet me at General Cunningham's, I proceeded towards home to bring off my wife and child on the 17 Jan [1781,] and found there was nothing left not even a blanket to keep off the inclement weather; or a change of garments; then leaving a pleasant situation in a lamentable state without a shilling in my pocket; proceeded for General Cunningham's, sleeping encamped that night at Fair-forest; As we could not preval [sic] on General Cunningham to use any exertions to embody his brigade of Militia we went to Edisto river in order to settle there having nothing but two horses and our clothes left, everything else being in the hands of the Americans and by them confiscated.[11]

I have not been at Pacholet since nor am I likely to be.

Source: E. Alfred Jones and Wilbur Henry Siebert, Eds., *The Journal of Alexander Chesney, A South Carolina Loyalist in the Revolution and After* (Columbus: Ohio State University, 1921, 20–22).

Tarleton's Account of the Battle of Cowpens

In 1787, Tarleton published A History of the Campaigns of 1780 and 1781 in the Southern Provinces of North America. *He described his defeat at the Battle of Cowpens. He refers to himself in third person.*

[In January 1780] the operations of the Americans to the westward of Broad river laid immediate claim to the attention of the British. General Morgan, with the continental light infantry, Colonel Washington's cavalry, and large detachments of militia, was reported to be advancing to Ninety Six. Although the fortifications were in tolerable condition at that place, and sufficiently strong to resist an assault, yet the preservation of the country in its neighbourhood was considered as so great an object for the garrison and the loyalists of the district, that Earl Cornwallis dispatched an aid-de-camp 1st of January, to order Lieutenant-colonel Tarleton over Broad river, with his corps of cavalry and light infantry, of five hundred and fifty men, the first battalion of the 71st, consisting of two hundred and two three-pounders, to counteract the designs of General Morgan, by protecting the country, and compelling him to repass [re-cross] Broad river. Tarleton received a letter the next day from his lordship [Cornwallis], communicating an earnest wish, that the American commander, if within his reach, "should be pushed to the utmost["]; and requiring, likewise, his opinion, whether any move of the main army [Cornwallis's main force] would be advantageous to the service. On the receipt of this letter, [Tarleton] directed his course to the westward, and employed every engine to obtain intelligence of the enemy. He had not proceeded above twenty miles from Brierley's ferry, before he had undoubted proofs, that the report which occasioned the order for the light light [sic] troops to march was erroneous. The secure state of Ninety Six, and the distance of General Morgan, immediately prompted Tarleton to halt the troops under his command, as well to allow time for the junction of the baggage of the different corps, which had been left on the ground when they first decamped, as to give information to Earl Cornwallis of the situation and force of Morgan, and to propose operations which required his [Cornwallis's] sanction and concurrence.

As Lieutenant-colonel Tarleton had been entrusted with the outline of the future campaign, he thought it incumbent on him to lay before his Lordship, by letter, the probable accounts of Morgan's force and designs; the necessity of waiting for the baggage of the light troops in their present situation, as any future delay might prove a great inconvenience to the army; and the plan of operation which struck him as equally necessary and advantageous for the King's service. He represented the course to be taken, which fortunately corresponded with the scheme of the campaign: He mentioned the mode of proceeding to be employed against General Morgan: He proposed the same time, for the army and light troops to commence their march: He explained the point to be attained by the main body: And he declared, that it should be his endeavour to push the enemy into that quarter.

Earl Cornwallis approving the suggested operations, the light troops only waited for their their baggage to proceed . . . On the arrival [of the baggage wagons], Lieutenant-colonel Tarleton crossed Indian, and afterwards Dunken creek, though both were considerably swelled by a late fall of rain: He hourly received accounts of the increase of Morgan's corps, which induced him to request Earl Cornwallis, who was moving on the east of Broad river, to give him permission to retain the 7th regiment, that the enemy might be sooner pressed over Broad river, or some favourable situation obtained, whence great advantage might be derived from additional numbers: Having received leave to carry forwards the 7th regiment, he continued his course on the 12th to the westward, in order to discover the most practicable fords for the passage of the Ennoree [sic] and Tyger [Rivers] and that the infantry might avoid the inconveniencies they had undergone in crossing the other waters. An useful expedient was concealed under this apparent necessity[:] In proportion to the approach of the light troops to the sources of the rivers, and the progress of the main army to King's mountain, General Morgan's danger would increase, if he remained to the westward of Broad river. The Ennoree and Tyger were passed on the 14th, above the Cherokee road, and Tarleton obtained information in the evening that General Morgan guarded all the fords upon the Pacolet. About the same time Earl Cornwallis advertised [advised] Tarleton that the main army had reached Bull's run [creek], and that General Leslie had surmounted the difficulties which had hitherto retarded his march. At this crisis Lieutenant-colonel Tarleton assured Earl Cornwallis that he would endeavour to pass the Pacolet, purposely to force General Morgan to retreat towards Broad river, and requested his lordship to proceed up the eastern bank without delay, because such a movement might perhaps admit of co-operation, and would undoubtedly stop the retreat of the Americans.[1]

On the 15th circumstantial intelligence was procured by Lieutenant-colonel Tarleton of the different guards stationed on the Pacolet. A march was commenced in the evening towards the iron works , which are situated high upon the river; but in the morning the course was altered, and the light troops secured a passage within six miles of the enemy's camp. As soon as the corps were assembled beyond the Pacolet, Lieutenant-colonel Tarleton thought it adviseable [sic] to advance towards some log houses, formerly constructed by Major Ferguson, which lay midway between the British and Americans, and were reported to be unoccupied by General Morgan. The necessity and utility of such a proceeding appeared so strong, that some dragoons and mounted infantry were sent with all possible expedition to secure them, lest a similar opinion should strike the American commander, which might be productive of great inconvenience. Tarleton intended to take post, with his whole corps, behind the log houses, and wait the motions of the enemy; but a patrol discovering that the Americans were decamped, the British fight troops were directed to occupy their position, because it yielded a good post, and afforded plenty of provisions, which they had left behind them, half cooked, in every part of their encampment.[2]

Patroles [sic] and spies were immediately dispatched to observe the Americans: The dragoons were directed to follow the enemy till dark, and the other emissaries to continue their inquiries till morning, if some material incident did not occur: Early in the night the patroles reported that General Morgan had struck into byways, tending towards Thicketty creek: A party of determined loyalists made an American colonel prisoner, who had casually left the line of march, and [the Loyalists] conducted him [the American colonel] to the British camp: The examination of the militia colonel, and other accounts soon afterwards received, evinced the propriety of hanging upon General Morgan's rear, to impede the junction of reinforcements, said to be approaching, and likewise to prevent his passing Broad river without the knowledge of the light troops, who could perplex his design, and call in the assistance of the main army if necessity required. Other reports at midnight of a corps of mountaineers being upon the march from Green river, proved the exigency of moving to watch the enemy closely, in order to take advantage of any favourable opportunity that might offer.

Accordingly, at three o'clock in the morning on the 17th, the pickets being called in, the British troops, under the command of Lieutenant-colonel Tarleton, were directed to follow the route the Americans had taken the preceding evening, and the baggage and waggons [sic] were ordered to remain upon their ground till daybreak, under the protection of a detachment from each corps. Three companies of light infantry, supported by the legion infantry, formed the advance; the 7th regiment, the guns, and the 1st battalion of the 71st, composed the center; and the cavalry and mounted infantry brought up the rear. The ground which the Americans had passed being broken, and much intersected by creeks and ravines, the march of the British troops during the darkness was exceedingly slow, on account of the time employed in examining the front and flanks as they proceeded. Before dawn, Thicketty creek was passed, when an advanced guard of cavalry was ordered to the front. The enemy's patrole approaching was pursued and overtaken: Two troops of dragoons, under Captain Ogilvie, of the legion, were then ordered to reinforce the advanced guard, and to harass the rear of the enemy. The march had not continued long in this manner, before the commanding officer in front reported that the American troops were halted and forming. The guides were immediately consulted relative to the ground which General Morgan then occupied, and the country in his rear. These people described both with great perspicuity: They said that the woods were open and free from swamps; that the part of Broad river, just above the place where King's creek joined the stream, was about six miles distant from the enemy's left flank, and that the river, by making a curve to the westward, ran parallel to their rear.

Lieutenant-colonel Tarleton having attained a position, which he certainly might deem advantageous, on account of the vulnerable situation of the enemy, and the supposed vicinity of the two British corps on the east and west of Broad river, did not hesitate to undertake those measures which the instructions of his commanding officer imposed, and his own judgment, under the present appearances, equally recommended. He ordered the legion dragoons to drive in the militia parties who covered the front, that General Morgan's disposition might be conveniently and distinctly inspected. He discovered that the American commander had formed a front line of about one thousand militia, and had composed his second line and reserve of five hundred continental light infantry, one hundred and twenty of Washington's cavalry, and three hundred back woodsmen. This accurate, knowledge being obtained, Tarleton desired the British infantry to disencumber themselves of everything, except their arms and ammunition: The light infantry were then ordered to file to the right till they became equal to the flank of the American front line:

The legion infantry were added to their left; and, under the fire of a three-pounder, this part of the British troops was instructed to advance within three hundred yards of the enemy. This situation being acquired, the 7th regiment was commanded to form upon the left of the legion infantry, and the other three-pounder was given to the right division of the 7th: A captain, with fifty dragoons, was placed on each flank of the corps, who formed the British front line, to protect their own, and threaten the flanks of the enemy: The 1st battalion of the 71st was desired to extend a little to the left of the 7th regiment, and to remain one hundred and fifty yards in the rear. This body of infantry, and near two hundred cavalry, composed the reserve. During the execution of these arrangements, the animation of the officers and the alacrity of the soldiers afforded the most promising assurances of success. The disposition being completed, the front line received orders to advance; a fire from some of the recruits of the 7th regiment was suppressed, and the troops moved on in as good a line as troops could move at open files. The militia, after a short contest, were dislodged, and the British approached the continentals. The fire on both sides was well supported and produced much slaughter: The cavalry on the right were directed to charge the enemy's left: They executed the order with great gallantry, but were drove back by the fire of the reserve, and by a charge of Colonel Washington's cavalry.

As the contest between the British infantry in the front line and the continentals seemed equally balanced, neither retreating, Lieutenant-colonel Tarleton thought the advance of the 71st into line, and a movement of the cavalry in reserve to threaten the enemy's right flank, would put a victorious period [conclusion] to the action. No time was lost in performing this maneuver. The 71st were desired to pass the 7th before they gave their fire, and were directed not to entangale [sic] their right flank with the left of the other battalion. The cavalry were ordered to incline to the left, and to form a line, which would embrace the whole of the enemy's right flank. Upon the advance of the 71st, all the infantry again moved on: The continentals and back woodsmen gave ground: The British rushed forwards: An order was dispatched to the cavalry to charge: An unexpected fire at this instant from the Americans, who came about as they were retreating, stopped the British, and threw them into confusion. Exertions to make them advance were useless. The part of the cavalry which had not been engaged fell likewise into disorder, and an unaccountable panic extended itself along the whole line. The Americans, who before thought they had lost the action, taking advantage of the present situation, advanced upon the British troops, and augmented their astonishment. A general flight ensued. Tarleton sent directions to his cavalry to form about four hundred yards to the right of the enemy, in order to check them, whilst he endeavoured to rally the infantry to protect the guns. The cavalry did not comply with the order, and the effort to collect the infantry was ineffectual: Neither promises nor threats could gain their attention; they surrendered or dispersed, and abandoned the guns to the artillery men, who defended them for some time with exemplary resolution. In this last stage of defeat Lieutenant-colonel Tarleton made another struggle to bring his cavalry to the charge. The weight of such an attack might yet retrieve the day, the enemy being much broken by their late rapid advance; but all attempts to restore order, recollection, or courage, proved fruitless. Above two hundred dragoons forsook their leader, and left the field of battle. Fourteen officers and forty horse-men were, however, not unmindful of their own reputation, or the situation of their commanding officer. Colonel Washington's cavalry were charged, and driven back into the continental infantry by this handful of brave men. Another party of the Americans, who had seized upon the baggage of the British troops on the road from the late encampment, were dispersed, and this detachment retired towards Broad river unmolested . . . The number of the killed and wounded, in the action at the Cowpens, amounted to near three hundred on both sides, officers and men inclusive: This loss was almost equally shared; but the Americans took two pieces of cannon, the colours of the 7th regiment, and near four hundred prisoners.

A diffuse comment upon this affair would be equally useless and tiresome: Two observations will be sufficient: One will contain the general circumstances which affected the plan of the campaign, and the other the particular incidents of the action. It appears that Earl Cornwallis intended to invade North Carolina: Before his march commenced, an irruption was made by the enemy into the western part of South Carolina: In order to expel hostility from that quarter, he directed Lieutenant-colonel Tarleton to proceed with a corps, and "push the enemy to the utmost"; at the same time desiring to know if any movement of the main army would be useful. Tarleton, finding the Americans not so far advanced as was reported, halted his troops, that he might convey his opinion, by letter, to his commanding officer. He proposed that the army under Earl Cornwallis, and the corps of light troops, would commence their march at the same time for King's mountain, and that he would endeavour to destroy the enemy, or push them over Broad river to that place. Earl Cornwallis replied, that Tarleton perfectly understood his intentions. After three days move from Wynnesborough [Winnsboro], his lordship sent intelligence that General Leslie was retarded by the waters, and that he imagined the light troops must be equally impeded. Tarleton shortened his marches till he heard that the reinforcement was out of the swamps, though he had more difficulties of that nature to struggle against than could possibly be found between the Catawba and Broad rivers: This delay being occasioned by General Leslie's corps, rather astonished him, because the troops under that officer's command were not mentioned in the first proposal; and if they were deemed necessary for the combination, one forced march would have brought them from the banks of the Catawba to the middle road, which Earl Cornwallis was then moving on, between the two great rivers, and where no creeks or waters could obstruct their advance towards Tryon county. On the 14th Earl Cornwallis informed Tarleton that Leslie had surmounted his difficulties, and that he imagined the enemy would not pass the Broad river, though it had fallen very much. Tarleton then answered, that he would try to cross the Pacolet to force them, and desired Earl Cornwallis to acquire as high a station as possible, in order to stop their retreat. No letter, order, or intelligence, from head quarters, reached Tarleton after this reply, previous to the defeat on the 17th, and after that event he found Earl Cornwallis on Turkey creek, near twenty-five miles below the place where the action had happened. The distance between Wynnesborough and King's mountain, or Wynnesborough and Little Broad river, which would have answered the same purpose, does not exceed sixty-five miles: Earl Cornwallis commenced his march on the 7th or 8th of January. It would be mortifying to describe the advantages that might have resulted from his lordship's arrival at the concerted point, or to expatiate upon the calamities which were produced by this event. If an army is acting where no co-operation can take place, it is necessary for the commander in chief to keep as near as possible to his detachments, if such a proceeding does not interfere with a maneuver which in itself would decide the event of the campaign. A steady adherence to that line of conduct would prevent the misfortunes which detachments are liable to, or soften their effects. Earl Cornwallis might have conceived, that, by attending to the situation of the enemy, and of the country, and by covering his light troops, he would, in all probability, have alternately brought Generals Morgan and Greene into his power by co-operative movements: He might also have concluded, that all his parties that were beaten in the country, if they had no corps to give them instant support or refuge, must be completely destroyed. Many instances of this nature occurred during the war. The fall of Ferguson was a recent and melancholy example: That catastrophe put a period to the first expedition into North Carolina; and the as fair of the Cowpens overshadowed the commencement of the second.

The particular incidents relative to the action arise from an examina tion of the orders, the march, the comparative situation of Morgan and Tarleton, the disposition, and the defeat. The orders were positive. The march was difficult, on account of the number of creeks and rivers; and circuitous, in consequence of such impediments: The Pacolet was passed by stratagem: The Americans to avoid an action, left their camp, and marched all night: The ground which General Morgan had chosen for the engagement, in order to cover his retreat to Broad river, was disadvantageous for the Americans, and convenient for the British: An open wood was certainly as proper a place for action as Lieutenant-colonel Tarleton could desire; America does not produce many more suitable to the nature of the troops under his command. The situation of the enemy was desperate in case of misfortune; an open country, and a river in their rear, must have thrown them entirely into the power of a superior cavalry; whilst the light troops, in cafe of repulse, had the expectation of a neighbouring force to protect them from destruction. The disposition was planned with coolness, and executed without embarrassment. The defeat of the British must be ascribed either to the bravery or good conduct of the Americans; to the loose manner of forming which had always been practised [sic] by the King's troops in America; or to some unforeseen event, which may throw terror into the most disciplined soldiers, or counteract the best-concerted designs. The extreme extension of the files always exposed the British regiments and corps, and would, before this unfortunate affair, have been attended with detrimental effect, had not the multiplicity of lines with which they generally fought rescued them from such imminent danger. If infantry who are formed very open, and only two deep, meet with opposition, they can have no stability: But when they experience an unexpected shock, confusion will ensue, and flight, without immediate support, must be the inevitable consequence. Other circumstances, perhaps, contributed to so decisive a rout, which, if the military system admitted the same judicious regulation as the naval, a court martial would, perhaps, have disclosed. Public trials of commanding officers after unfortunate affairs, are as necessary to one service as the other, and might, in some instances, be highly beneficial to the military profession. Influenced by this idea, Lieutenant-colonel Tarleton, some days after the action, required Earl Cornwall's approbation of his proceedings, or his leave to retire till inquiry could be instituted, to investigate his conduct. The noble Earl's decided support of Lieutenant-colonel Tarleton's management of the King's troops, previous to and during the action, is fully expressed in a letter from his lordship.

Source: Banastre Tarleton, *A History of the Campaigns of 1780 and 1781 in the Southern Provinces of North America* (Dublin: Collis, Exshaw, White, et al., 1787), 216–29.

Notes

1 The Southern Backcountry Before the American Revolution

Epigraphs: Robert Stansbury Lambert, *South Carolina Loyalists in the American Revolution* (Columbia: University of South Carolina Press, 1987), 16 and Charles Woodmason, *The Carolina Backcountry on the Eve of the Revolution: The Journal and Other Writings of Charles Woodmason, Anglican Itinerant*, Richard James Hooker, Ed. (Chapel Hill: University of North Carolina Press, 1953), 214.

1 Michael C. Scoggins, *The Day It Rained Militia: Huck's Defeat and the Revolution in the South Carolina Backcountry*, May–July 1780 (Charleston: History Press, 2005), 92.

2 John W. Gordon, *South Carolina and the American Revolution: A Battlefield History* (Columbia: University of South Carolina Press, 2003), 1; Wilma Dykeman, *With Fire and Sword: The Battle of Kings Mountain, 1780* (Washington, D.C.: National Park Service, n.d.), n.p.

3 Walter Edgar, *Partisans and Redcoats: The Southern Conflict that Turned the Tide of the American Revolution* (New York: Perennial, 2001), xi.

4 Edgar, *Partisans and Redcoats*, xii, 2–3; Philip N. Racine, *Seeing Spartanburg: A History in Images* (Spartanburg: Hub City Writers Project, 1999): 19–21; Melissa Walker and Tom Moore Craig, "Introduction," in Tom Moore Craig, Ed., *Upcountry South Carolina Goes to War*, xiii–xv; Walter Edgar, *South Carolina: A History* (Columbia: University of South Carolina Press, 1998), 205; Richard Maxwell Brown, *The South Carolina Regulators* (Cambridge: The Belknap Press of Harvard University, 1963), 2–3; Rachel N. Klein, *Unification of a Slave State: The Rise of the Planter Class in the South Carolina Backcountry, 1760–1808* (Chapel Hill: University of North Carolina Press, 1990), 19, 9; Jack M. Sosin, *The Revolutionary Frontier, 1763–1783* (New York: Holt Rinehart, and Winston, 1967), 61–8.

5 Edgar, *South Carolina: A History*, 205.

6 Jim Piecuch, *Three Peoples, One King: Loyalists, Indians, and Slaves in the Revolutionary South, 1775–1782* (Columbia: University of South Carolina Press, 2008), 26; Cole Cheek, "'Let South Carolina Deal Justly By The Catawbas': The Catawba Struggle

To Survive In The Upstate In The Nineteenth Century," in *Piedmont Portraits: Unexplored Moments in the History of the Nineteenth Century South Carolina Upcountry,* Timothy P. Grady and Melissa Walker, Eds. (Columbia: University of South Carolina Press, forthcoming 2012); Edgar, *South Carolina: A History,* 205; Richard Maxwell Brown, *South Carolina Regulators,* 3.

7 Tom Hatley, *The Dividing Paths: Cherokees and South Carolinians through the Era of Revolution* (New York: Oxford, 1993), 70; Richard Maxwell Brown, *South Carolina Regulators,* 3–4; Edgar, *South Carolina: A History,* 206.

8 Piecuch, *Three Peoples, One King,* 31–2.

9 Richard Maxwell Brown, *The South Carolina Regulators,* 4; Edgar, *South Carolina: A History,* 206.

10 Richard Maxwell Brown, *The South Carolina Regulators,* 4; Edgar, *South Carolina: A History,* 206; Piecuch, *Three Peoples, One King,* 28; Hatley, *The Dividing Path,* 82, 99–101, 105–7, 112–15, 123–4.

11 Richard Maxwell Brown, *The South Carolina Regulators,* 5–7, quotes on p. 7; Edgar, *Partisans and Redcoats,* 12–13; Hatley, *The Dividing Path,* 127.

12 Richard Maxwell Brown, *The South Carolina Regulators,* 4–12; Edgar, *South Carolina: A History,* 206–7; Edgar, *Partisans and Redcoats,* 13; Hatley, *The Dividing Path,* 128–34, 138–40.

13 Richard Maxwell Brown, *The South Carolina Regulators,* 10–20, 31, 72; Edgar, *South Carolina: A History,* 212; Edgar, *Partisans and Redcoats,* 14.

14 Richard Maxwell Brown, *The South Carolina Regulators,* 34–6; Edgar, *Partisans and Redcoats,* 14.

15 Richard Maxwell Brown, *The South Carolina Regulators,* 24; Edgar, *South Carolina: A History,* 212.

16 Richard Maxwell Brown, *Strain of Violence: Historical Studies of American Violence and Vigilantism* (New York: Oxford University Press, 1975), 72; Edgar, *South Carolina: A History,* 205; Piecuch, *Three Peoples, One King,* 14; Hatley, *The Dividing Path,* 179.

17 Richard Maxwell Brown, *The South Carolina Regulators,* 72; Edgar, *South Carolina: A History,* 212.

18 Richard Maxwell Brown, *The South Carolina Regulators,* 38–41; Edgar, *South Carolina: A History,* 212–13; Jack M. Sosin, *The Revolutionary Frontier, 1763–1783* (New York: Holt Rinehart, and Winston, 1967), 68–70; Edgar, *Partisans and Redcoats,* 15–16.

19 Edgar, *South Carolina: A History,* 212–13; Sosin, *The Revolutionary Frontier,* 68–70.

20 Quotations from Richard J. Hooker, Ed., *The Carolina Backcountry on the Eve of the Revolution: The Journal and Other Writings of Charles Woodmason,* Anglican Itinerant (Chapel Hill: University of North Carolina Press, 1953), 60, 56.

21 Charles Woodmason, *The Carolina Backcountry on the Eve of the Revolution: The Journal and Other Writings of Charles Woodmason, Anglican Itinerant,* Richard James Hooker, Ed. (Chapel Hill: University of North Carolina Press, 1953), 214; Richard Maxwell Brown, *The South Carolina Regulators,* 41–2.

22 Woodmason and Hooker, 215; Edgar, *Partisans and Redcoats,* 16.

23 Richard Maxwell Brown, *The South Carolina Regulators,* 44–6, 49–50, 53–63; Edgar, *South Carolina: A History,* 213; Edgar, *Partisans and Redcoats,* 17.

24   Edgar, *Partisans and Redcoats*, 17–19; Hatley, *The Dividing Path*, 181–3; Richard Maxwell Brown, *The South Carolina Regulators*, 53–82, 113–34; Edgar, *South Carolina: A History*, 213, 215; Sosin, *The Revolutionary Frontier*, 68–70.

25   Richard Maxwell Brown, *The South Carolina Regulators*, 83–111; Edgar, *South Carolina: A History*, 215–16; Edgar, *Partisans and Redcoats*, 19.

26   Richard Maxwell Brown, *The South Carolina Regulators*, 9–10; Sosin, *The Revolutionary Frontier*, 68–70.

27   Richard Maxwell Brown, *The South Carolina Regulators*, 9–10; Sosin, *The Revolutionary Frontier*, 68–70.

28   Scoggins, *The Day It Rained Militia*, 23.

2 Imperial Crisis in the South

Epigraph: Ray Raphael, *A People's History of the American Revolution: How Common People Shaped the Fight for Independence* (New York: The New Press, 2001), author quote, 246, quote from General Committee, 313.

1   Scoggins, *The Day It Rained Militia*, 23.
2   Gordon, *South Carolina and the American Revolution*, 15.
3   Edgar, *South Carolina: A History*, 207–8.
4   Edgar, *South Carolina: A History*, 209.
5   Edgar, *South Carolina: A History*, 209–10.
6   Edgar, *South Carolina: A History*, 210–11.
7   Edgar, *South Carolina: A History*, 211, 216, 218; Piecuch, 15.
8   Carol Berkin, *Revolutionary Mothers: Women in the Struggle for American Independence* (New York: Vintage, 2005), 15–17; Cynthia A. Kierner, *Beyond the Household: Women's Place in the Early South, 1700–1835* (Ithaca: Cornell University Press, 1998), 75–6.
9   Edgar, *South Carolina: A History*, 211, 217.
10   Edgar, *South Carolina: A History*, 219; Piecuch, 16.
11   Edgar, *South Carolina: A History*, 219; Edgar, *Partisans and Redcoats*, 27.
12   Peter N. Moore, *World of Toil and Strife: Community Transformation in Backcountry South Carolina, 1750–1805* (Columbia: University of South Carolina Press, 2007), 61.
13   Piecuch, *Three Peoples, One King*, 19–21.
14   Edgar, *South Carolina: A History*, 219; Piecuch, 16; Edgar, *Partisans and Redcoats*, 27–8.
15   Berkin, *Revolutionary Mothers*, 21.
16   Berkin, *Revolutionary Mothers*, 21–2; Cynthia A. Kierner, *Beyond the Household: Women's Place in the Early South, 1700–1835* (Ithaca: Cornell University Press, 1998), 78–86.
17   Edgar, *South Carolina: A History*, 219; Edgar, *Partisans and Redcoats*, 28.
18   Edgar, *South Carolina: A History*, 219–20; Piecuch, *Three Peoples, One King*, 17, 21.
19   Edgar, *South Carolina: A History*, 219–22; Piecuch, 17.
20   Edgar, *South Carolina: A History*, 222; Edgar, *Partisans and Redcoats*, 29.
21   Piecuch, *Three Peoples, One King*, 22.

22   Raphael, *A People's History*, 245–6; Gordon, *South Carolina and the American Revolution*, 17.
23   Douglas R. Egerton, *Death or Liberty: African Americans and Revolutionary America* (New York: Oxford University Press, 2009), 53.
24   *Somerset v. Stewart*, 1772; Egerton, 70; Raphael, 247–8.
25   Piecuch, *Three Peoples, One King*, 28, 33, 20; Brown, *Strain of Violence*, 71–2.
26   Raphael, *A People's History*, 221; Piecuch, *Three Peoples, One King*, 26–30.

3 Revolutionary War and the Challenge of Winning Hearts and Minds

Epigraph: Rachel N. Klein, *Unification of a Slave State: The Rise of the Planter Class in the South Carolina Backcountry, 1760–1808* (Chapel Hill: University of North Carolina Press, 1990), 18; David Fanning, *The Narrative of Colonel David Fanning (a Tory in the Revolutionary War with Great Britain) Written by Himself detailing astonishing events in No. Ca.* (Richmond, Virginia: privately printed, 1861): 3.

1   Scoggins, *The Day It Rained Militia*, 25–6; Gordon, *South Carolina and the American Revolution*, 20, 22; Hatley, *The Dividing Path*, 187.
2   Edgar, *South Carolina: A History*, 222; Piecuch, *Three Peoples, One King*, 17–19, 48; Edgar, *Partisans and Redcoats*, 29; "A Circular Letter To The Committees In The Several Districts And Parishes Of South Carolina," in Robert W. Gibbes, *Documentary History of the American Revolution: Consisting of Letters and Papers Relating to the Contest for Liberty, Chiefly in South Carolina, from Originals in the Possession of the Editor, and Other Sources* (New York: D. Appleton & Co, 1853), 107–16.
3   Edgar, *Partisans and Redcoats*, 29–30; Scoggins, *The Day It Rained Militia*, 25; Piecuch, *Three Peoples, One King*, 17.
4   Edgar, *Partisans and Redcoats*, 29; Raphael, *A People's History*, 153; Klein, *Unification of a Slave State*, 84–5.
5   Piecuch, *Three Peoples, One King*, 50–1; Edgar, *Partisans and Redcoats*, 30–2; Brown, *Strain of Violence*, 73; Edgar, *South Carolina: A History*, 223; Scoggins, 25–9. Throughout the colonial period, geographic designations were evolving in the southern colonies. For example, South Carolina was divided into only four counties until the passage of the 1769 judiciary act established seven judicial districts. In 1776, the new state constitution created new boundaries for twenty-seven election districts. Backcountry election districts were called "districts" while the lowcountry districts were called "parishes."
6   Sosin, *The Revolutionary Frontier*, 100–1.
7   Piecuch, *Three Peoples, One King*, 49; Sosin, *The Revolutionary Frontier*, 100; Lambert, *South Carolina Loyalists*, 28; John Gordon, *South Carolina and the American Revolution*, 22–3.
8   Edgar, *Partisans and Redcoats*, 32–3; Edgar, *South Carolina: A History*, 223; Piecuch, *Three Peoples, One King*, 52.
9   Richard M. Brown, *Strain of Violence*, 73; Raphael, *A People's History*, 154–5; Edgar, *South Carolina: A History*, 229; Robert Stansbury Lambert, *South Carolina Loyalists in the American Revolution* (Columbia: University of South Carolina Press, 1987), 28.

10 Klein, *Unification of a Slave State*, 81–2, 87, 89, 107; Raphael, *A People's History*, 153–5; Lambert, *South Carolina Loyalists*, 28.

11 Piecuch, *Three Peoples, One King*, 22.

12 Edgar, *South Carolina: A History*, 226–7; Piecuch, *Three Peoples, One King*, 22; Gordon, *South Carolina and the American Revolution*, 25–6.

13 Edgar, *Partisans and Redcoats*, 32; Piecuch, *Three Peoples, One King*, 63; John W. Gordon, *South Carolina and the American Revolution*, 29.

14 Scoggins, *The Day It Rained Militia*, 31; Brown, *Stain of Violence*, 73; Edgar, *Partisans and Redcoats*, 33; Hatley, *The Dividing Path*, 187–8; Raphael, *A People's History*, 155. John W. Gordon put the number of Loyalist militia at the siege at 1,900. Gordon, *South Carolina and the American Revolution*, 30.

15 Scoggins, *The Day It Rained Militia*, 31–2; Sosin, *The Revolutionary Frontier*, 99–100; Edgar, *South Carolina: A History*, 226; Edgar, *Partisans and Redcoats*, 33; Hatley, *The Dividing Path*, 188; Raphael, *A People's History*, 155; John W. Gordon, *South Carolina and the American Revolution*, 31–3.

16 Alexander E. Chesney, *The Journal of Alexander Chesney, A South Carolina Loyalist in the Revolution and After*, Alfred Jones and Wilbur Henry Siebert, Eds. (Columbus: Ohio State University, 1921), 6–7.

17 Scoggins, *The Day It Rained Militia*, 32.

18 Raphael, *A People's History*, 260–3.

19 Douglas R. Egerton, *Death or Liberty: African Americans and Revolutionary America* (New York: Oxford University Press, 2009), 75.

20 Raphael, *A People's History*, 290–1; Egerton, *Death or Liberty*, 80–4.

21 Edgar, *Partisans and Redcoats*, 34; Edgar, *South Carolina: A History*, 227; Pauline Maier, *American Scripture: Making the Declaration of Independence* (New York: Knopf, 1997), 48.

22 Edgar, *South Carolina: A History*, 227; Edgar, *Partisans and Redcoats*, 34–6.

23 Quote in Ray Raphael, *A People's History of the American Revolution: How Common People Shaped the Fight for Independence* (New York: The New Press, 2001), 234.

24 Raphael, *A People's History*, 231.

25 Hatley, *The Dividing Path*, 191; John W. Gordon, *South Carolina and the American Revolution*, 46–7.

26 Scoggins, *The Day It Rained Militia*, 33; Cynthia A. Kierner, *Southern Women in Revolution, 1776–1800: Personal and Political Narratives* (Columbia: University of South Carolina Press, 1998), 36–7.

27 Hatley, *The Dividing Path*, 194–7; John W. Gordon, *South Carolina and the American Revolution*, 49–51.

28 Scoggins, *The Day It Rained Militia*, 33; John W. Gordon, *South Carolina and the American Revolution*, 52–3; "Arthur Fairies' Journal of the Expedition Against the Cherokee Indian from July 8, 1776 to October 11, 1776," transcribed by Cynthia C. Faris from the RG 15: Records of the Veterans Administration, National Archives and Records Administration, College Park, MD; E. F. Rockwell, "The Historical Magazine and Notes and Queries" (Morrisania NY: Henry B. Dawson, 1867), 212–20; Chesney, *The Journal of Alexander Chesney*, 7; Raphael, *A People's History*, 224.

29 Scoggins, 34; Edgar, *South Carolina: A History*, 229; Brown, *Stain of Violence*, 74; Edgar, *Partisans and Redcoats*, 36–7.

30   Edgar, *South Carolina: A History*, 229; Edgar, *Partisans and Redcoats*, 38–40.

31   Edgar, *South Carolina: A History*, 229–30.

32   Edgar, *South Carolina: A History*, 231; Edgar, *Partisans and Redcoats*, 40–3.

33   Piecuch, *Three Peoples, One King*, 93–100; Edgar, *Partisans and Redcoats*, 44.

34   Scoggins, *The Day It Rained Militia*, 34–5; John W. Gordon, *South Carolina and the American Revolution*, 56–7; Piecuch, *Three Peoples, One King*, 93.

35   John Ferling, *Almost a Miracle: The American Victory in the War of Independence* (New York: Oxford University Press, 2007), 269–70, 410.

36   Edgar, *South Carolina: A History*, 231; Scoggins, 35–7; Edgar, *Partisans and Redcoats*, 44–5; John W. Gordon, *The American Revolution and South Carolina*, 62–3.

37   Ferling, *Almost a Miracle*, 410; Edgar, *South Carolina: A History*, 231; Edgar, *Partisans and Redcoats*, 49; John W. Gordon, *South Carolina and the American Revolution*, 66–7.

38   Ferling, *Almost a Miracle*, 411–13; Edgar, *South Carolina: A History*, 232.

4 The South's First Civil War: The Fall of Charles Town and its Aftermath

Epigraphs: John W. Gordon, *South Carolina and the American Revolution: A Battlefield History* (Columbia: University of South Carolina Press, 2003), 137; Lambert, *South Carolina Loyalists in the American Revolution*, 121.

1   Ferling, *Almost a Miracle*, 411–17; John W. Gordon, *South Carolina and the American Revolution*, 73.

2   Ferling, *Almost a Miracle*, 417; John W. Gordon, *South Carolina and the American Revolution*, 75–8.

3   Ferling, *Almost a Miracle*, 416; Egerton, *Death or Liberty*, 80, 85; Edgar, *South Carolina: A History*, 232; John W. Gordon, *South Carolina and the American Revolution*, 75–8.

4   Eliza Wilkinson, *Letters of Eliza Wilkinson*, Caroline Howard Gilman, comp. (New York: New York Times, 1969).

5   Ferling, *Almost a Miracle*, 418–19, Edgar, *South Carolina: A History*, 233; Gordon, *South Carolina and the American Revolution*, 81.

6   Ferling, *Almost a Miracle*, 419–21; Gordon, *South Carolina and the American Revolution*, 81.

7   Ferling, *Almost a Miracle*, 421–7; Gordon, *South Carolina and the American Revolution*, 80–3.

8   Ferling, *Almost a Miracle*, 421–7; Gordon, *South Carolina and the American Revolution*, 80–3; Scoggins, *The Day It Rained Militia*, 41; Edgar, *South Carolina: A History*, 233.

9   Ferling, *Almost a Miracle*, 425–7; Scoggins, *The Day It Rained Militia*, 41; Edgar, *South Carolina: A History*, 233.

10   Egerton, *Death or Liberty*, 85; Boston King, *The Life of Boston King*. Ruth Holmes Whitehead, and Carmelita Robertson, Eds. (Halifax, N.S.: Nimbus Pub, 2003), 170, available online at http://site.ebrary.com/id/10215232.

11   Ferling, 427; Edgar, *South Carolina: A History*, 233; Lambert, *South Carolina Loyalists in the American Revolution*, 94, 96.

12   Scoggins, *The Day It Rained Militia*, 39, 43; Gordon, *South Carolina and the American Revolution*, 86–8.

13   Scoggins, *The Day It Rained Militia*, 45–6; Peter N. Moore, *World of Toil and Strife: Community Transformation in Backcountry South Carolina, 1750–1805* (Columbia: University of South Carolina Press, 2007), 60–1; Ferling, *Almost a Miracle*, 437; Gordon, *South Carolina and the American Revolution*, 86–8.

14   Edgar, *South Carolina: A History*, 234; Scoggins, *The Day It Rained Militia*, 44; Lambert, *South Carolina Loyalists in the American Revolution*, 121.

15   Edgar, *South Carolina: A History*, 233; Scoggins, *The Day It Rained Militia*, 49–50; Gordon, *South Carolina and the American Revolution*, 88.

16   Moore, *World of Toil and Strife*, 64–5.

17   Ferling, *Almost a Miracle*, 417.

18   Scoggins, *The Day It Rained Militia*, 49; Ferling, *Almost a Miracle*, 417, 435, 455; Lambert, *South Carolina Loyalists in the American Revolution*, 104–20. Lambert says that Loyalist militias enrolled 2,500 officers and men in the first two months.

19   John Buchanan, *The Road to Guilford Courthouse: The American Revolution in the Carolinas* (New York: John Wiley & Sons, 1997, 142–50, quote on 142; Ferling, *Almost a Miracle*, 437–8.

20   Ferling, *Almost a Miracle*, 51–2; Buchanan, *The Road to Guilford Courthouse*, 142–50.

21   Ferling, *Almost a Miracle*, 452–5; Edgar, *Partisans and Redcoats*, 68–70, quote on 69.

22   Moore, *World of Toil and Strife*, 61, 63; Edgar, *Partisans and Redcoats*, 71; Scoggins, *The Day It Rained Militia*, 61–2, 67, 85–6; Lambert, *South Carolina Loyalists*, 127; Buchanan, *The Road to Guilford Courthouse*, 106–10.

23   Scoggins, *The Day It Rained Militia*, 52.

24   Edgar, *Partisans and Redcoats*, 67.

25   Richard Maxwell Brown, *Strain of Violence*, 78–80.

26   Berkin, *Revolutionary Mothers*, 38–9; Kierner, *Southern Women in Revolution*, 30.

27   Egerton, *Death or Liberty*, 86–7.

28   Benjamin Quarles, *The Negro in the American Revolution* (Chapel Hill: University of North Carolina Press, 1961), 108–9, 115–17, 132–3, 156.

29   Scoggins, *The Day It Rained Militia*, 92.

30   Scoggins, *The Day It Rained Militia*, 51–2.

31   Scoggins, *The Day It Rained Militia*, 68–70.

32   Edgar, *Partisans and Redcoats*, 75–6; Scoggins, *The Day It Rained Militia*, 103–7.

33   Edgar, *Partisans and Redcoats*, 77–9; Scoggins, *The Day It Rained Militia*, 109–11.

34   Ferling, *Almost a Miracle*, 456; Scoggins, *The Day It Rained Militia*, 111–20; Edgar, *Partisans and Redcoats*, 78–83; William Hill, *Col. William Hill's Memoirs of the Revolution* A.S. Salley, Jr., Ed. (Columbia: The Historical Commission of the State of South Carolina, 1921), 10.

35   John B. O. Landrum, *Colonial and Revolutionary History of Upper South Carolina*, (Greenville: Shannon & Co. Printers and Binders, 1897), 110–11; Gordon, *South Carolina and the American Revolution*, 89; Buchanan, *The Road to Guilford Courthouse*, 112.

36   Edgar, *Partisans and Redcoats*, 89–90.

37   Ferling, *Almost a Miracle*, 457; Edgar, *South Carolina: A History*, 235; Charles Cornwallis, and Charles Derek Ross, *Correspondence of Charles, First Marquis Cornwallis*, vol. 1, (London: J. Murray, 1859).

38   Scoggins, 39; Edgar, *South Carolina: A History*, 235; Dykeman, Wilma, *With Fire and Sword: The Battle of Kings Mountain, 1780* (Washington, D.C.: National Park Service, n.d.), n.p.

39   Ferling, *Almost a Miracle*, 439–40; Buchanan, *The Road to Guilford Courthouse*, 153–5.

40   Ferling, *Almost a Miracle*, 441–2; Edgar, *South Carolina: A History*, 234–5, Robert W. Brown, *Kings Mountain and Cowpens*, 41; Edgar, *Partisans and Redcoats*, 110; Gordon, *South Carolina and the American Revolution*, 92–4; Buchanan, *The Road to Guilford Courthouse*, 157–72.

41   Edgar, *Partisans and Redcoats*, 114–15; Buchanan, *The Road to Guilford Courthouse*, 176–80; "Battle of Musgrove's Mill Historic Site," National Historic Register application, n.d. ca. 1975, available online at www.nationalregister.sc.gov/union/S10817744014/S10817744014.pdf

42   Sosin, *The Backcountry Frontier*, 128; Buchanan, *The Road to Guilford Courthouse*, 179–80.

43   Lambert, *South Carolina Loyalists*, 131.

5 Kings Mountain: "First Link in a Chain"

Epigraph: Robert W. Brown, Jr., *Kings Mountain and Cowpens: Our Victory Was Complete* (Charleston: The History Press, 2009), 14–15; Isaac Shelby quoted in Lyman Copeland Draper, *King's Mountain and Its Heroes: History of the Battle of King's Mountain, October 7th, 1780, and the Events Which Led to It* (Cincinnati: P.G. Thomson, 1881), 196.

1   Ferling, *Almost a Miracle*, 459; Robert W. Brown, *Kings Mountain and Cowpens*, 44; Cornwallis to Clinton, 6 August and 29 August 1780, in Charles Cornwallis, *Correspondence of Charles, First Marquis Cornwallis*, Charles Derek Ross, Ed. (London: J. Murray, 1859): 54, 58.

2   Ferling, *Almost a Miracle*, 459; Robert W. Brown, *Kings Mountain and Cowpens*, 44; Bucahanan, *The Road to Guilford Courthouse*, 194.

3   Robert W. Brown, *Kings Mountain and Cowpens*, 47–8; Edgar, *Partisans and Redcoats*, 116; Draper, *King's Mountain and Its Heroes*, 169.

4   Robert W. Brown, *Kings Mountain and Cowpens*, 48–9.

5   Robert W. Brown, *Kings Mountain and Cowpens*, 48–9, 59, Shelby quoted by Brown, 49; Draper, *King's Mountain and Its Heroes*, 174; Dykeman, *With Fire and Sword*, n.p.; Ferling, *Almost a Miracle*, 460. Accounts vary as to the number of men who mustered with the Overmountain men. Leland Draper said that Sevier and Shelby had about 240 each while William Campbell had 200. Robert W. Brown says Sevier and Shelby had 800 men and Campbell 400.

6   Draper, *King's Mountain and Its Heroes*, 195; Stephen W. Foster, "The Battle of Kings Mountain," *American Historical Magazine* 1:1 (January 1896): 26.

7   Robert W. Brown, *Kings Mountain and Cowpens*, 50, 59–60; Draper, *King's Mountain and Its Heroes*, 203, 207–8; Lambert, *South Carolina Loyalists*, 140; Dykeman, *With Fire and Sword*, n.p.

8   Wilma Dykeman, *With Fire and Sword*, n.p.; Robert W. Brown, *Kings Mountain and Cowpens*, 65; Lambert, *South Carolina Loyalists*, 139.

9   Draper, *Kings Mountain and Its Heroes*, 209–10; Dykeman, *With Fire and Sword*, n.p; Edgar, *Partisans and Redcoats*, 118; Robert M. Dunkerly, *Kings Mountain Walking Tour Guide* (Pittsburgh: Dorrance Publishing Company, 2003), 9.

10   Dykeman, *With Fire and Sword*, n.p.

11   Dykeman, *With Fire and Sword*, n.p.; Draper, *Kings Mountain and Its Heroes*, 195.

12   Draper, *Kings Mountain and Its Heroes*, 195.

13   Draper, *Kings Mountain and Its Heroes*, 196.

14   Hunter, C. L., *Sketches of Western North Carolina, Historical and Biographical: Illustrating Principally the Revolutionary Period of Mecklenburg, Rowan, Lincoln, and Adjoining Counties, Accompanied with Miscellaneous Information, Much of It Never Before Published.* Raleigh: Raleigh News Steam Job Print, 1877, 120–2.

15   Edgar, *Partisans and Redcoats*, 117.

16   William Hill, *Memoirs of the Revolution*, A.S. Salley, Ed. (Columbia: State Historical Commission of South Carolina, 1921): 22.

17   Robert W. Brown, *Kings Mountain and Cowpens*, 59–60; Draper, *Kings Mountain and Its Heroes*, 227–8; John W. Gordon, *South Carolina and the American Revolution*, 114; Hill, *Memoirs of the Revolution*, 22–3.

18   Robert W. Brown, *Kings Mountain and Cowpens*, 60–4.

19   Robert W. Brown, *Kings Mountain and Cowpens*, 64–7; John W. Gordon, *South Carolina and the American Revolution*, 115–7; Hill, *Memoirs of the Revolution*, 23.

20   Draper, *Kings Mountain and Its Heroes*, 247; Robert Campbell, "Another Account of the Battle of Kings Mountain," *American Historical Magazine* 1:1 (January 1896): 42.

21   Robert W. Brown, *Kings Mountain and Cowpens*, 68–72; Hill, *Memoir of the Revolution*, 24.

22   Robert W. Brown, *Kings Mountain and Cowpens*, 68–74; Ferling, *Almost a Miracle*, 462; John W. Gordon, *South Carolina and the American Revolution*, 116–7.

23   Robert W. Brown, *Kings Mountain and Cowpens,* 64, 75.

24   Robert W. Brown, *Kings Mountain and Cowpens*, 74–6, 80–5; Dykeman, *With Fire and Sword*, n.p.

25   Robert W. Brown, *Kings Mountain and Cowpens*, 83.

26   Robert W. Brown, *Kings Mountain and Cowpens*, 85; Draper, *Kings Mountain and Its Heroes*, 308.

27   Robert W. Brown, *Kings Mountain and Cowpens*, 86; Dykeman, *With Fire and Sword*, n.p.

28   Robert W. Brown, *Kings Mountain and Cowpens*, 85–7; "A letter from a Royalist officer," Charlestown, January 30th, 1781, published in Rivington's *Royal Gazette*, New York, February 24, 1781, www.tngenweb.org/revwar/kingsmountain/17810130.html; Banastre Tarleton, *A History of the Campaigns of 1780 and 1781 in the Southern Provinces of North America.* (New York: New York Times, 1968, reprint of 1807 edition); 169; Campbell, 44.

29   Draper, *Kings Mountain and Its Heroes*, 339–40.

30   Draper, *Kings Mountain and Its Heroes*, 340, Brown, *Kings Mountain and Cowpens*, 89; Hill, *Memoir of the Revolution*, 24.

31   Dykeman, *With Fire and Sword*, n.p.

32   Robert W. Brown, *Kings Mountain and Cowpens*, 89–90; Edgar, *South Carolina: A History*, 235; Cornwallis to Clinton, December 3, 1780, in Charles Cornwallis, *Correspondence of Charles, First Marquis Cornwallis*, Charles Derek Ross, Ed. (London: J. Murray, 1859), 71; Tarleton quoted in Robert W. Brown, 87.

33   Dykeman, *With Fire and Sword*, n.p.

34   Ferling, *Almost a Miracle*, 463; Lawrence E. Babits, *A Devil of a Whipping: The Battle of Cowpens* (Chapel Hill: University of North Carolina Press, 1998), 5; Lambert, *South Carolina Loyalists*, 198.

6 The Battle of Cowpens: Victory for "The Flying Army"

Epigraph: Lawrence E. Babits, *A Devil of a Whipping: The Battle of Cowpens* (Chapel Hill: University of North Carolina Press, 1998), 1.

1   Dykeman, *With Fire and Sword*, n.p.; Edgar, *South Carolina: A History*, 236; Ferling, *Almost a Miracle*, 477.

2   Robert W. Brown, *Kings Mountain and Cowpens*, 91; Ferling, *Almost a Miracle*, 464.

3   Ferling, *Almost a Miracle,* 464. Fabian tactics take their name from Fabius Maximus, the Roman general who defeated Hannibal of Carthage in the third century B.C.E. using exactly these tactics.

4   Ferling, *Almost a Miracle*, 464–5; Edgar, *South Carolina: A History*, 236; Babits, *A Devil of a Whipping*, 5.

5   Ferling, *Almost a Miracle*, 465–6; Edgar, *South Carolina: A History*, 236; Babits, *A Devil of a Whipping*, 6–7; Don Higginbotham, *Daniel Morgan: Revolutionary Rifleman* (Chapel Hill: University of North Carolina Press, 1961), 121; Greene quoted in Lawrence E. Babits and Joshua B. Howard, *Long, Obstinate, and Bloody: The Battle of Guilford Courthouse* (Chapel Hill: University of North Carolina Press, 2009), 9.

6   Ferling, *Almost a Miracle*, 477–9.

7   Ferling, *Almost a Miracle*, 479; Babits, *A Devil of a Whipping*, 9; Charles Cornwallis, Correspondence of Charles, First Marquis Cornwallis, 71, 76, 81.

8   Robert W. Brown, *Kings Mountain and Cowpens*, 93; Ferling, *Almost a Miracle*, 480; Babits, *A Devil of a Whipping*, 23–4; Higginbotham, *Daniel Morgan*, 3–7, 27–41, 55–77.

9   Babits, *A Devil of a Whipping*, 25–8, 150–2; Ferling, *Almost a Miracle*, 480.

10   Robert W. Brown, *Kings Mountain and Cowpens*, 97.

11   Robert W. Brown, *Kings Mountain and Cowpens*, 94–7, 100, 102.

12   Banastre Tarleton, *A History of the Campaigns of 1780 and 1781 in the Southern Provinces of North America* (New York: New York Times, 1968, reprint of 1807 edition), 217–9.

13   Babits, *A Devil of a Whipping*, 8–9, 48–50; Ferling, *Almost a Miracle*, 479–80.

14   Robert W. Brown, *Kings Mountain and Cowpens*, 101; Ferling, *Almost a Miracle*, 479–80; Babits, *A Devil of a Whipping*, 50–1.

15   Ferling, *Almost a Miracle*, 479–80; Babits, *A Devil of a Whipping*, 50–1; John W. Gordon, *South Carolina and the American Revolution*, 133; Higginbotham, *Daniel Morgan*, 130.

16   Robert W. Brown, *Kings Mountain and Cowpens*, 102–3; Babits, *A Devil of a Whipping*, 52–3.

17   Robert W. Brown, *Kings Mountain and Cowpens*, 102–3; Babits, *A Devil of a Whipping*, 53–4; Ferling, *Almost a Miracle*, 480; John W. Gordon, *South Carolina and the American Revolution*, 129.

18   Robert W. Brown, *Kings Mountain and Cowpens*, 104–5.

19   Ferling, *Almost a Miracle*, 482–3; Babits, *A Devil of a Whipping*, 55–6; John W. Gordon, *South Carolina and the American Revolution*, 129–31.

20   Young quoted in Babits, *A Devil of a Whipping*, 54–5.

21   Ferling, *Almost a Miracle*, 481–3, Robert W. Brown, *Kings Mountain and Cowpens*, 104; Babits, *A Devil of a Whipping*, 56–7; John W. Gordon, *South Carolina and the American Revolution*, 132–3, Tarleton, *A History of the Campaigns of 1780 and 1781*, 221.

22   Babits, *A Devil of a Whipping*, 58–9.

23   Babits, *A Devil of a Whipping*, 58–60.

24   Tarleton, *A History of the Campaigns of 1780 and 1781*, 221–2; Collins quoted in Babits, *A Devil of a Whipping*, 72.

25   Babits, *A Devil of a Whipping*, 72, 81–4; Ferling, *Almost a Miracle*, 484; Tarleton, *A History of the Campaigns of 1780 and 1781*, 222.

26   Babits, *A Devil of a Whipping*, 84–99; Ferling, *Almost a Miracle*, 484–6; John W. Gordon, *South Carolina and the American Revolution*, 134.

27   Babits, *A Devil of a Whipping*, 100–36, quotes on 101, 102, 123; Ferling, *Almost a Miracle*, 484–7; Tarleton, *A History of the Campaigns of 1780 and 1781*, 223.

28   Babits, *A Devil of a Whipping*, 100–36, quotes on 101, 102, 123; Ferling, *Almost a Miracle*, 484–7; Gordon, *South Carolina and the American Revolution*, 134–5.

29   Chesney, *The Journal of Alexander Chesney*, 21.

30   Babits, *A Devil of a Whipping*, 159–60; Babits, personal communication with author, July 2009.

31   Babits, *A Devil of a Whipping*, 137, 141; Ferling, *Almost a Miracle*, 487.

32   Babits, *A Devil of a Whipping*, 143; Ferling, *Almost a Miracle*, 487

33   Babits, *A Devil of a Whipping*, 144–5, Ferling, *Almost a Miracle*, 488; Buchanan, *Road to Guilford Courthhouse*, 332–3.

34   Greene quoted in Morrill, *Southern Campaigns of the American Revolution*, 136.

7 Denouement

Epigraphs: Dan L. Morrill, *Southern Campaigns of the American Revolution* (Baltimore, Md: Nautical & Aviation Pub. Co. of America, 1993), 3; Charles O'Hara quoted in Buchanan, *Road to Guilford Courthouse*, 337.

1   Babits and Howard, *Long, Obstinate, and Bloody*, 11, 14; Babits, *A Devil of a Whipping*, 144–5, Ferling, *Almost a Miracle*, 488.

2   Angus Konstam, *Guilford Courthouse, 1781: Lord Cornwallis's Ruinous Victory* (Oxford, England: Osprey Publishing, 2002), 42; Buchanan, *Road to Guilford Courthouse*, 341.

3   Morill, *Southern Campaigns of the American Revolution*, 136–8; Konstam, *Guilford Courthouse, 1781*, 42–3; Buchanan, *Road to Guilford Courthouse*, 339, 341.

4   Morrill, *Southern Campaigns of the American Revolution*, 136; Ferling, *Almost a Miracle*, 490; Buchanan, *Road to Guilford Courthouse*, 336–7.

5   Buchanan, *Road to Guilford Courthouse*, 341–4.

6   Konstam, *Guilford Courthouse*, 1781, 45–8; Babits and Howard, *Long, Obstinate, and Bloody*, 23–7; Ferling, *Almost a Miracle*, 490; Buchanan, *Road to Guilford Courthouse*, 357.

7   Collins, *Autobiography of a Soldier*, 270; Buchanan, *Road to Guilford Courthouse*, 243–4; Ferling, *Almost a Miracle*, 491–2.

8   Konstam, *Guilford Courthouse, 1781*, 45; Babits and Howard, *Long, Obstinate, and Bloody*, 27; Morrill, *Southern Campaigns of the American Revolution*, 149–50; Greene quoted in Buchanan, *Road to Guilford Courthouse*, 351.

9   Konstam, *Guilford Courthouse, 1781*, 45–8; Babits and Howard, *Long, Obstinate, and Bloody*, 23–7.

10 Buchanan, *The Road to Guilford Courthouse*, 357–9; Ferling, *Almost a Miracle*, 493–4.

11 Buchanan, *Road to Guilford Courthouse*, 359–60; Ferling, *Almost a Miracle*, 494.

12 Ferling, *Almost a Miracle*, 495–6; Buchanan, *Road to Guilford Courthouse*, 362–6.

13 Ferling, *Almost a Miracle*, 496; Gordon, *South Carolina and the American Revolution*, 144–8.

14 Ferling, *Almost a Miracle*, 496–7; Buchanan, *Road to Guilford Courthouse*, 368–9.

15 Buchanan, *Road to Guilford Courthouse*, 370–1.

16 Ferling, *Almost a Miracle*, 497–9; Buchanan, *Road to Guilford Courthouse*, 372–80; Morrill, *Southern Campaigns of the American Revolution*, 149–57.

17 Gordon, *South Carolina and the American Revolution*, 144–8; Morrill, *Southern Campaigns of the American Revolution*, 149–57; Ferling, *Almost a Miracle*, 498; Buchanan, *Road to Guilford Courthouse*, 377, 380.

18 Morrill, *Southern Campaigns of the American Revolution*, 159; Edgar, *South Carolina: A History*, 237; Babits, *A Devil of a Whipping*, 5–6; Lambert, *South Carolina Loyalists*, 169; Ferling, *Almost a Miracle*, 499.

19 Edgar, *South Carolina: A History*, 237–8, Morrill, *Southern Campaigns of the American Revolution*, 159–61; Piecuch, *Three Peoples, One King*, 276–9; John W. Gordon, *South Carolina and the American Revolution*, 141–5, 148–51, 154.

20 Gordon, *South Carolina and the American Revolution*, 155–7; Edgar, *South Carolina: A History*, 237; Marvin Cann, *Old Ninety Six in the South Carolina Backcountry, 1780–1781* (Eastern National: 2000), 20; Cornwallis, *Correspondence of Charles, First Marquis Cornwallis*, 84.

21 Cann, *Old Ninety Six*, 20–24; Gordon, *South Carolina and the American Revolution*, 155–7; Lambert, *South Carolina Loyalists*, 170–3.

22 Cann, *Old Ninety Six*, 24–5, Greene quoted on 25.

23 Cann, *Old Ninety Six*, 25.

24 Cann, *Old Ninety Six*, 26–31; Gordon, *South Carolina and the American Revolution*, 155–7; Lambert, *South Carolina Loyalists*, 170–3.

25 Lambert, *South Carolina Loyalists*, 229–30.

26 Piecuch, *Three Peoples, One King*, 299–308.

27 Edgar, *South Carolina: A History*, 237–6.

28 Ferling, *Almost a Miracle*, 508–9.

29 Ferling, *Almost a Miracle*, 510–16 and 523–39; Edgar, *South Carolina: A History*, 239; Morrill, *Southern Campaigns of the American Revolution*, 177–83.

30 Edgar, *South Carolina: A History*, 239; Lambert, *South Carolina Loyalists*, 169–70; Greene quoted in Piecuch, *Three Peoples, One King*, 284.

31 Edgar, *South Carolina: A History*, 239; Piecuch, *Three Peoples, One King*, 280–2.

32 Richard Maxwell Brown, *Strain of Violence*, 81; Piecuch, *Three Peoples, One King*, 282, 291.

33 Lambert, *South Carolina Loyalists*, 230–1.

34 Kierner, *Beyond the Household*, 97–100, 70.

35 Edgar, *South Carolina: A History*, 240–1; Lambert, *South Carolina Loyalists*, 175; Egerton, *Death or Liberty*, 151.

36 Egerton, *Death or Liberty*, 89–90, 151–2; Gary B. Nash, *The Forgotten Fifth*, 43; Ray Raphael, *A People's History*, 268–70.

37 Morrill, *Southern Campaigns of the American Revolution*, 3.

Document 1 Colonel William Hill on the Battle of Huck's Defeat

Excerpted from William Hill, *Col. William Hill's Memoirs of the Revolution* A.S. Salley, Jr., Ed. (Columbia: The Historical Commission of the State of South Carolina, 1921), 8–10.

1 Christian Huck, a former Philadelphia lawyer who had joined the British Army early in the Revolution. Huck quickly rose to the rank of Captain, commanding a unit of Loyalist forces detached from Tarleton's command.

2 Hill's Iron Works, owned by Colonel William Hill, author of this document, was an important backcountry manufacturing facility.

3 Wives of Patriot militiamen that Huck brought to the Williamsons' home as hostages.

4 Actually July 12, 1780.

Document 6 Alexander Chesney Describes the Battle of Kings Mountain

Source: E. Alfred Jones and Wilbur Henry Siebert, Eds., *The Journal of Alexander Chesney, A South Carolina Loyalist in the Revolution and After* (Columbus: Ohio State University, 1921), 14–20.

1 The area around the Holston River where the Overmountain men were mustering.

2 Probably a reference to a pass or "gap" in the Blue Ridge Mountains.

3 Colonel Benjamin Cleveland, Colonel Isaac Shelby, and General William Campbell.

4 He implies that Ferguson's choice of a hunting shirt should have made him look like any other militia man—Loyalist or Whig. Of course, few militiamen wore plaid hunting shirts.

5 Col. James Williams.

6 Ferguson had lost the use of his right arm after being wounded at the Battle to Brandywine.

7 Ferguson's second-in-command.

8 Present-day Winston-Salem.

9 By disguising themselves as Whig militia.

Document 9 Alexander Chesney describes the Battle of Cowpcnɔ

Source: E. Alfred Jones and Wilbur Henry Siebert, Eds., *The Journal of Alexander Chesney, A South Carolina Loyalist in the Revolution and After* (Columbus: Ohio State University, 1921), 20–2.

1   Col. James Williams, who had been mortally wounded at the Battle of Kings Mountain.
2   Brig. General Robert Cunningham.
3   Benjamin Roebuck who would soon be promoted to rose from the rank of lieutenant to that of lieutenant-colonel in the American service during the Revolutionary war. He served in numerous backcountry actions including Musgrove's Mills, King's Mountain, and Cowpens.
4   Captain John Clarke, son of Colonel Elijah Clarke. Chesney is referring to a common practice of prisoner exchange which led to men being repeatedly captured and then set free to fight again.
5   Chesney's farm was on the Pacolet River, and he was familiar with the territory where Morgan was then encamped.
6   Morgan's men had left their camp at Grindal Shoals headed for The Cowpens.
7   Another term for The Cowpens.
8   Some of Morgan's camp was on Chesney's farm, and the Whig soldiers had looted Chesney's property.
9   Some of Tarleton's soldiers were Americans who had been captured at Camden and given the option of joining the British forces rather than languishing in prison or worse. These men were quick to flee to the Continentals when they had the opportunity at Cowpens.
10   Actually, he probably did not "break" the rifleman. Chesney was witnessing Morgan's plan of taking three shots and moving back.
11   Chesney was able to escape after the defeat and take his wife and child to safety.

Document 10 Tarleton's Account of the Battle of Cowpens

1   The plan was for Tarleton to back Morgan's force up to the Broad River where General Cornwallis's troops would guard the other side, preventing his crossing and forcing him to surrender or be destroyed.
2   Morgan had roused his men to abandon their camp quickly, leaving behind some of their provisions.

Bibliography

Lawrence E. Babits, *A Devil of a Whipping: The Battle of Cowpens* (Chapel Hill: University of North Carolina Press, 1998).

Lawrence E. Babits and Joshua B. Howard, *Long, Obstinate, and Bloody: The Battle of Guilford Courthouse* (Chapel Hill: University of North Carolina Press, 2009).

Carol Berkin, *Revolutionary Mothers: Women in the Struggle for American Independence* (New York: Vintage, 2005).

Richard Maxwell Brown, *The South Carolina Regulators* (Cambridge: The Belknap Press of Harvard University, 1963).

Richard Maxwell Brown, *Strain of Violence, Historical Studies of American Violence and Vigilantism* (New York: Oxford University Press, 1975).

Robert W. Brown, Jr., *Kings Mountain and Cowpens: Our Victory Was Complete* (Charleston: The History Press, 2009).

John Buchanan, *The Road to Guilford Courthouse: The American Revolution in the Carolinas* (New York: John Wiley & Sons, 1997).

Marvin Cann, *Old Ninety Six in the South Carolina Backcountry, 1780–1781* (Eastern National: 2000).

Robert Campbell, "Another Account of the Battle of Kings Mountain," *American Historical Magazine* 1:1 (January 1896): 40–4.

Alexander Chesney, *The Journal of Alexander Chesney, A South Carolina Loyalist in the Revolution and After.* E. Alfred Jones, and Wilbur Henry Siebert, Eds. (Columbus: Ohio State University, 1921).

Charles Cornwallis, *Correspondence of Charles, First Marquis Cornwallis,* Charles Derek Ross, Ed. (London: J. Murray, 1859).

Lyman Copeland Draper, *King's Mountain and Its Heroes: History of the Battle of King's Mountain, October 7th, 1780, and the Events Which Led to It.* Cincinnati: P.G. Thomson, 1881.

Wilma Dykeman, *With Fire and Sword: The Battle of Kings Mountain, 1780* (Washington, D.C.: National Park Service, n.d.).

Robert M. Dunkerly, *Kings Mountain Walking Tour Guide.* (Pittsburgh: Dorrance Publishing Company, 2003).

Walter Edgar, *Partisans and Redcoats: The Southern Conflict that Turned the Tide of the American Revolution* (New York: Perennial, 2001).

Walter Edgar, *South Carolina: A History* (Columbia: University of South Carolina Press, 1998).

Douglas R. Egerton, *Death or Liberty: African Americans and Revolutionary America* (New York: Oxford University Press, 2009).

John Ferling, *Almost a Miracle: The American Victory in the War of Independence* (New York: Oxford University Press, 2007).

Stephen W. Foster, "The Battle of Kings Mountain," *American Historical Magazine* 1:1 (January 1896): 22–39.

Robert W. Gibbes, *Documentary History of the American Revolution: Consisting of Letters and Papers Relating to the Contest for Liberty, Chiefly in South Carolina, from Originals in the Possession of the Editor, and Other Sources*. New York: D. Appleton & Co, 1853.

Grant Gordon, *From Slavery to Freedom: The Life of David George, Pioneer Black Baptist Minister*. (Hantsport, N.S: Published by Lancelot Press for Acadia Divinity College and the Baptist Historical Committee of the United Baptist Convention of the Atlantic Provinces, 1992).

John W. Gordon, *South Carolina and the American Revolution: A Battlefield History* (Columbia: University of South Carolina Press, 2003).

Tom Hatley, *The Dividing Paths: Cherokees and South Carolinians through the Era of Revolution* (New York: Oxford, 1993).

Alexia Jones Helsley, *South Carolinians in the War for American Independence* (Columbia: South Carolina Department of Archives and History, 2000).

Don Higginbotham, *Daniel Morgan: Revolutionary Rifleman* (Chapel Hill: University of North Carolina Press, 1961).

William Hill, *Memoirs of the Revolution*, A.S. Salley, Ed. (Columbia: State Historical Commission of South Carolina, 1921).

Richard J. Hooker, Ed., *The Carolina Backcountry on the Eve of the Revolution: The Journal and Other Writings of Charles Woodmason*, Anglican Itinerant (Chapel Hill: University of North Carolina Press, 1953).

Cynthia A. Kierner, *Beyond the Household: Women's Place in the Early South, 1700–1835* (Ithaca: Cornell University Press, 1998).

Cynthia A. Kierner, *Southern Women in Revolution, 1776–1800: Personal and Political Narratives* (Columbia: University of South Carolina Press, 1998).

Rachel N. Klein, *Unification of a Slave State: The Rise of the Planter Class in the South Carolina Backcountry, 1760–1808* (Chapel Hill: University of North Carolina Press, 1990).

Angus Konstam, *Guilford Courthouse, 1781: Lord Cornwallis's Ruinous Victory* (Oxford: Osprey Publishing, 2002).

Robert Stansbury Lambert, *South Carolina Loyalists in the American Revolution* (Columbia: University of South Carolina Press, 1987).

John B. O. Landrum, *Colonial and Revolutionary History of Upper South Carolina*, (Greenville: Shannon & Co. Printers and Binders, 1897).

Peter N. Moore, *World of Toil and Strife: Community Transformation in Backcountry South Carolina, 1750–1805* (Columbia: University of South Carolina Press, 2007).

Dan L. Morrill, *Southern Campaigns of the American Revolution* (Baltimore: Nautical & Aviation Pub. Co. of America, 1993).

Gary B. Nash, *The Forgotten Fifth: African Americans in the Age of Revolution,* (Cambridge: Harvard University Press, 2006).

Jim Piecuch, *Three Peoples, One King: Loyalists, Indians, and Slaves in the Revolutionary South, 1775–1782* (Columbia: University of South Carolina Press, 2008).

Benjamin Quarles, *The Negro in the American Revolution* (Chapel Hill: University of North Carolina Press, 1961).

Ray Raphael, *A People's History of the American Revolution: How Common People Shaped the Fight for Independence* (New York: The New Press, 2001).

Michael C. Scoggins, *The Day It Rained Militia: Huck's Defeat and the Revolution in the South Carolina Backcountry, May-July 1780* (Charleston: History Press, 2005).

Jack M. Sosin, *The Revolutionary Frontier, 1763–1783* (New York: Holt Rinehart, and Winston, 1967).

Banastre Tarleton, *A History of the Campaigns of 1780 and 1781 in the Southern Provinces of North America* (New York: New York Times, 1968, reprint of 1807 edition).

Index